Solicitors and Financial Services

3RD EDITION

LOWE & GORDON SEMINARS

Solicitors and Financial Services

A Compliance Handbook

3RD EDITION

Peter Camp LL.B., Solicitor

Member of the Law Society's
working party on financial services

The Law Society

Material in Appendices A1–A4 is Crown copyright. Crown copyright legislation is reproduced with the permission of the Controller of Her Majesty's Stationery Office.
Material in Appendix C1 is FSA copyright.

ISBN 1 85328 805 5

This third edition published in 2002 by the Law Society
113 Chancery Lane, London WC2A 1PL
and
Lowe & Gordon Seminars
3 Palace Court, 250 Finchley Road, London NW3 6DN

Typeset by J&L Composition Ltd, Filey, North Yorkshire
Printed by Antony Rowe Ltd, Chippenham, Wilts

Contents

Preface   *ix*
List of abbreviations   *x*
Tables of cases and legislation   *xii*

PART I   REGULATORY FRAMEWORK

1   Financial services framework   **3**

Introduction   3
Regulatory framework   5

2   Regulated activities   **9**

Introduction   9
Regulated activities   10
Conclusion   25

3   Statutory exclusions   **26**

Introduction   26
Specific exclusions under the RAO   27
General exclusions under the RAO   39
Conclusion   46

4   Exempt regulated activities   **47**

Introduction   47
Definition under the FSMA   47
Solicitors' Financial Services (Scope) Rules 2001   52
Conclusion   61

PART II COMPLIANCE

5 Compliance requirements — 65

Introduction — 65
Compliance applicable to all solicitors involved in financial services — 65

6 Solicitors' Financial Services (Conduct of Business) Rules 2001 — 78

Introduction — 78
Solicitors' Financial Services (Conduct of Business) Rules 2001 — 79
Solicitors authorised by the FSA – non-mainstream activities — 87
Monitoring and complaints — 88

7 Financial promotions — 90

Introduction — 90
Types of financial promotion — 92
Exemptions under the FPO — 94
Marketing a solicitor's practice — 105

8 Probate and administration — 107

Introduction — 107
Statutory exclusions — 108
FMSA, Part XX régime — 112
Will trusts — 115
Beneficiaries — 116
Compliance — 116
Financial promotions — 117

9 Trusts — 118

Introduction — 118
Statutory exclusions — 120
Nominee companies — 123
FSMA, Part XX régime — 124
Compliance — 127
Financial promotions — 128

10 Powers of attorney — 129

Introduction — 129
Statutory exclusions — 130

FSMA, Part XX régime 132
Compliance 134
Financial promotions 135

11 Receivers **136**

Introduction 136
Statutory exclusions 136
FSMA, Part XX régime 137
Compliance 138
Financial promotions 138

12 Property department **139**

Introduction 139
Regulated mortgage contracts 141
Contractually based investments 143
Shares in a management or service company 146
Compliance 147
Financial promotions 147

13 Corporate department **148**

Regulated activities 148
Statutory exceptions 149
FSMA, Part XX régime 151
Insolvency practitioners 155
Compliance 155
Financial promotions 155

14 Litigation department (including matrimonial work) **157**

Regulated activities 157
Statutory exceptions 157
FSMA, Part XX régime 159
Compliance 162
Financial promotions 162

15 Private clients **163**

Introduction 163
Tax, pensions and school fees 163
Costs versus commission 164

16 Management of investment business   168

Introduction   168
Policy decisions   168
The compliance manual   171

APPENDICES

A   Statutory material   173

A1 Financial Services and Markets Act 2000, sections 19–26   174
A2 Financial Services and Markets Act 2000, Part XX   178
A3 Financial Services and Markets Act 2000 (Regulated Activities) Order 2001, SI 2001/544 (as amended by the Financial Services and Markets Act 2000 (Regulated Activities) (Amendment) Order 2001, SI 2001/3544)   184
A4 Financial Services and Markets Act 2000 (Financial Promotion) Order 2001, SI 2001/1335 (as amended by the Financial Services and Markets Act 2000 (Financial Promotion) (Amendment) Order 2001, SI 2001/2633 – extracts)   230

B   Rules of practice   239

B1 Solicitors' Financial Services (Scope) Rules 2001   240
B2 Solicitors' Financial Services (Conduct of Business) Rules 2001   247

C   Guidance   251

C1 Professional firms – the need for authorisation under the Financial Services and Markets Act 2000: FSA Guidance – August 2001 (extracts)   252
C2 Financial Services and Solicitors: Law Society Professional Ethics information pack (extracts)   278

Index   *285*

Preface

Financial services regulation has undergone an enormous change with the coming into force of the Financial Services and Markets Act 2000. This Act has not only changed the way in which the industry generally has been regulated but has had a significant impact on solicitors' practices. The Law Society is no longer able to regulate solicitors for the purposes of investment activities. However, most firms of solicitors will not need regulation under the new régime. A number of exclusions and exemptions should ensure that solicitors can avoid the need for regulation.

This new edition of the Handbook concentrates upon assisting those firms of solicitors which are not authorised under the Act. It will also assist authorised firms in respect of their non-investment departments where investment activities fall into the 'non-mainstream' category.

The format of this edition follows the same pattern as the two previous editions. The first part (Chapters 1–5) contains an overview of the Financial Services Act 2000 (together with the appropriate secondary legislation) and a detailed look at the way the statutory exclusions and exemptions apply to solicitors.

The second part (Chapters 5–15) covers compliance with the Law Society's Scope Rules, their Conduct of Business Rules and other Law Society Rules applicable to solicitors undertaking investment activities. This part also looks at compliance within particular departments of a solicitor's firm. Having looked at the principles solicitors can then turn their attention to the appropriate chapter to ascertain how the detailed obligations apply to their particular area of practice.

Chapter 16 deals with management aspects of compliance.

My thanks are due to Jackie Corcoran from the Legal Services department at the Law Society for her invaluable help with the manuscript.

Peter Camp
May 2002

List of abbreviations

COBS	FSA Conduct of Business Sourcebook
DPB	Designated Professional Body
FPO	Financial Services and Markets Act 2000 (Financial Promotions) Order 2001
FSA	Financial Services Authority
FSA Guidance	*Professional Firms – the need for authorisation under the Financial Services and Markets Act 2000*
FSMA	Financial Services and Markets Act 2000
IMRO	Investment Management Regulatory Organisation
ISD	Investment Services Directive
NEA Order	Financial Services and Markets Act 2000 (Professions) (Non-Exempt Activities) Order
N2	30 November 2001
OEIC	Open Ended Investment Company
PIA	Personal Investment Authority
PR	Personal representative(s)
RAO	Regulated Activities Order
RPB	Recognised Professional Body
SAYE	Save As You Earn
Scope Rules	Solicitors' Financial Services (Scope) Rules 2001

SFA	Securities and Futures Authority
SIB	Securities and Investment Board
SIBR	Solicitors' Investment Business Rules 1995
SRO	Self Regulating Organisation

Tables of cases and legislation

CASES

Smith *v.* Anderson (1880) 15 Ch 247 . . . . 2.2

STATUTES

Building Society Act 1986
    s.119 . . . . 2.5
Financial Services Act 1986 . . . . . . 1.1,
    3.29–3.30
Financial Services and Markets Act 2000
    Part II
    s.19 . . . . 7.8
        (1) 1.2, 2.1,
        4.2, 7.8
    ss.19–26 . . . . **App A1**
    s.21 . . . . . . 1.5–1.7, 7.1, 7.15
        (8) 7.1
    s.22 . . . . 2.2
    s.23 . . . . 4.25
    Part III
    s.31 . . . . 1.3
    s.23 . . . . 1.6–1.7, 6.11
    s.24 . . . . 1.6
    s.25 . . . . 7.1
    ss.26–8 . . . . 1.7
    s.32 . . . . 1.3
    ss.38–9 . . . . 1.4
    Part IV 1.3
    Part XVII
    s.235 . . . . 2.10, 2.34
    s.323(3)–(5) 4.6
    Part XX 2.1, 3.34, 4.1, 4.2,
    4.6, 4.7, 4.9, 4.12,

    4.17, 4.18, 4.20, 4.23,
    4.25, 4.26, 5.1, 5.8, 5.9,
    5.12, 6.1, 6.10, 6.11,
    7.9–7.11, 7.20, 7.21, 8.18,
    8.19, 8.23, 8.25, 8.26,
    9.21–9.28, 10.7–10.13,
    11.4–11.9, 12.10, 12.12,
    12.15, 12.16, 13.7–13.13,
    14.6–14.10, 15.3, 16.3,
    App A2
    s.325(2) 4.3
    s.327 . . . . . . 4.2, 4.3, 4.8, 6.6,
    6.10, 7.6, 7.8
        (4) 4.5
        (3) 4.4
        (6) 4.16
        (8) 4.5
    s.328 . . . . 4.18
    s.329 . . . . 4.18, 4.25
    s.422 . . . . 4.22, 13.7
Income and Corporation Taxes Act 1988
    s.630 . . . . 4.21
Solicitors Act 1974
    s.33 . . . . 2.26
    s.57 . . . . 15.4
        (5) 15.4
Welfare Reform and Pensions Act 1999
    s.1 . . . . 2.11

STATUTORY INSTRUMENTS

Banking Act 1987 (Exempt Transactions) Reulations 1997, SI 1997/817
    art. 8 . . . . 3.3
Financial Services and Markets Act 2000 (Designated Professional Bodies)
    Order 2001, SI 2001/1226 . . . . 4.1
Financial Services and Markets Act 2000 (Exemption) Order 2001,
    2001/3623 . . . . .1.4, 13.12
Financial Services and Markets Act 2000 (Financial Promotion) Order 2001,
    SI 2001/1335 . . . . .1.5, 4.5, 5.4, 7.3, 12.17, **App A4**
      art. 7(1), (2), (5) 7.2
      art. 8(1), (3) 7.2
      art. 14 . . . . 7.13, 7.15, 7.22, 8.27, 9.29, 10.14, 11.10, 12.17, 13.14, 14.11
        (2) 7.13
      art. 15 . . . . 7.14, 7.22, 8.27, 9.29, 10.14, 11.10, 12.17, 13.14, 14.11
      art. 28 . . . . 7.11, 7.21, 7.22, 8.27, 9.29, 10.14, 11.10, 12.17, 13.14, 14.11
        (2)–(3) 7.11
        (4) 7.2
      art. 28A 7.12, 7.22, 8.27, 9.29, 10.14, 11.10, 12.17, 13.14, 14.11
      art. 48 . . . . 7.15, 7.16
        (4) 7.15
      art. 49 . . . . 7.16
        (4) 7.16
      art. 53 . . . . 7.17, 8.27
      art. 54 . . . . 7.18, 8.27, 9.29
      art. 55 . . . . 7.4, 7.5, 7.9, 7.21, 7.22, 8.27, 9.29,
                                    10.14, 11.10, 12.17, 13.14, 14.11
        (3) 7.8
      art. 55A 7.9, 7.10, 7.13, 7.20–7.22, 8.27, 9.29,
                                    10.14, 11.10, 12.17, 13.14, 14.11
        (2) 7.10
      Schedules 1 and 2 . . . . 7.1
Financial Services and Markets Act 2000 (Financial Promotion) (Amendment)
    Order 2001, SI 2001/2633 . . . . 7.10, 7.12, **App A4**
Financial Services and Markets Act 2000 (Professions) (Non-Exempt Activities)
    Order, SI 2001/1227 . . . . 4.7, 4.9, 4.11, 4.16, 4.22, 6.10,
                                 8.19, 9.22, 9.27, 11.4, 12.11
Financial Services and Markets Act 2000 (Professions) (Non-Exempt Activities)
    (Amendment) Order 2001, SI 2001/682 . . . . 4.7, 9.27
Financial Services and Markets Act 2000 (Regulated Activities) Order 2001,
    SI 2001/544 . . . . **App A3**
      art. 3 . . . . 2.4, 2.12–2.13, 2.22
      art. 5 . . . . 2.20, 2.26
      art. 7 . . . . 2.26, 3.3
      art. 10 . . . . 2.27
      art. 14 . . . . 2.28, 3.4, 9.2
      art. 15 . . . . 2.28, 3.4, 3.24
      art. 16 . . . . 2.28, 3.4
      art. 21 . . . . 2.29, 3.5, 3.32, 9.2
      art. 22 . . . . 2.29, 3.5, 3.7, 3.9, 5.8, 8.16, 9.18, 14.4

Financial Services and Markets Act 2000 (Regulated Activities) Order 2001 (*cont.*)
  art. 25 . . . . 2.30, 3.10, 3.12–3.15, 3.32, 3.33, 9.5
  art. 26 . . . . 3.11, 5.8
  art. 29 . . . . 3.12, 4.20, 8.16, 9.18, 10.5, 12.12, 13.5, 13.8, 14.4, 14.7
  art. 32 . . . . 3.13
  art. 33 . . . . 3.14, 7.14, 12.11, 13.3, 14.3
  art. 34 . . . . 3.15, 13.1
  art. 37 . . . . 2.31, 3.16, 8.2, 10.1–10.2
      (a), (b) 10.1
  art. 38 . . . . 3.16, 4.23, 10.2, 11.2, 13.12
  art. 40 . . . . 2.32, 3.17, 3.25, 3.32, 9.6
  art. 41 . . . . 3.17
  art. 43 . . . . 3.17
  art. 45 . . . . 2.33
  arts. 46–8 . . . . 3.18
  art. 51 . . . . 2.34
  art. 52 . . . . 2.35
  art. 53 . . . . 2.36, 3.19, 3.30, 9.4, 10.4
  art. 54 . . . . 2.36, 3.19
  art. 56–8 . . . . 2.37
  art. 59 . . . . 2.38
  art. 61 . . . . 2.39, 3.20
      (1) 12.7
      (2) 12.7–12.8
      (3) 2.21, 12.7
  art. 62 . . . . 2.39, 3.20, 12.8
      (2) 12.8
  art. 66 . . . . . 3.23–3.30, 3.32, 3.34, 4.23, 7.17, 7.20, 8.9–8.13, 8.16, 8.19, 8.21,
                  8.25, 9.10–9.12, 9.14, 9.15, 9.18, 9.22, 9.24, 10.4–10.6, 11.2
  art. 67 . . . . 3.32, 3.32, 7.8–7.10, 7.21, 8.9–8.11, 8.15–8.17, 9.11–9.13,
                  9.17–9.19, 9.21, 10.4–10.6, 12.11, 12.14, 13.6, 14.5, 15.1
  art. 70 . . . . 3.33, 7.9, 13.4
  art. 74 . . . . 2.20
  art. 75 . . . . 2.6, 2.13, 2.22
  art. 76 . . . . 2.5, 2.8–2.9, 12.13
  art. 77 . . . . 2.6–2.9
  art. 78 . . . . 2.7–2.8
  art. 79 . . . . 2.8
  art. 81 . . . . 2.5, 2.10
  art. 82 . . . . 2.11
  art. 83 . . . . 2.9, 2.14
  arts. 83–87 . . . . 2.12
  art. 84 . . . . 2.15
  art. 85 . . . . 2.16
  art. 86 . . . . 2.17
  art. 87 . . . . 2.18
  art. 88 . . . . 2.21, 2.23
  art. 89 . . . . 2.12, 2.23
Sched. 1
  Part I 2.22
  Part II 2.13

Financial Services and Markets Act 2000 (Regulated Activities) (Amendment)
    Order 2001, SI 2001/3544 .... 2.39, 3.20, 12.7, **App A3**
Solicitors' (Non-Contentious Business) Remuneration Order 1994,
    SI 1994/2616(16) 15.4
Uncertificated Securities Regulations 1995, SI 1995/3272 .... 2.33, 3.18

EUROPEAN

Capital Adequacy Directive 4.14
Investment Services Directive 4.14
Money Laundering Directive 5.12

LAW SOCIETY REGULATIONS, RULES AND CODES

Money Laundering Regulations 1993 .... 5.12
    reg. 5(1) 5.13–5.16
    reg. 7 .... 5.13
    reg. 9 .... 5.13
    regs. 10(1)(d), (f), (g) 5.13
    reg. 11 .... 5.13
    reg. 12 .... 5.14
    reg. 14 .... 5.15
Solicitors' Accounts Rules 1998 .... 4.15
    Part C 5.11
    r.19 .... 15.4
Solicitors' Costs Information and Client Care Code 1999 .... 5.10, 6.3, 16.7
Solicitors' Financial Services (Scope) Rules 2001 .... 4.4, 4.6, 4.7, 4.9, 4.19,
                6.10, 8.18, 8.21–8.23, 9.21–9.28, 10.7–10.12, 11.7, 11.8,
                13.7–13.13, 14.6–14.10, 15.4, 15.5, 16.3, 16.6, 16.9, **App B1**
    r.2 .... 4.10, 6.10
    r.3 .... 4.11, 12.9
    r.4 .... 4.12
        (a) 4.13, 4.14
        (b) 4.14
        (c) 4.15, 5.8
        (d) 4.16
        (e) 4.17
        (f) 4.18
        (g) 4.19
    r.5(1) 4.20, 12.12, 13.8, 14.7
        (2) 4.21, 12.12, 13.9, 14.8
        (3) 4.22, 13.7, 14.6
            (b) 13.7
        (4) 4.23, 12.12, 13.8, 14.7
        (5) 4.24, 13.10

Solicitors' Financial Services (Scope) Rules 2001 (*cont.*)
    r.7(1) 6.5
    r.8 . . . . 4.20, 4.21
    r.12 . . . . 6.8
Solicitors' Financial Services (Conduct of Business) Rules 2001 . . . . . 4.6, 5.1, 5.14,
    5.19, 6.1–6.11, 8.26, 9.28, 10.13, 13.13, 14.10, 16.3, 16.6, 16.7, 16.9, **App B2**
    r.2(a) 6.2
    r.3 . . . . 6.2, 6.3
          (2) 6.3
    r.4 . . . . 6.4
    r.5 . . . . 6.5
    r.6 . . . . 6.6
    r.7 . . . . 6.7
    r.8 . . . . 6.8
    r.9 . . . . 6.5, 6.6
    r.10 . . . . 6.9
Solicitors' Financial Services (Amendment) Rules 2001 . . . . 5.6, 5.9
Solicitors' Incorporated Practice Rules 2001 . . . . 5.6
Solicitors' Introduction and Referral Code 1990 . . . . 3.14, 5.2, 5.5, 12.11
Solicitors' Investment Business Rules 1995 . . . . 4.9, 5.18, 6.4, 6.7
Solicitors' Practice Rules 1990 . . . . 5.2
    r.1 . . . . 3.7, 5.3, 5.9, 6.4, 6.8
    r.2 . . . . 5.4
    r.3 . . . . 5.5
    r.5 . . . . 5.6, 5.9
    r.7 . . . . 5.7
    r.10 . . . . 3.9, 3.14, 4.15, 5.8, 6.6, 7.14, 15.3–15.5, 16.8
    r.12 . . . . 1.4, 5.6, 5.9
          (1)(b) 5.9
    r.15 . . . . 5.10, 6.4, 16.7
Solicitors' Publicity Code 2001 . . . . 5.2, 5.4, 6.3
Solicitors' Separate Business Code 1994 . . . . 5.6

PART I

Regulatory framework

CHAPTER 1

Financial services framework

INTRODUCTION

The Financial Services Act 1986 was brought to the statute books following **1.1** the collapse of two investment businesses in 1981. The Secretary of State commissioned Professor L.C.B. Gower to undertake a review of the then current investor protection provision and to advise on the need for any new legislation. In January 1984 Professor Gower published a report (Cmnd No. 9125) which recommended a new system of statute-backed self regulation, subject to supervision by a Government Regulator.

Although Professor Gower's report received widespread support, two outstanding matters still had to be settled: the number and kind of self-regulatory bodies and the nature of the Government Regulator. Accordingly advisory groups were set up by the Government and following their reports, the Government issued a White Paper in January 1985 entitled *Financial Services in the United Kingdom: A New Framework for Investor Protection* (Cmnd No. 9432). This White Paper was based largely upon Professor Gower's report and formed the basis of the system adopted by the Financial Services Act 1986 which came into effect in April 1988.

Under this system, providers of *investment business* (as defined) had to seek authorisation or claim exempt person status in order to provide defined services. Many professions became subject to the requirement to obtain authorisation despite the fact that they only provided financial services ancillary to their other business. The solicitors' profession fell into this category – few firms of solicitors could avoid authorisation. The Law Society became a Recognised Professional Body (RPB) (as defined in the Financial Services Act 1986) and as such could authorise firms of solicitors for the purposes of the 1986 Act. Other professional bodies were also RPBs capable of authorising their members. Mainstream providers of financial services sought authorisation through membership of an appropriate Self Regulating Organisation (SRO) such as the Securities and Futures Authority (SFA), the Investment Management Regulatory Organisation (IMRO) or the Personal Investment Authority (PIA).

In 1997 the new Labour Government announced the end of self regulation, with a view to bringing the financial services industry under the control of one regulator. The Securities and Investments Board (SIB) (which had overall responsibility for the SROs and the RPBs) was renamed the Financial Services Authority (FSA) with a view to becoming the regulator for the whole industry.

The Financial Services and Markets Act 2000 (FSMA) received the Royal Assent on 14 June 2000. This was the enabling legislation which allowed the new system of regulation to be put into effect. Much of the detail is, however, contained in secondary legislation. The FSA's functions are very wide-ranging. The FSMA provides for the FSA to regulate businesses involved in investments, deposit taking, insurance, mortgages and investment markets.

The FSA also, under the Act, takes responsibility for making rules and issuing codes of practice for those involved in regulated activities. It has wide powers of enforcement and is the prosecuting authority for those criminal activities contained in the FSMA and other regulating statutes.

The FSMA (and thus the new regulatory régime) came into force at midnight on 30 November 2001 (termed N2 by the industry). At that time RPBs ceased to function and in relation to solicitors, the Law Society ceased to be in a position to authorise members of the profession. From that date the requirement to be authorised and the means of authorisation became subject to the terms of the FSMA and appropriate secondary legislation.

Like previous editions of this handbook, the material contained in this publication is limited to those parts of the legislation relevant to solicitors practising as such. Under the previous statutory régime, few solicitors could avoid the need for authorisation. However the Law Society could authorise firms with either a category 1 certificate (restricting firms to undertaking non-discrete investment business only) or a category 2 certificate (allowing firms to undertake both non-discrete and mainstream or discrete investment business). At N2 just over 200 firms of solicitors had category 2 certificates – the vast majority of members of the profession did not carry out (nor did they wish to carry out) mainstream investment business.

Under the new régime *discrete investment business* and non-*discrete* investment business disappear as concepts. Firms of solicitors who wish to undertake *regulated activities* will need authorisation from the only authorising authority, the FSA. However the intention of the legislators is that members of professions (including solicitors) should not be required to be authorised simply to undertake regulated activities which are ancillary to their professional activities. The legislation, therefore, contains a number of exclusions which, potentially, could take solicitors outside the need for authorisation.

It therefore becomes essential for solicitors to understand exactly what activities require authorisation and what exclusions may apply. Further, it must be appreciated that interpreting the legislation incorrectly and carrying out regulated activities without either authorisation or an appropriate exclusion applying, could lead to a criminal offence being committed.

Since only those firms of solicitors who were authorised under the old régime with a category 2 certificate from the Law Society (i.e. those who undertook discrete investment business) are likely to require authorisation from FSA, and these firms number just over 200, this handbook concentrates on the requirements applicable to the vast majority of solicitors' firms, explaining what activities potentially give rise to the requirement for authorisation; what relevant exclusions apply and what compliance obligations arise from the use of these exclusions.

Solicitors who are authorised by FSA become subject to the FSA's Conduct of Business Sourcebook (COBS). This handbook is not intended to provide a commentary on the obligations imposed by the FSA's COBS. However, firms subject to FSA authorisation may find that regulated activities provided to clients ancillary to their legal services may be capable of benefiting from the exclusions available to other firms, despite their mainstream investment activities. Details of this can be found in Chapter 3 below.

THE REGULATORY FRAMEWORK

The general prohibition

FSMA, section 19(1) provides: 1.2

'No person may carry on a regulated activity in the United Kingdom, or purport to do so, unless he is:

(a) an authorised person; or
(b) an exempt person.'

This prohibition is referred to in the FSMA as the *general prohibition*.

Authorised persons

FMSA, section 3.1 defines an authorised person broadly as someone who has   1.3
permission under FSMA, Part IV from the FSA to carry on one or more regulated activities (there are other provisions relating to certain overseas persons). If a firm is authorised (e.g. a firm of solicitors), section 32 provides that the authorisation is in the name of the firm and the authorisation is not affected by any change in membership of the firm. (There are also provisions in section 32 relating to *successor* firms.)

Exempt persons

Section 38 provides that exempt status can be conferred on specified persons   1.4
or on a specified class of person by an *exemption order* made by the Treasury. An order has been made by the Treasury which exempts activities undertaken by the Bank of England, the European Central Bank and the International Monetary Fund.

FSMA, section 39 specifically provides that *appointed representatives* shall be exempt. An appointed representative is someone who has contracted with an Authorised Person (his principal) under the terms of which the appointed representative is permitted or required to carry on business of a prescribed nature and required to comply with prescribed requirements. The principal will have accepted responsibility for the acts and omissions of the appointed representative in relation to the carrying on of that business. Effectively, therefore, the appointed representative will sell the products of his principal. In doing so the appointed representative will be undertaking regulated activities but provided such regulated activities are within the scope of the contract between the appointed representative and his principal, there is no need for the appointed representative to be separately authorised.

Solicitors who wish to undertake regulated activities generally do not have the choice of seeking exempt status as an appointed representative. (This should not be confused with the provision of exempt regulated activities by professions which solicitors will benefit from – see Chapter 3 below.) Solicitors' Practice Rules 1990, Rule 12(1) (as amended by Solicitors' Financial Services (Amendment) Rules 2001) provides, *inter alia*:

> 'Without prejudice to the generality of the principles embodied in rule 1 of these rules, solicitors shall not in connection with investment business:
>
> (a) be appointed representatives; . . . .'

Investment business is defined in Rule 12(5) as any regulated activity defined by FSMA.

For further details of Solicitors' Practice Rules 1990, Rule 12 and the other practice rules applicable to financial services, see below, para. 5.2.

Solicitors may, however, benefit from the provisions of FSMA, section 38 and the Financial Services and Markets Act 2000 (Exemption) Order 2001 which provide exempt status for insolvency practitioners for most regulated activities.

Financial promotions

1.5 FSMA, section 21(1) and (2) provide that no person must, in the course of business communicate an invitation or inducement to engage in investment activity unless that person is authorised or the content of the communication is approved by an authorised person. Under section 21(4) and (5), the Treasury is authorised to make rules regarding the definition of *in the course of business* for the purpose of section 21. The Treasury is also empowered to specify circumstances (including compliance with financial promotion rules) when section 21 does not apply.

The Financial Services and Markets Act 2000 (Financial Promotions) Order 2001, SI 2001/1335 sets out the detailed rules relating to financial promotions and the need for compliance with FSMA, section 21. These details, as they apply to solicitors, appear in Chapter 7 below.

Criminal offences

1.6 FSMA creates three criminal offences arising from a breach of these provisions. First, under section 23, a person who contravenes the general prohibition commits a criminal offence. That is a person who undertakes regulated activities (as defined) without being an authorised or exempt person or otherwise excluded from the provisions of the requirement will commit a criminal offence. The penalty, on summary conviction, is imprisonment for a term not exceeding six months or a fine not exceeding the statutory maximum or both; on indictment, to imprisonment for a term not exceeding two years or a fine, or both. However in proceedings for such an offence it is a defence for the accused to show that he took all reasonable precautions and exercised all due diligence to avoid committing the offence.

Secondly, under FSMA, section 24 a person who is neither an authorised person nor, in relation to the regulated activity in question, an exempt person is guilty of an offence if he:

(a) describes himself (in whatever terms) as an authorised person; or
(b) describes himself (in whatever terms) as an exempt person in relation to the regulated activity; or
(c) behaves, or otherwise holds himself out, in a manner which indicates (or which is reasonably likely to be understood as indicating) that he is an authorised person or an exempt person in relation to that activity.

A person guilty of an offence under this section is liable on summary conviction to imprisonment for a term not exceeding six months or a fine not exceeding level 5 on the standard scale, or both. However if the description is on public display, the maximum fine is level 5 on the standard scale multiplied by the number of days the display continued.

Again the defence of reasonable precaution and due diligence applies.

Thirdly a person who contravenes section 21 (restrictions on financial promotion) is guilty of an offence. For details of this offence see Chapter 7 below.

Civil remedies

1.7 In addition to the criminal offences created by FSMA, the Act also provides for civil remedies for clients or customers who have suffered as a result of breaches of the terms of FSMA. Any agreement made by a person carrying on a regulated activity in contravention of FSMA is unenforceable against the other party (FSMA, section 26). Further the other party in these circumstances may recover any money or property paid or transferred under the agreement and compensation for any loss sustained as a result of parting with money or property.

Of particular note for solicitors is FSMA, section 27. This section provides that an agreement made by an authorised person (who is not in breach of section 21 – the general prohibition) but made in consequence of something said or done by another person in the course of regulated activities carried out by that other person in breach of section 21 is unenforceable against the other party to the agreement. As with section 26, the other party to the agreement may recover any money or property paid or transferred under the agreement and compensation for any loss sustained as a result of parting with money or property.

As is noted in subsequent chapters of this handbook, solicitors should, generally, be able to avoid the need for authorisation, providing appropriate conditions are satisfied. A failure to comply with these conditions will mean that the solicitor is at risk of being in breach of the general prohibition where the solicitor is not an authorised person. The possible effect of being in breach of the general prohibition is:

(a) a criminal offence is committed (section 23);
(b) the contract with the client is unenforceable and compensation can be ordered (section 26); and
(c) if the contract is made between the client and an authorised person, that contract may be unenforceable if entered into as a result of something said or done by the solicitor (section 27).

However, under FSMA, section 28 a breach of sections 26 and 27 need not always lead to the agreement being declared unenforceable. On an application to the court, where the court is satisfied that it is just and equitable, the court may enforce the agreement and any money or property paid may be retained. In determining whether to exercise its discretion, the court must have regard to whether the person carrying out the regulated activity reasonably believed that he was not breaching the general prohibition, or in the case of section 27, whether the authorised person knew that the other person was contravening the general prohibition.

CHAPTER 2

Regulated activities

INTRODUCTION

In order to ascertain whether a solicitor requires authorisation as a result **2.1**
of FSMA, section 19 (the general prohibition), three conditions need to be
satisfied:

(a) there must be a business;
(b) there must be a regulated investment; and
(c) there must be a regulated activity.

Even if, on the face of it, it appears that a solicitor is required to be authorised under the Act (i.e. the three conditions referred to above are satisfied)
there are possible exclusions or exemptions which will avoid the need for
authorisation by FSA. These are dealt with in detail elsewhere in this handbook, but by way of an overview, the three areas of legislation where exclusions or exemptions relevant to solicitors appear are:

(a) in the definition of certain regulated activities. Specific exclusions in the
definitions, if applicable, will ensure that the activity is not regulated;
(b) in the general exclusions. The legislation contains some general
exclusions which if applicable will ensure that the activity is not regulated;
(c) in FSMA, Part XX. This allows certain persons who are regulated by
Designated Professional Bodies (DPBs) to undertake regulated activities
without being authorised by the FSA subject to rules made by the DPB.
These are referred to as *exempt regulated activities*.

All three possibilities need to be taken into account by solicitors in
determining whether they require authorisation under the Act.

REGULATED ACTIVITIES

A business

2.2 FSMA, section 22 provides that

'an activity is a regulated activity for the purposes of this Act if it is an activity of a specified kind *which is carried on by way of business* and relates to an investment of a specified kind'.

There is no definition of *business* in the Act. Business was defined for other purposes in the case of *Smith* v. *Anderson* (1880) 15 Ch 247 as

'a series of acts which if successful produce gain'.

There is no doubt that persons may carry on more than one business and that a business carried on as a sideline may nonetheless be caught and potentially require authorisation.

In some limited circumstances solicitors may be able to show that they have been appointed as a trustee (which may involve them in certain regulated activities) but that the appointment has been in their personal capacity and not in their capacity as a solicitor. In these circumstances, provided that none of the work relating to the administration of the trust fund is carried on by the solicitor from his office, activities in relation to the trust fund should not be regulated.

Note, however, that the absence of a fee for work done within a solicitor's firm will not take that work outside the requirements of the FSMA.

Regulated Activities Order

Details of what amounts to a *regulated activity* and what is defined as an *investment of a specified kind* within the meaning of section 22 do not appear in the FSMA. These items are defined in the Financial Services and Markets Act 2000 (Regulated Activities) Order 2001, SI 2001/544. The full text of the Regulated Activities Order (RAO) appears in Appendix A3.

Specified investments

2.3 Specified investments are defined in RAO, articles 74–89. Any activity relating to investments not defined in the RAO will be outside the scope of regulation by the FSMA. The 16 investments listed in the RAO are grouped into three categories:

(a) Securities;
(b) Contractually based investments; and
(c) Others (i.e. investments which are neither securities nor contractually based investments).

Solicitors generally, will be involved in the first (securities) and second (con-tractually based investments). Solicitors' involvement in the third category of investments will be less common.

Securities

Securities are defined in RAO, article 3 as meaning (except where the context **2.4** otherwise requires) any investment of the kind specified by any of articles 76–82 or, so far as relevant to any such investment, article 89.

Shares (article 76)

These include shares or stock in the share capital of: **2.5**

(a) any body corporate (wherever incorporated), and
(b) any unincorporated body constituted under the law of a country or territory outside the United Kingdom.

Thus private and public, listed and unlisted shares are caught. Excluded from the definition are shares in Open Ended Investment Companies (OEICs), shares in building societies (unless they are deferred shares for the purposes of the Building Society Act 1986, section 119) and shares in industrial or provident societies and credit unions (unless transferable shares).

It should, however be noted that shares in OEICs, although not caught as investments under article 76 will be caught as investments under article 81 (see below, para. 2.10).

Instruments creating or acknowledging indebtedness (article 77)

These include debentures, debenture stock, loan stock, bonds and certificates **2.6** of deposit or any other instrument creating or acknowledging indebtedness.
Excluded from this article are:

(a) an instrument acknowledging or creating indebtedness for, or for money borrowed to defray, the consideration payable under a contract for the supply of goods or services;
(b) a cheque or other bill of exchange, a banker's draft or a letter of credit (but not a bill of exchange accepted by a banker);
(c) a banknote, a statement showing a balance on a current, deposit or savings account, a lease or other disposition of property, or a heritable security; and
(d) a contract of insurance.

As a result of the exceptions, solicitors who act for bankers and who arrange for a debenture to be issued to enable a company to borrow money to buy, for example plant and machinery, will be outside the scope of the

FSMA's regulation. Further, since it could be argued that a bank statement acknowledges indebtedness, the exclusion ensures that this is not the case. As a result of this provision (and the previous exception applying to building societies) bank and building society deposit accounts are not investments for the purposes of the Act's definition.

It should be noted, however, that contracts of insurance which acknowledge indebtedness (for example a single premium bond issued by an insurance company) although not caught as an investment under article 77 will be caught under article 75 (see below para. 2.13).

Government and public securities (article 78)

2.7   These include loan stock, bonds and other instruments creating or acknowledging indebtedness, issued by or on behalf of any of the following:

(a)   the government of the United Kingdom;
(b)   the Scottish Administration;
(c)   the Executive Committee of the Northern Ireland Assembly;
(d)   the National Assembly for Wales;
(e)   the government of any country or territory outside the United Kingdom;
(f)   a local authority in the United Kingdom or elsewhere.

The exclusions referred to above (see para. 2.6) relating to article 77 also apply to this category of investments. Further, any instrument creating or acknowledging indebtedness in respect of deposits or otherwise in connection with the National Savings Bank is excluded.

As a result of this provision, the following investments are outside the scope of the Act:

(a)   National Savings Certificates;
(b)   yearly plan contracts;
(c)   income bonds;
(d)   capital bonds;
(e)   premium bonds;
(f)   SAYE (linked to share option schemes, which are not themselves covered).

Instruments giving entitlement to investments (article 79)

2.8   Warrants and other instruments entitling the holder to subscribe for any investments of the kind specified by article 76, 77 or 78. It is immaterial whether the investments are for the time being in existence or identifiable. Any investment falling within this article is deemed not to be covered by the articles relating to options, futures, or contracts for differences (see below, paras. 2.14–16).

Certificates representing certain securities (article 80)

These are certificates which confer contractual or property rights in respect **2.9** of any investment specified by articles 76–79, being an investment held by someone (the owner) other than the certificate holder, where the transfer may be effected without the consent of the owner. Excluded from this article are those rights consisting of an investment falling within article 83 (options) – see below, para. 2.14.

Units in a collective investment scheme (article 81)

A *collective investment scheme* is defined in FSMA, section 235. The definition **2.10** covers any arrangements with respect to property of any description (including money) the purpose or effect of which is to enable participants taking part in the arrangements (whether by becoming owners of the property or any part of it or otherwise) to participate in or receive profits or income arising from the acquisition, holding, management or disposal of the property or sums paid out of such profits or income. The arrangements must be such that the participants do not have day-to-day control over the management of the property. The arrangements must also have either or both of the following characteristics:

(a) the contributions of the participants and the profits or income out of which payments are to be made to them are pooled;
(b) the property is managed as a whole by or on behalf of the operator of the scheme.

Units in a collective investment scheme and shares in and securities of an open-ended investment company are caught under this heading. The most common forms of investment under this heading are units in a regulated unit trust scheme and shares in an open-ended investment company.

Rights under a stakeholder pension scheme (article 82)

A stakeholder pension scheme is defined in Welfare Reform and Pensions Act **2.11** 1999, section 1.

Contractually based investments

RAO, article 3 defines a *contractually based investment* as meaning: **2.12**

(a) rights under a qualifying contract of insurance;
(b) any investment of the kind specified by any of articles 83, 84, 85 and 87; or
(c) any investment of the kind specified by article 89 so far as relevant to an investment falling within (a) or (b).

Rights under a contract of insurance (article 75)

2.13 A contract of insurance is defined in RAO, article 3 as a contract of long-term insurance or a contract of general insurance. Only *qualifying contracts of insurance* are caught as contractually based investments. These are defined in RAO as meaning contracts of long-term insurance which are not:

(a) reinsurance contracts; or

(b) contracts in respect of which the following conditions are met:

    (i) the benefits under the contract are payable only on death or in respect of incapacity due to injury, sickness or infirmity;

    (ii) the contract provides that benefits are payable on death (other than death due to an accident) only where the death occurs within ten years of the date on which the life of the person in question was first insured under the contract, or where the death occurs before that person attains a specified age not exceeding 70 years;

    (iii) the contract has no surrender value, or the consideration consists of a single premium and the surrender value does not exceed that premium; and

    (iv) the contract makes no provision for its conversion or extension in a manner which would result in it ceasing to comply with any of the above conditions).

Long-term insurance is important for solicitors as it catches such insurance contracts as endowment or pension policies and single premium bonds issued by insurance companies. The full definition of long-term insurance is to be found in RAO, Schedule 1, Part II (see Appendix A3).

The exclusions to the definition ensure that term assurance contracts are not caught as long-term insurance. The intention of the Act as it applies to solicitors is to catch contracts of insurance or annuities which include an investment element. Thus life policies having an endowment or investment element will be caught as long-term; those which are pure term assurance are not.

Options (article 83)

2.14 Options to acquire or dispose of investments which include:

(a) a security or contractually based investment (for the definition of these terms, see above paras. 2.4, 2.12);

(b) currency of the United Kingdom or any other country or territory;

(c) palladium, platinum, gold or silver; or

(d) an option to acquire or dispose of an investment of the kind specified by this article by virtue of paragraph (a), (b) or (c).

Solicitors who advise on or make arrangements in respect of share options may find themselves involved in a regulated activity (subject to what is said later about regulated activities and exclusions).

Futures (article 84)

Rights under a contract for the sale of a commodity or property of any other **2.15** description under which delivery is to be made at a future date at a price agreed upon when the contract is made, is itself an investment. However the article does not apply if the contract is made for commercial and not investment purposes. The common form of investments caught by this article are commodity and financial futures. Article 84(4)–(7) expand upon the basic exclusion giving indications as to whether a contract is to be taken as being made for a commercial or other purpose.

Contracts for differences (article 85)

This article covers rights under a contract for differences or under any other **2.16** contract the purpose or pretended purpose of which is to secure a profit or avoid a loss by reference to fluctuations in the value or price of property of any description or in an index or other factor designed for that purpose in the contract. There is an exception which applies to contracts where it is intended that the property to which it relates is to be delivered. Examples of contracts likely to fall within this paragraph would be currency or interest rate swaps or futures on stock exchange indices.

Lloyd's syndicate capacity and syndicate membership (article 86)

This article covers the underwriting capacity of a Lloyd's syndicate and a **2.17** person's membership (or prospective membership) of a Lloyd's syndicate.

Funeral plan contracts (article 87)

A funeral plan contract is a contract under which: **2.18**

(a) a customer makes one or more payments to the provider; and
(b) the provider undertakes to provide, or secure that another person provides, a funeral in the United Kingdom for the customer (or some other person who is living at the date when the contract is entered into) on his death;

unless, at the time of entering into the contract, the customer and the provider intend or expect the funeral to occur within one month.

Other specified investments

2.19 There are some investments which fall neither into the definition of *securities* nor into the definition of *contractually based investments*. These are noted as follows:

Deposits (article 74)

2.20 A *deposit* is defined in RAO, article 5 as a sum of money paid on terms under which it will be repaid, with or without interest or a premium, either on demand or at a time or in circumstances agreed by or on behalf of the person making the payment and the person receiving it. Note, however the important exclusion for practising solicitors – see below, para. 2.26.

Regulated mortgage contracts (article 88)

2.21 A contract is a regulated mortgage contract if, at the time it is entered into, the following conditions are met:

(a) the contract is one under which a person (the lender) provides credit to an individual or to trustees (the borrower);

(b) the contract provides for the obligation of the borrower to repay to be secured by a first legal mortgage on land (other than timeshare accommodation) in the United Kingdom;

(c) at least 40 per cent of that land is used, or is intended to be used, as or in connection with a dwelling by the borrower or (in the case of credit provided to trustees) by an individual who is a beneficiary of the trust, or by a related person (RAO, article 61(3) as amended).

Contracts of insurance (article 75)

2.22 As noted above (para. 2.13) a contract of insurance is defined in RAO, article 3 as a contract of long-term insurance or a contract of general insurance. Long-term insurance contracts are generally caught as *contractually based investments*; general insurance contracts, although regulated by FSMA, are neither *securities* nor *contractually based investments*. For the full definition of general insurance, see RAO, Schedule 1, Part I (Appendix A3 below). The definition includes accident and sickness policies, motor insurance policies and property insurance.

Rights and interests in investments

Rights and interests in investments (Article 89)

As a *catch all* provision the definition of investments also includes *any right* **2.23**
to and interests in anything which is specified by any other provision of this Part
(other than article 88). Regulation under the Act cannot be avoided by
dealing in interests in investments rather than in the investments themselves.
In these circumstances the interests are investments.

Where the rights or interests are in investments which are *securities* the
rights and interests themselves will be securities; where the rights and interests are in *contractually based investments*, the rights and interests will be
contractually based investments.

Certain rights and interests are excluded from the definition. First, as can
be seen from the wording of the definition, rights and interests in article 88
investments (regulated mortgage contracts) are excluded. Further, article 89
does not apply to interests under the trusts of an occupational pension
scheme.

Conclusion

It should be noted that only those investments noted above fall to be regu- **2.24**
lated by the FSMA provisions. Any activity in relation to an investment not
defined in the RAO will give rise to no regulation. The most common
unregulated investments are:

(a) bank deposit accounts and building society deposit or share accounts;
(b) land (although a unitised property fund may be a collective investment
    scheme and thus caught by the Act's regulatory framework);
(c) currency and precious metals (although currency options and certain
    precious metal options are caught as investments); and
(d) tangible assets such as works of art, stamp collections, vintage cars, etc.

The most common investments from the point of view of a solicitor's
practice are:

(a) shares;
(b) debentures;
(c) government and public securities;
(d) unit and investment trusts and shares in open-ended investment
    companies;
(e) endowment/pension policies; and
(f) single premium bonds issued by life companies.

Regulated activities and the need for authorisation

2.25 The regulated activities are set out in RAO, Part II (see Appendix A3). These activities, if they involve specified investments as defined, and constitute business activities, will potentially involve the solicitor in the need for authorisation. However, as noted above, some of the definitions contain specific exclusions. In addition there are further general exclusions and the possibility of solicitors using the *exempt regulated activities* route to avoid authorisation. It is, though vital for solicitors to understand what activities potentially give rise to the need for authorisation.

Accepting deposits (article 5(1))

2.26 The acceptance of deposits (defined above, see para. 2.20) is a regulated activity if the money received is lent to others or if the business is financed wholly or to a material extent out of the capital or interest on the money received by way of deposit.

The Law Society expressed concern over the possible impact on solicitors of this activity. They believed that in certain circumstances solicitors could be caught by article 5 through holding client money in their client bank account. Since under Solicitors Act 1974, section 33 interest on client money belongs to the solicitor, there was a possibility that some practices could be financed to a material extent out of interest on the money received by way of deposit.

To avoid any possible difficulties RAO, article 7 excludes sums received by practising solicitors from this activity if the sum is received in the course of their profession. *Practising solicitors*, for these purposes, include recognised bodies (i.e. incorporated practices), registered foreign lawyers who are members of multinational partnerships, and registered European lawyers.

Effecting and carrying out contracts of insurance as principal (article 10)

2.27 Effecting a contract of insurance as principal is a regulated activity as is carrying out a contract of insurance as principal. Although, as noted above (para. 2.13) both long-term and general insurance are caught by these provisions, neither of these activities should cause problems for solicitors. Article 10 catches insurance companies acting as principal in the provision of insurance services.

Dealing in investments as principal (article 14)

2.28 This activity is defined as buying, selling, subscribing for or underwriting securities or contractually based investments as principal. Article 14 does not apply where the investment is funeral plan contract.

Further, under an exclusion contained in article 15, article 14 will not apply to transactions which relate to securities or to an assignment of a qualifying contract of insurance, unless a person:

(a) holds himself out as willing to buy, sell, etc. such investments at prices determined by him generally and continuously; or
(b) holds himself out as engaging in the business of buying such investments with a view to selling them; or
(c) holds himself out as engaging in the business of underwriting such investments; or
(d) regularly solicits members of the public for the purpose of inducing them to enter into transactions specified by article 14.

Article 16 provides that article 14 will not apply to transactions relating to a contractually based investment where the transaction is entered into with or through an authorised person.

Solicitors will rarely deal in investments as principal. In the vast majority of cases where solicitors buy, sell or subscribe for investments they will do so on behalf of clients (and as such may be caught under the *dealing as agent* activity – see below para. 2.29). Where, however, solicitors are trustees or personal representatives and they buy or sell securities or contractually based investments in their own name (albeit in their capacity as either trustee or personal representative) they could be said to be dealing as principal. However the articles 15 and 16 exclusions noted above should ensure that in these circumstances no regulated activity is undertaken.

Dealing in investments as agent (article 21)

Again this involves buying, selling, subscribing for or underwriting securities **2.29** or contractually based investments (excluding funeral plan contracts). Buying or selling investments as agent could catch those situations where a solicitor purchases investments in his own name for the account of a client or where solicitors instruct, e.g. stockbrokers to buy or sell investments on behalf of clients and the contract note is made out in the solicitor's name. However, where solicitors are instructed by a client simply to submit the client's application to buy or sell investments they may be caught by the *arrangements* activity (see below, para. 2.30).

Article 22 excludes this activity if the person enters into a transaction as agent for a client with or through an authorised person and:

(a) the transaction is entered into on advice given to the client by an authorised person; or
(b) it is clear in all the circumstances that the client, in his capacity as an investor, is not seeking and has not sought advice from the solicitor as to the merits of the client entering the transaction (or if the client has

sought advice the solicitor has declined to give it but has recommended the client to seek advice from an authorised person).

The above exclusion does not apply if the agent receives from any person other than the client any pecuniary reward or advantage, for which he does not account to the client, arising out of his entering into the transaction.

For details of the practical application of this important exclusion, see below, para. 3.5.

Arranging deals in investments (article 25)

2.30 This activity is defined as

'(1) Making arrangements for another person (whether as principal or agent) to buy, sell, subscribe for or underwrite a particular investment which is –

(a) a security,

(b) a contractually based investment . . . [or]

(2) Making arrangements with a view to a person who participates in the arrangements buying, selling, subscribing for or underwriting investments falling within paragraph (1)(a), (b) . . .'

Clearly these arrangements will be common in a solicitor's office. Solicitors who arrange for their clients to buy or sell investments (e.g. shares or endowment policies) will be caught by this paragraph. However, it is important to note that the solicitor must be involved in some activity, for example the completion of an application form, or the submission of an application form, before there is an arrangement.

Excluded from article 25 are:

(a) arrangements which do not or would not bring about the transaction to which the arrangements relate;

(b) arrangements made with or through an authorised person (a similar exclusion to that noted above (dealing as agent). The exclusion will not apply where the person receives any pecuniary reward, etc. as noted above, para. 2.29;

(c) introductions where a person introduces a client to an authorised or exempt person and the introduction is made with a view to the provision of independent advice;

(d) arrangements made by a company for the purposes of issuing its own shares or share warrants; and

(e) arrangements made by any person for the purposes of issuing his own debentures or debenture warrants.

For details of the practical application of this important exclusion, see below, para. 3.10.

Article 25(2) catches commission agreements. If a solicitor has a commission agreement under the terms of which the life office agrees to pay the solicitor a commission when the solicitor introduces a client to the life office, this commission agreement is an arrangement with a view to a person who participates in the arrangement (i.e. the life office) selling investments (i.e. the life policy). However, excluded from article 25(2) are arrangements which a person makes with a view to transactions into which he enters (or is to enter) as principal or agent for some other person (article 28(2)). This exclusion should ensure solicitors (entering into arrangements as principal or agent for their clients) will not be caught, even if commission agreements are in place. It is, however, unlikely to be of concern to most unauthorised firms.

Managing investments (article 37)

This activity is defined as managing assets belonging to another in circum- **2.31**
stances involving the exercise of discretion where:

> '(a) the assets consist of or include any investment which is a security or a contractually based investment; or
> (b) the arrangements for their management are such that the assets may consist of or include such investments, and either the assets have at any time since 29th April 1988 done so, or the arrangements have at any time (whether before or after that date) been held out as arrangements under which the assets would do so'.

Excluded from this activity is management arising under a power of attorney where all routine or day-to-day decisions relating to the investments are taken by an authorised or exempt person (for the practical application of this exclusion, see below, para. 3.16).

Management is an important head as far as solicitors are concerned since it will catch, in many circumstances, solicitors who are trustees, personal representatives, donees under powers of attorney, and receivers appointed by the Court of Protection. It should be noted that only *discretionary* management is caught; administrative activities (such as simply acting for trustees and personal representatives) do not constitute *management*. However, it is likely that firms carrying on non-discretionary management will also be involved in other activities which could potentially be regulated activities, e.g. dealing as agent for their clients or arranging deals.

Safeguarding and administering investments (article 40)

The activity consists of both: **2.32**

(a) the safeguarding of assets belonging to another, and
(b) the administration of those assets

or arranging for one or more other persons to carry on that activity.

The assets in question must consist of securities or contractually based investments or the arrangements for their safeguarding and administration are such that the assets may consist of or include such investments, and either the assets have at any time since 1 June 1997 done so, or the arrangements have at any time (whether before or after that date) been held out as ones under which such investments would be safeguarded and administered.

For the purposes of this article it is immaterial that title to the assets safeguarded and administered is held in uncertificated form.

The safeguarding of materials (i.e. documents of title to investments) by itself is not sufficient. It is necessary for some other act of administration to be undertaken by a firm before the regulated activity applies. This could include collecting dividends relating to the investment, preparing tax returns or proxy voting.

Arrangements with a *qualifying* custodian (i.e. one authorised or exempt under FSMA) will be excluded where the custodian has accepted responsibility for safeguarding and administration or where a solicitor has merely introduced a client to a qualifying custodian. Further, for the purposes of article 40, the following activities do not constitute administration:

(a) providing information regarding the number of units or value of any assets in custody;

(b) converting currency; or

(c) receiving documents solely for the purpose of onward transmission to, from or at the direction of the person to whom the investment belongs.

Sending dematerialised instructions (article 45)

2.33 Sending, on behalf of another person, dematerialised instructions relating to a security is a specified kind of activity, where those instructions are sent by means of a relevant system in respect of which an operator is approved under the Uncertificated Securities Regulations 1995.

Article 48 contains details of an exclusion where the person on whose behalf the instructions are sent is an offeror making a takeover offer. For details of this exclusion, see RAO, article 45 (Appendix A3).

Establishing, etc. a collective investment scheme (article 51)

2.34 Collective investment schemes are defined in FSMA, section 235 (see above para. 2.10). The following activities in relation to collective investment schemes are caught as regulated activities:

(a) establishing, operating or winding up a collective investment scheme;

(b) acting as a trustee of an authorised unit trust scheme; and

(c) acting as the depositary or sole director of an open-ended investment company.

There are no relevant exclusions and solicitors wishing to undertake any of these activities will require authorisation.

Establishing, etc. a stakeholder pension scheme (article 52)

Establishing, operating or winding up a stakeholder pension scheme is a regulated activity. Again, there are no relevant exclusions and solicitors wishing to undertake this activity will require authorisation. **2.35**

Advising on investments (article 53)

This activity is defined as where advice is: **2.36**

(a) given to a person in his capacity as an investor or potential investor, or in his capacity as agent for an investor or a potential investor; and

(b) advice on the merits of his doing any of the following (whether as principal or agent):

   (i) buying, selling, subscribing for or underwriting a particular investment which is a security or a contractually based investment, or

   (ii) exercising any right conferred by such an investment to buy, sell, subscribe for or underwrite such an investment.

Certain newspaper and broadcast advice is excluded from this article – see RAO, article 54 (Appendix A3).

Thus, as drafted, the article is extremely wide. It will catch any form of advice given to clients by solicitors on the merits of, for example, buying or selling investments. However the inclusion of the word *particular* in the article makes it clear that generic advice is not caught, i.e. general advice on the benefits of an endowment mortgage compared to say a straight repayment mortgage will be outside the scope of this article.

In many ways, this activity is the most dangerous activity for solicitors who may be tempted to give advice without realising the consequences of such advice. Off-the-cuff advice to clients on the merits of buying or selling investments must be avoided unless the solicitor is authorised or is able to bring the advice within one of the appropriate exclusions. (For details of the exclusions, see below, para. 3.19.) Note however, the activity only applies to advice on securities or contractually based investments. Advice given on the merits of entering into, for example, general insurance policies or regulated mortgage contracts will not be caught by this article.

Activities relating to Lloyd's (articles 56, 57 and 58)

2.37 Advising a person to become or continue or cease to be a member of a particular Lloyds' syndicate is a regulated activity. So too is managing the underwriting capacity of a Lloyd's syndicate as a managing agent at Lloyd's.

No appropriate exclusions apply to these activities. Thus, to advise a person to become a member of a particular Lloyd's syndicate, for example, a solicitor will need authorisation.

Funeral plan contracts (article 59)

2.38 Entering as provider into a funeral plan contract is a regulated activity.

Regulated mortgage contracts (article 61)

2.39 Regulated mortgage contracts are defined in article 61(3) (see above para. 2.21). Under article 61(1), entering into a regulated mortgage contract as lender is a regulated activity. Further under article 61(2), administering a regulated mortgage contract is also a specified kind of activity, but only where the contract is entered into by way of business after the coming into force of this article. The words *by way of business* were inserted by the Financial Services and Markets Act 2000 (Regulated Activities) (Amendment) Order 2001, SI 2001/3544. This amendment ensures that administering *private* mortgages will not be caught by this article.

Administering a regulated mortgage contract means either or both of:

(a) notifying the borrower of changes in interest rates or payments due under the contract, or of other matters of which the contract requires him to be notified; and

(b) taking any necessary steps for the purposes of collecting or recovering payments due under the contract from the borrower.

Unlike most of the provisions contained in FSMA and RAO, it was intended that this particular article would not come into force until 1 September 2002. However, the government has announced its intention to extend the regulation of mortgages in the future and has decided not to bring in the limited regulation contained in FSMA until full regulation applies (probably sometime in 2004).

There are exclusions contained in RAO, article 62. A person who is not an authorised person does not administer a regulated mortgage contract in accordance with article 62(2) where he:

(a) arranges for an authorised person with permission to carry on an activity of that kind, to administer the contract; or

(b) administers the contract himself during a period of not more than one month beginning with the day on which any such arrangement comes to an end.

Further a person who is not an authorised person does not carry on an activity of the kind specified by article 61(2) in relation to a regulated mortgage contract where he administers the contract pursuant to an agreement with an authorised person who has permission to carry on an activity of that kind.

CONCLUSION

It is likely that solicitors will be most commonly involved in the following regulated activities: **2.40**

(a) dealing as agent;
(b) arranging deals;
(c) managing investments;
(d) safeguarding and administering investments; and
(e) investment advice.

CHAPTER 3

Statutory exclusions

INTRODUCTION

3.1 Solicitors who undertake any of the regulated activities defined in Chapter 2 above will potentially require authorisation from the FSA. However, in most cases an appropriate exclusion or exemption should ensure that solicitors can avoid the need for authorisation. The RAO contains a number of exclusions – some incorporated into the definitions of regulated activities (as briefly noted in Chapter 2); others of a more general nature. Both types of exclusions are dealt with in detail in this chapter. In Chapter 4 the exempt regulated activities régime is considered. Solicitors must bear in mind that where regulated activities are undertaken they must be able to show that either any exclusion will apply or that the activity can be treated as exempt. A failure to do so could lead to both criminal and civil liability (see above paras. 1.6–7).

The FSA has issued guidance to the professions (including the solicitors' profession). This guidance has been issued as FSA Guidance – August 2001, and is called *Professional firms – the need for authorisation under the Financial Services and Markets Act 2000* (see Appendix C1). The guidance is extremely helpful in interpreting the various exclusions and the exempt régime. It is referred to throughout this handbook as FSA Guidance and is quoted with the kind permission of the FSA. The Preface to the Guidance states:

'The Guidance contains views expressed by the FSA as to the meaning and interpretation of various statutory provisions. The FSA's views will not bind a court of law and it will remain the responsibility of each firm to satisfy itself as to whether or not it will need authorisation under the Act.'

However, in paragraph 1.1.1 G of the FSA Guidance it provides:

'Nevertheless, any person acting in line with the guidance may have recourse to the defence provided in section 23(3) of the Act that he took all reasonable precautions and exercised all due diligence to avoid committing an offence'

(see also above, para. 1.6).

SPECIFIC EXCLUSIONS UNDER THE RAO

A number of the definitions of regulated activities contained in the RAO **3.2** contain specific exclusions. If solicitors are able to bring themselves within the scope of these specific exclusions, they will not be undertaking regulated activities and, in respect of those activities to which the specific exclusions apply, they will not need to be authorised.

Accepting deposits (article 5(1))

As noted above, para. 2.26, the acceptance of deposits (defined above, see **3.3** para. 2.20) is a regulated activity if the money received is lent to others or if the business is financed wholly or to a material extent out of the capital or interest on the money received by way of deposit.

RAO, article 7 excludes sums received by practising solicitors from this activity if the sum is received in the course of their profession. This continues the exemption contained in the Banking Act 1987 (Exempt Transactions) Regulations 1997, article 8. *Practising solicitors*, for these purposes, include recognised bodies (i.e. incorporated practices), registered foreign lawyers who are members of multinational partnerships, and registered European lawyers. As a result of this exclusion, solicitors should not be concerned about any possible regulated activity arising from the acceptance of deposits.

Dealing in investments as principal (article 14)

As noted above (para. 2.28) this activity is defined as buying, selling, sub- **3.4** scribing for or underwriting securities or contractually based investments as principal.

There are three statutory exclusions which can be applied to avoid dealing as principal being a regulated activity.

(a) Article 14 expressly states that this activity does not apply where the investment is a funeral plan contract (it is, perhaps, unlikely in any event that a solicitor would be involved in dealing as principal in relation to funeral plan contracts);

(b) Article 15 provides that article 14 will not apply to transactions which relate to securities or to an assignment of a qualifying contract of insurance, unless a person:

(i) holds himself out as willing to buy, sell, etc. such investments at prices determined by him generally and continuously; or

(ii) holds himself out as engaging in the business of buying such investments with a view to selling them; or

(iii) holds himself out as engaging in the business of underwriting such investments; or

(iv)   regularly solicits members of the public for the purpose of inducing them to enter into transactions specified by article 14; and

(c)   Article 16 provides that article 14 will not apply to transactions relating to a contractually based investment where the transaction is entered into with or through an authorised person.

Where a solicitor is a trustee and buys investments in his own name for the trust fund he will *prima facie* be dealing as principal within article 14. However the exclusion noted in (b) or (c) above is likely to exclude this activity from being a regulated activity. Further, firms of solicitors who invest their profits in short-term investments in order, for example to create a tax reserve, will be excluded by this same provision from the necessity of authorisation arising out of that activity.

Dealing in investments as agent (article 21)

3.5   This activity, as noted above (para. 2.29) involves buying, selling, subscribing for or underwriting securities or contractually based investments (excluding funeral plan contracts). Buying or selling investments as agent could catch those situations where a solicitor purchases investments in his own name for the account of a client or where solicitors instruct, e.g. stockbrokers to buy or sell investments on behalf of clients and the contract note is made out in the solicitor's name.

There is a very important exclusion contained in article 22. The dealing as agent activity will be excluded if a solicitor enters into a transaction as agent for a client with or through an authorised person and one of two alternative conditions are satisfied together with, in either case, a further condition relating to pecuniary reward. The alternative conditions are:

(a)   the transaction is entered into on advice given to the client by an authorised person; or

(b)   it is clear in all the circumstances that the client, in his capacity as an investor, is not seeking and has not sought advice from the solicitor as to the merits of the client entering the transaction (or if the client has sought advice the solicitor has declined to give it but has recommended the client to seek advice from an authorised person).

The further condition provides that the exclusion does not apply if the agent receives from any person other than the client any pecuniary reward or advantage, for which he does not account to the client, arising out of his entering into the transaction.

These points will be dealt with individually.

Authorised person

An authorised person is someone who is authorised by FSA. It is necessary **3.6**
that the dealing is undertaken as agent for the client with or through an
authorised person. However, paragraph 1.16.3 G of the FSA Guidance provides that, in the FSA's view, an agent will be entering into a transaction
through an authorised person where:

(a) the authorised person also enters into the transaction as agent (whether
     for the agent's client or the counterparty to the trade) or arranges for the
     transaction to be effected; or
(b) where the transaction is arranged lawfully by an appointed representative
     of an authorised person.

Advice given to the client by an authorised person

It is not necessary for the advice to be obtained by the firm from the auth- **3.7**
orised person. The requirement is that the authorised person has given advice
to the client. The client may have received the advice directly from the
authorised person or through the agency of some other third party.

Further, where a firm of solicitors merely passes on the advice of an
authorised person without any comment or endorsement, the solicitor has
not given investment advice and the client will be deemed to have been given
the advice by the authorised person. Solicitors must be very careful to avoid
commenting on the advice of the authorised person. Whilst the advice would
still be treated as the advice of the authorised person (thus allowing the exclusion in article 22 to apply), the solicitor would, in these circumstances, have
given investment advice and, without authority, would have to be satisfied
that another appropriate exclusion or exemption applied.

Although article 22 does not require the authorised person to be independent, a solicitor who obtained or passed on the advice of a non-independent
authorised person would not be discharging his or her obligations under
Practice Rule 1 regarding independence (see below, para. 5.3).

The FSA Guidance provides, however, that a solicitor may give legal
advice, not being advice on the merits of entering into the transaction as an
investor, and still be able to use this exclusion.

The client has not sought the advice of solicitor as to merits, etc.

If the client has not received the advice of an authorised person it may still **3.8**
be possible to rely upon this exclusion if the alternative condition set out in
paragraph 22 applies. This requires the solicitor to be satisfied that in all the
circumstances the client, in his capacity as an investor, is not seeking and has
not sought advice from the solicitor as to the merits of the client entering the
transaction (or if the client has sought advice the solicitor has declined to

give it but has recommended the client to seek advice from an authorised person). This is, in essence, an *execution-only* transaction.

Whilst it might be possible in limited circumstances for solicitors to bring themselves within the requirements of this condition, it should be remembered that the solicitor/client relationship could suggest that in some cases, the client might reasonably expect the firm to indicate if the transaction was inappropriate. If this is the case, it would not be possible for the solicitor to rely upon this condition being satisfied unless the solicitor has recommended the client to seek advice from an authorised person and the client has declined to do so. (For further comment on *execution-only* transactions, see below, para. 6.8.)

Pecuniary reward or advantage

3.9   Even if the conditions noted above are satisfied, a solicitor will not be able to use this exclusion if the solicitor receives from any person other than the client any pecuniary reward or advantage, for which he does not account to the client, arising out of his entering into the transaction. Clearly this envisages the solicitor retaining commission from the dealing activity. If commission is retained there is a danger that the solicitor will not be able to bring himself within the terms of the exclusion. It is vital, therefore, that the firm's commission policy is reviewed and is capable of ensuring that this exclusion is available to the firm.

The starting point with regard to commissions must be the Solicitors' Practice Rules 1990, Rule 10. This provides:

> 'Solicitors shall account to their clients for any commission received of more than £20 unless, having disclosed to the client in writing the amount or basis of calculation of the commission or (if the precise amount or basis cannot be ascertained) an approximation thereof, they have their client's agreement to retain it.'

Practice Rule 10 applies to any commission received by a solicitor (it is not limited to commissions received from investment activities). Firms should already have in place systems for dealing with the receipt of commissions. Many firms will wish to use the exclusion in article 22 to avoid the *dealing as agent* activity giving rise to a requirement for authorisation. It is important that a proper system for commissions is adopted by all fee-earners – getting it wrong could lead to the loss of the article 22 exclusion and criminal liability.

Paragraph 1.9.1 G of FSA Guidance provides:

> 'The FSA considers that, in order for a professional firm to be accounting to his client . . ., the firm must treat any commission or other pecuniary benefit received from third parties . . . as held to the order of the client. A professional firm will not be accounting to his client simply by telling the client that the firm will receive commission. Unless the client agrees to the firm keeping the commission it belongs

to the client and must be paid to the client. There is no de minimis below which the professional firm may retain the sum. In the FSA's opinion, the condition would be satisfied by the professional firm paying over to the client any third party payment it receives. Otherwise, it would be satisfied by the professional firm informing the client of the sum and that he has the right to require the firm to pay the sum concerned to the client, thus allowing the sum to be used to offset fees due from the client in respect of professional services. However it does not permit a professional firm to retain third party payments by seeking its client's agreement through standard terms and conditions. Similarly mere notification to the client that a particular sum has been received coupled with the professional firm's request to retain it does not satisfy the condition.'

The Law Society has also given guidance on the treatment of commission for these purposes. The guidance is contained in the information pack produced by Professional Ethics and entitled *Financial Services and Solicitors* (August 2001). Extracts from the information pack can be found in Appendix C2. Section 4, clause 3 deals with the question of commission as follows:

'3.1 ... if a firm receives commission (or any financial benefit) from a third party because of acting for or giving advice to a client, the firm must account for the commission (or other financial benefit) to the client. Accounting to the client does not mean simply telling the client that the firm will receive commission. It means that the commission or reward must be held to the order of the client. This is similar to the requirement under rule 10 of the Solicitors' Practice Rules 1990 ... The Society believes that solicitors will still account to the client if they have the client's **informed consent** to keep the commission.

3.4 There is one important difference between Practice Rule 10 and the condition [in article 22] in that Practice Rule 10 includes a de minimis provision whereby firms are allowed to keep commission of £20 or less. **This £20 de minimis provision does not apply in relation to [article 22].** Therefore commissions of £20 or less, which arise out of *regulated activities*, must be treated in the same way as commissions of more than £20.'

Arranging deals in investments (article 25)

As noted above (para. 2.30) this activity is defined as: **3.10**

'(1) Making arrangements for another person (whether as principal or agent) to buy, sell, subscribe for or underwrite a particular investment which is –

(a) a security,
(b) a contractually based investment ... [or]

(2) Making arrangements with a view to a person who participates in the arrangements buying, selling, subscribing for or underwriting investments falling within paragraph (1)(a), (b) ...'

There are a number of statutory exclusions from article 25. Solicitors will frequently make arrangements for clients to acquire or dispose of securities or contractually based investments. Consequently it is important that they are aware of the various means to avoid carrying on a regulated activity. It should be noted, however, that the article 25 activity only applies to securities and contractually based investments. Arrangements made by solicitors to assist their clients to acquire regulated mortgage contracts or general insurance policies will not be regulated activities and therefore will not give rise to the need for authorisation.

The most helpful exclusions are dealt with below.

Arrangements not causing a deal (article 26)

3.11 Arrangements which do not or would not bring about the transaction to which the arrangements relate are excluded from article 25. This confirms that in order to be caught by article 25 a solicitor must undertake activities which do or would bring about the transaction in question. Anything falling short of this would not be caught by article 25.

Arranging deals with or through an authorised person (article 29)

3.12 Article 29 excludes the article 25 activity if the solicitor makes arrangements with a view to a transaction which is or is to be entered into by a client with or through an authorised person if:

(a) the transaction is entered into on advice given to the client by an authorised person; or

(b) it is clear in all the circumstances that the client, in his capacity as an investor, is not seeking and has not sought advice from the person as to the merits of the client entering into the transaction (or if the client has sought advice the solicitor has declined to give it but has recommended the client to seek advice from an authorised person).

The above exclusion does not apply if the agent receives from any person other than the client any pecuniary reward or advantage, for which he does not account to the client, arising out of his entering into the transaction.

This is a similar exclusion to that noted above (dealing as agent – see above, paras. 3.5 *et seq*.). The same conditions apply and the points above regarding:

(a) authorised persons;

(b) advice;

(c) execution-only transactions; and

(d) pecuniary rewards and commissions;

must be carefully noted to ensure that the *authorised person* exclusion can properly apply to arrangements as well as to *dealing as agent*.

Provision of finance (article 32)

Where the sole purpose of an arrangement is the provision of finance to enable a person to buy, sell, underwrite or subscribe for investments, such an arrangement is excluded from article 25.   **3.13**

Introducing (article 33)

Where a solicitor introduces a client to an authorised or exempt person and the introduction is made with a view to the provision of independent advice, this will not be caught by article 25. However, it must be noted that introductions to advisers who are not independent (i.e. to a tied agent of a life office) will not be excluded by this article. Such introductions may involve the solicitor in regulated activities. They may also be a breach of the Solicitors' Introduction and Referral Code 1990 which provides in Section 4, clauses 2 and 3:   **3.14**

'(2) The referral to a tied agent of a client requiring life insurance would not discharge the solicitor's duty to give his client independent advice. In such circumstances, any referral should be to an independent intermediary.

(3) If the best interests of the client require it, a solicitor may refer a client requiring a mortgage to a tied agent, provided that the client is informed that the agent offers products from only one company.'

Solicitors introducing clients to authorised and independent advisers may be offered a commission as a result of such introductions. Whilst Practice Rule 10 (see above para. 3.9) will apply to such commission, the exclusion in article 33 is not subject to the *no pecuniary or other reward* condition which appears elsewhere in the RAO. Consequently, although commissions from introductions must be accounted for in accordance with Practice Rule 10, the £20 *de minimis* provision in Practice Rule 10 will apply. However, note the position where the solicitor's communication amounts to a financial promotion. There is an exemption for *introducers* in the FPO but this is subject to a condition requiring no pecuniary reward (see below Chapter 7).

Arrangements made by a company for the purposes of issuing its own shares or share warrants (article 34)

These arrangements are expressly excluded from article 25. Further article 34(1)(a) states clearly that for the purposes of article 25 a company is not, by reason of issuing its own shares to be treated as selling them. Consequently a company cannot be said to be dealing or arranging deals when it issues its own shares.   **3.15**

Article 34 also excludes arrangements made by any person for the purposes of issuing his own debentures or debenture warrants.

Managing investments (article 37)

3.16 As noted above (see para. 2.31) this activity is defined as managing assets belonging to another in circumstances involving the exercise of discretion where:

> '(a) the assets consist of or include any investment which is a security or a contractually based investment; or
>
> (b) the arrangements for their management are such that the assets may consist of or include such investments, and either the assets have at any time since 29th April 1988 done so, or the arrangements have at any time (whether before or after that date) been held out as arrangements under which the assets would do so.'

Management will catch, in many circumstances, solicitors who are trustees, personal representatives, donees under powers of attorney, and receivers appointed by the Court of Protection. It should be noted that only *discretionary* management is caught; administrative activities (such as simply acting for trustees and personal representatives (PRs)) do not constitute *management*.

In order to ascertain whether the solicitor, in his capacity as trustee, PR, etc. is likely to be involved in discretionary management, it is necessary to identify whether investment decisions can be made within the firm with no reference to others outside the firm. Trust and probate work can be divided into three categories for these purposes:

(a) Outside trustees or PRs: where the firm is merely acting for outside trustees/PRs there will be no discretionary management by the firm unless the outside trustees/PRs have delegated their discretion to the firm.

(b) Outside and in-house trustees/PRs jointly: where there are co-trustees/PRs inside and outside the firm there will be no discretionary management by the firm unless discretion has been delegated to the solicitor trustee/PR or the firm.

(c) In-house trustees or PRs: there will be discretionary management where the sole trustee/PR (or all the trustees/PRs) are in-house.

Only category (c) is likely to give rise to management in practice and this will potentially give rise to the need for authorisation. There is no specific exclusion in article 37 for trustees (although there are some important general exclusions available to trustees, nominees and personal representatives. For details of these, see para. 3.23 below).

However, it is not just solicitor trustees or PRs who risk undertaking discretionary management. This activity could also arise where a solicitor acts under a power of attorney. In these circumstances article 38 provides for a specific exclusion from management where:

'all routine or day-to-day decisions, so far as relating to investments of a kind mentioned in article 37, are taken on behalf of that person by –

(i)   an authorised person with permission to carry on activities of the kind specified by article 37;

(ii) a person who is an exempt person in relation to activities of that kind or

(iii) an overseas person'.

The FSA Guidance (Appendix C1) assists in the definition of the words *routine* and *day-to-day* for these purposes. Paragraph 1.18.2 G provides:

'(1) a "routine" decision is any decision other than one which may properly be regarded as exceptional. In determining whether or not decisions are routine, due account would need to be taken of the usual types of decision which the attorney takes or expects to be taking. Examples of possible non-routine decisions which an attorney might take include where the appointed fund manager has a conflict of interest or decisions relating to certain specified situations (for example, where the appointed fund manager proposes to invest in a particular type of investment such as a company associated with the tobacco or arms supply industries);

(2) a "day-to-day" decision is a decision which relates to the everyday management of the assets in question. It will not include strategic decisions such as decisions on the proportion of the assets which should be invested in equities as compared to fixed interest securities, or decisions on which investment manager(s) to appoint or to whom to apportion cash for investment purposes from time to time;

(3) the exclusion requires that the attorney takes only decisions which are neither "routine" nor "day-to-day" in nature.'

Consequently providing the attorney restricts his decisions to those which are non routine and not day to day, the discretionary management arising from such decisions will not be a regulated activity. However, one further question arises: is it the firm or the attorney who benefits from this exclusion? It might be argued that the strict wording of article 38 excludes the attorney only. If the attorney is acting as a partner or member of the firm, then the firm too, could be said to be undertaking discretionary management and therefore require authorisation.

Paragraph 1.18.3 G of the FSA Guidance (Appendix C1) assists again. It provides:

'It is usually the case that where a professional firm provides attorney services it will be an individual partner or employee of the firm who becomes the attorney. The question then arises as to whether it is the firm or the actual attorney who is potentially covered by the exclusion. It is the FSA's view that, provided it is the case that the firm has offered to provide the services of a partner or employee to act as attorney and that the client accounts to the firm for fees payable for the services of the attorney, it will be the firm which has and needs the benefit of the exclusion. This is because the attorney will be carrying on the firm's business and not his own business. It follows that if the attorney, in implementing a decision which is not a routine or day-to-day decision uses other employees, offices or partners of the firm to execute or arrange the transaction, the firm would be entitled to make use of any exclusion which may be available to a person acting as attorney.'

This guidance now makes it clear that anyone in the firm who undertakes discretionary management on behalf of an attorney will be capable of benefiting from the exclusion, if the management was undertaken in such a way that, if undertaken by the attorney would have been excluded by article 38.

Safeguarding and administering investments (article 40)

3.17   As noted above (see para. 2.32) the activity consists of both:

(a)   the safeguarding of assets belonging to another, and

(b)   the administration of those assets

or arranging for one or more other persons to carry on that activity.

The assets in question must consist of securities or contractually based investments or the arrangements for their safeguarding and administration are such that the assets may consist of or include such investments, and either the assets have at any time since 1 June 1997 done so, or the arrangements have at any time (whether before or after that date) been held out as ones under which such investments would be safeguarded and administered.

Article 41 excludes arrangements made with a *qualifying* custodian where the custodian has accepted responsibility for safeguarding and administration or where a solicitor has merely introduced a client to a qualifying custodian. A qualifying custodian is defined as

'an authorised person who has permission to carry on an activity of the kind specified by article 40 (safeguarding and administration) or an exempt person acting in the course of a business comprising a regulated activity in relation to which he is exempt'.

Further, for the purposes of article 40, the following activities do not constitute administration:

(a)   providing information regarding the number of units or value of any assets in custody;

(b)   converting currency; or

(c)   receiving documents solely for the purpose of onward transmission to, from or at the direction of the person to whom the investment belongs (article 43).

Sending dematerialised instructions (article 45)

As noted above (para. 2.33) sending, on behalf of another person, demateri- **3.18**
alised instructions relating to a security is a specified kind of activity, where
those instructions are sent by means of a relevant system in respect of which
an operator is approved under the Uncertificated Securities Regulations
1995.

Articles 46 and 47 exclude from this activity the act of sending or causing
to be sent a dematerialised instruction where the person on whose behalf the
instruction is sent or caused to be sent is a participating issuer (within the
meaning of the Uncertificated Securities Regulations 1995) or a settlement
bank in its capacity as such.

Article 48 contains details of an exclusion where the person on whose
behalf the instructions are sent is an offeror making a takeover offer. For
details of this exclusion, see RAO, article 48 (Appendix A3).

Advising on investments (article 53)

As noted above (para. 2.36) this activity is defined as where advice is: **3.19**

(a) given to a person in his capacity as an investor or potential investor, or
     in his capacity as agent for an investor or a potential investor; and
(b) advice on the merits of his doing any of the following (whether as
     principal or agent) –

  (i)   buying, selling, subscribing for or underwriting a particular
        investment which is a security or a contractually based investment,
        or
  (ii) exercising any right conferred by such an investment to buy, sell,
        subscribe for or underwrite such an investment.

Article 54 excludes certain written newspaper and broadcast advice if the
principal purpose of the publication or service, taken as a whole and including any advertisements or other promotional material contained in it is
neither the giving of investment advice (within the meaning of article 53)
nor leading to or enabling persons to buy, sell, subscribe for or underwrite
securities or contractually based investments.

Some solicitors write for advice columns in local newspapers. This exclusion may be of benefit to them, if, in the course of their written advice, they
mention the merits of buying particular investments.

Regulated mortgage contracts (article 61)

Regulated mortgage contracts are defined in article 61(3) (see above para. **3.20**
2.21). Under article 61(1), entering into a regulated mortgage contract as
lender is a regulated activity. Further under article 61(2), administering a

regulated mortgage contract is also a specified kind of activity, but only where the contract is entered into by way of business after the coming into force of this article (note the delay in bringing this article into force – see para. 2.39). The words *by way of business* were inserted by the Financial Services and Markets Act 2000 (Regulated Activities) (Amendment) Order 2001, SI 2001/3544. This amendment ensures that administering *private* mortgages will be excluded from this article. (For the definition of *administering* for these purposes, see para. 2.32 above.)

There are exclusions contained in RAO, article 62. A person who is not an authorised person does not administer a regulated mortgage contract in accordance with article 62(2) where he:

(a) arranges for an authorised person with permission to carry on an activity of that kind, to administer the contract; or

(b) administers the contract himself during a period of not more than one month beginning with the day on which any such arrangement comes to an end.

This exclusion permits a solicitor to simply arrange for the administration of a regulated mortgage contract to be undertaken by an authorised person with permission to undertake that activity. It further allows the solicitor to administer the contract himself for a period of one month after the arrangement comes to an end and before a new administrator is appointed.

Further a person who is not an authorised person does not carry on an activity of the kind specified by article 61(2) in relation to a regulated mortgage contract where he administers the contract pursuant to an agreement with an authorised person who has permission to carry on an activity of that kind. This exclusion will permit an unauthorised solicitor to accept instructions from a lending institution (who will be authorised for these purposes), where those instructions involve the solicitor in, for example, collecting or recovering payments due under the contract from the borrower.

Conclusion

3.21 The exclusions from dealing and arranging deals are important. In some cases these exclusions are the only way in which solicitors can avoid the need for authorisation. Firms need to ensure that they have systems in place which will allow the benefit of these exclusions to be obtained. The exclusions for the other activities will have limited impact upon solicitors' firms. Occasionally they may prove useful, but for the most part, solicitors are going to have to look elsewhere to avoid the need for authorisation arising from discretionary management, custody services and investment advice.

GENERAL EXCLUSIONS UNDER THE RAO

In addition to the specific exclusions noted above, the RAO contains a **3.22** number of general exclusions, the effect of which will remove a number of activities from the definition of regulated (and hence remove the need for authorisation). The relevant general exclusions arise under the following heads:

(a) Trustees, nominees and personal representatives;
(b) Activities carried on in the course of a profession;
(c) Activities carried on in connection with the sale of a body corporate.

Each is dealt with in more detail below.

Trustees, nominees and PRs (article 66)

RAO, art.66 contains exclusions applicable to trustees, nominees and per- **3.23** sonal representatives. Where these apply, solicitors will be able to avoid regulated activities and thus avoid the need for authorisation. However, it should be noted that these exclusions are subject to certain conditions, which must be satisfied before the exclusion can benefit the firm. Unfortunately the conditions are not universal to all the exclusions contained in article 66. Solicitors using these exclusions must carefully consider if they can satisfy the relevant conditions and ensure that systems are in place so that all relevant members of staff are aware of how the firm complies with the conditions.

Sole trustees/PRs or joint trustees/PRs where all come from within the firm are likely to be involved in discretionary management if the trust fund or estate involves specified investments. They are also likely to be buying and/or selling investments in their own name and thus dealing as principal.

Solicitors, or their employees, who are joint trustees/PRs with outsiders will not generally be involved in discretionary management (see above para. 3.16). However the in-house trustees/PRs may be advising external trustees or PRs on the purchase or sale of investments or arranging deals on behalf of themselves and the outsiders.

In both the above paragraphs in-house trustees/PRs could be providing safekeeping and administration services and possibly sending dematerialised instructions.

All of the activities noted above are capable of benefiting from the exclusions in the RAO, provided the appropriate conditions apply. However, article 66 is not capable of excluding activities where the firm is simply acting for outside trustees/PRs. For the article to apply a member of the firm (partner or employee) must be a trustee or PR. It is not necessary, however, for all the trustees or PRs to come from within the firm.

Dealing as principal

3.24   If in-house trustees/PRs deal in their own name (i.e. as principal), they are unlikely to be undertaking regulated activities because of the exclusion from dealing as principal contained in article 15 (see above para. 3.4). However, if the exclusion cannot apply for any reason, article 66 provides that the activity of dealing as principal is not a regulated activity if:

(a)   a person enters into a transaction as a bare trustee for another;

(b)   he is acting on that other's instructions; and

(c)   he does not hold himself out as providing a service of buying and selling securities or contractually based investments.

Arranging deals

3.25   Article 66 excludes arrangements where they are made by an in-house trustee/PR acting as such for or with a view to a transaction which is to be entered into:

(a)   by that in-house trustee/PR and a fellow trustee or PR (acting in that capacity); or

(b)   by a beneficiary under the trust, will or intestacy.

There is a further condition which requires that the person carrying on the activity is not remunerated for what he does in addition to any remuneration he receives as trustee or PR (for further details of this condition, see below, para. 3.31).

Discretionary management

3.26   Article 66 excludes discretionary management carried on by a person acting as trustee/PR unless he holds himself out as providing a management service (for further details of what is meant by *holds himself out as providing a management service*, see below para. 3.30). The additional condition, which requires that the person carrying on the activity is not remunerated for what he does in addition to any remuneration he receives as trustee or PR, also applies to this exclusion.

Safeguarding and administration

3.27   Article 66 excludes the activity of safeguarding and administration where a person acting as trustee or PR carries on the activity, unless he holds himself out as providing a safe custody service. Again, the additional condition, which requires that the person carrying on the activity is not remunerated for what he does in addition to any remuneration he receives as trustee or PR, applies to this exclusion.

Sending dematerialised instructions

This activity is excluded by article 66 if the instructions relate to an investment which that person holds as trustee or PR.   **3.28**

Investment advice

This activity is excluded by article 66 where the advice is given by a person acting as trustee or PR and the advice is given to: **3.29**

(a)   A fellow trustee or PR for the purpose of the trust or estate; or
(b)   A beneficiary under the trust, will or intestacy concerning his interest in the trust fund or estate.

Again, the additional condition, which requires that the person carrying on the activity is not remunerated for what he does in addition to any remuneration he receives as trustee or PR, applies to this exclusion.

Holding out

To benefit from the article 66 exclusions applicable to: **3.30**

(a)   dealing in investments;
(b)   managing investments; and
(c)   safeguarding and administration of investments,

it is necessary that the trustee or PR does not hold himself out as providing such services. The FSA Guidance gives further advice on the meaning of holding out for these purposes. It provides:

> 'In the FSA's opinion trustees (or personal representatives) will be holding themselves out as providing services of this kind only where they offer to provide services over and above those which trustees normally provide; and professional trustees will so hold themselves out where they offer to provide services over and above those provided by trustees generally, rather than those provided by professional trustees.'

If solicitors wish to benefit from these specific exclusions in article 66, they must ensure that they do not hold out themselves as providing a service over and above those services provided by lay trustees. Care must be taken to avoid any wording in the firm's brochures or websites which might be taken as holding out a provision of services beyond that permitted. For example, solicitors should not suggest in their brochures that clients should appoint members of the firm as trustees because of their specialist skills.

Additional remuneration

3.31 To benefit from the article 66 exclusions relating to:

(a) arranging deals in investments;
(b) managing investments;
(c) safeguarding and administration of investments; and
(d) advising on investments,

the trustee or PR must not receive remuneration for providing these services in addition to any remuneration he might receive for providing the services of trustee or PR. This is a similar condition to the trustee/PR exclusion contained in the Financial Services Act 1986 which solicitors rarely used. Counsel instructed by the Law Society suggested that solicitors who charged for their trust work using a time recording system were receiving additional remuneration. The RAO addresses this point specifically. Article 66(7) provides that a person is not to be regarded as receiving additional remuneration merely because his remuneration is calculated by reference to time.

This point is dealt with further in the FSA Guidance (Appendix C1 below). Paragraph 1.20.2 G states

> '. . . the mere fact that a trustee may spend, for example, an hour of his time taking part in a meeting at which decisions are made does not, of itself, mean that a trustee is additionally remunerated for undertaking investment management duties by virtue of his being paid by the hour for providing trustee services'.

This condition will, however, preclude trustees from retaining any commission over and above the fees charged for acting as trustees.

A further problem under the Financial Services Act 1986 was that in many cases the activities were carried out not by the individual solicitor who was the trustee or PR, but by other members of the firm. Counsel again advised the Law Society that this fact would generally preclude the use of the exclusion by solicitors. This point has been addressed by the FSA in its Guidance. Paragraph 1.20.4 G (Appendix C1 below) states

> 'It is the FSA's view that where a firm provides the services of a trustee or personal representative it is, for similar reasons to those given in 1.18.3.G, the firm itself which benefits from the trustees' exclusion (on the basis, that amongst other things, that the individual partner or employee is not himself carrying on a business of any kind)'.

The reference to 1.18.3 G is a reference to the FSA Guidance on attorneys (which is reproduced in para. 3.16 above). However it is so important for solicitors to understand the guidance that the paragraph is reproduced below with the reference to attorneys being replaced by trustees (my amendments):

> 'It is usually the case that where a professional firm provides *trustee* services it will be an individual partner or employee of the firm who becomes the *trustee*. The ques-

tion then arises as to whether it is the firm or the actual *trustee* who is potentially covered by the exclusion. It is the FSA's view that, provided it is the case that the firm has offered to provide the services of a partner or employee to act as *trustee* and that the client accounts to the firm for fees payable for the services of the *trustee*, it will be the firm which has and needs the benefit of the exclusion. This is because the *trustee* will be carrying on the firm's business and not his own business.'

For further details of the practical implications of the trustee/PR exclusions contained in article 66 see below, Chapter 9 (Compliance and Trusts) and Chapter 8 (Compliance and Probate and Administration).

Activities carried on in the course of a profession (article 67)

Article 67 contains exclusions where the activities are carried on in the course of a profession or non-investment business. These exclusions apply to regulated activities otherwise caught by articles 21 (dealing as principal), 25 (arranging deals), 40 (safe custody) and 53 (advice) and apply where: **3.32**

(a) the activity is carried on in the course of carrying on any profession or business which does not otherwise consist of regulated activities; and
(b) the activity may reasonably be regarded as a necessary part of other services provided in the course of the profession or business.

The activity concerned must not be separately remunerated from the other services.

Three conditions must be satisfied before this exclusion can apply. First, the activities must be carried on in the course of a profession which does not otherwise consist of regulated activities. In other words the activity cannot be a necessary part of other regulated activities.

Secondly, the activities must reasonably be regarded as a necessary part of the other services (i.e. legal services) provided. A similar (but not identical) condition applied to the exclusion in the Financial Services Act 1986 and was interpreted in a very narrow way. Indeed the Law Society advised solicitors that it would rarely be possible for them to rely upon this exclusion. Article 67 differs from the exclusion in the 1986 Act. The requirement that the activities must be *a necessary* part of other services is qualified by a reasonableness test, not present in the 1986 Act. The FSA Guidance states (paragraph 1.20.5 G)

'... if it should turn out that something done by a professional firm was not, in fact, necessary, the firm will not have conducted a regulated activity provided it was reasonable for it to have regarded the action to be necessary at the time it was taken'.

Clearly it is still necessary for firms to approach this exclusion with caution and only rely upon it where there are clear indications at the time of the proposed activity that such activity was a necessary part of other services.

However, the reasonableness test does mean that firms may now be able to use this exclusion, where, in the past there was some slight doubt over its use. Further Guidance has been given by the FSA. Paragraph 1.20.6 G provides:

> 'Examples of situations where the "necessary" exclusion may apply for professional firms include an accountant advising a client on the tax implications of entering into an investment agreement or a lawyer advising a client of the legal implications of doing so. Much of the work undertaken by lawyers in negotiating and putting into effect matrimonial or structured settlements may reasonably be regarded to be a necessary part of their professional services. For example, following the provision of necessary advice in a matrimonial dispute it may be reasonably regarded to be necessary for the solicitor to instigate the sale of an insurance policy by instructing an authorised intermediary to find a buyer at the best price and then to arrange the deal. It would be unlikely, however, that it would reasonably be regarded as necessary for the solicitor to undertake the role of that authorised intermediary.'

The third condition is that the activity must not be separately remunerated from the other services. *Separate* remuneration differs from *additional* remuneration (for example, article 66 talks about *additional* remuneration). The requirement that the activity is not *separately* remunerated is simply complied with by not showing the remuneration for this service as a separate item on the solicitor's bill of costs.

Activities in connection with sale of body corporate (article 70)

3.33 Solicitors acting on the acquisition or disposal of a company are likely to be involved in activities which potentially could be regulated. They are likely to give advice on the merits of buying or selling the shares in the company and, in making arrangements for the transfer of the shares, they could be caught by article 25 (arranging deals). It may be that the advice and subsequent arrangements are a further example of activities which could reasonably be treated as being a necessary part of the corporate and legal work.

However, a further exclusion appears in article 70. Dealing as principal or agent, arranging deals and investment advice in connection with the sale of a body corporate are all excluded if:

(a) the shares acquired or disposed are not shares in an open-ended investment company;

(b) the following conditions are met:

    (i) the shares consist of or include 50 per cent or more of the voting shares in the company; or

    (ii) the shares together with those already held by the person acquiring them consist of at least 50 per cent or more of the voting shares; and

(iii)   the acquisition or disposal is between parties each of whom is a body corporate, a partnership, a single individual or a group of connected individuals.

A group of connected individuals, for the purposes of article 70 means: in relation to a party disposing of shares in a body corporate, a single group of persons each of whom is –

(a)   a director or manager of the body corporate;
(b)   a close relative of any such director or manager;
(c)   a person acting as trustee for any person falling within paragraph (a) or (b) above.

In relation to a party acquiring shares in a body corporate, a group of connected individuals means a single group of persons each of whom is:

(a)   a person who is or is to be a director or manager of the body corporate;
(b)   a close relative of any such person; or
(c)   a person acting as trustee for any person falling within paragraph (a) or (b) above.

A *close relative* is defined, for the purpose of article 70 above as meaning:

(a)   his spouse;
(b)   his children and stepchildren, his parents and stepparents, his brothers and sisters and his stepbrothers and stepsisters; and
(c)   the spouse of any person falling within (b) above.

Even if the above conditions are not met the activities will be excluded if the object of the transaction may, nevertheless be reasonably regarded as the acquisition of day to day control of the affairs of the body corporate. The FSA has provided guidance on this aspect of the exclusion. Paragraph 1.20.13 G states:

'In any case where the conditions referred to in [article 70] are not met, it will be necessary to consider the circumstances in which the transaction takes place in order to determine whether the objective is the acquisition of day to day control. In situations where the 50 per cent holding of voting shares test is not met it remains possible that the objective of a transaction could still be the acquisition of day to day control – for instance, because the remaining shareholders represent a large number of small shareholders who it is reasonable to suppose will not regularly act in concert.'

The Guidance further deals with the position where the test regarding the status of the parties is not met. It states:

'Where the nature of the parties test is not met (typically because there are two or more parties involved as buyer or seller and they do not collectively represent a group of connected individuals as defined) it may still be the case that the objective

45

of the transction is the acquisition of day to day control when due account is taken of the purpose for which the person concerned holds or proposes to hold the voting shares. This may typically occur, for example, where shares are to be held by:

(1) a person (of either sex) with whom a manager or director cohabits;

(2) a venture capital company which has invested, or proposes to invest, in the company and which provides or is to provide a representative to act as manager or director of the company; or

(3) a private company used as a vehicle to hold shares by a person who is or is to be a manager or director of the company (or a close relative).'

CONCLUSION

3.34 The specific and general exclusions contained in the RAO will go some way to ensure that solicitors are able to avoid undertaking regulated activities and thus the need for authorisation. However these exclusions are unlikely to ensure that all activities are excluded. For example, solicitors acting for outside trustees/PRs will not be able to use the exclusion in article 66. They may wish to give advice, make arrangements and undertake custody services for outside trustees. These activities will not be a necessary part of the legal work provided and article 67 will not therefore apply. It may be possible for the dealing and arrangements to be excluded using the *authorised person* route, but only if advice was given by an authorised person and the other conditions applied. There are no helpful exclusions in the definition of investment advice or in the provision of custody services. Consequently for these and other activities, solicitors must look elsewhere to avoid the need for authorisation. They will need to consider the provisions of FSMA, Part XX which are dealt with in the next chapter.

CHAPTER 4

Exempt regulated activities

INTRODUCTION

Solicitors who are not able to avoid the need for authorisation through the **4.1** use of the exclusions contained in the RAO (see Chapter 3 above) will need to consider whether they are able to bring themselves within the concept of exempt regulated activities, contained in FSMA, Part XX.

FSMA, Part XX allows members of certain professions (including solicitors) to undertake regulated activities without the need for authorisation. These activities are referred to as *exempt regulated activities*. It is the activity which is exempt, not the solicitor. In other words, solicitors using this method to avoid authorisation do not become exempt persons.

Part XX applies to members of a profession which is supervised and regulated by a designated professional body (DPB).

Under the Financial Services and Markets Act 2000 (Designated Professional Bodies) Order 2001, the following bodies are designated as DPBs for these purposes:

(a) the Law Society;
(b) the Law Society of Scotland;
(c) the Law Society of Northern Ireland;
(d) the Institute of Chartered Accountants in England and Wales;
(e) the Institute of Chartered Accountants of Scotland;
(f) the Institute of Chartered Accountants in Ireland;
(g) the Association of Chartered Certified Accountants;
(h) the Institute of Actuaries.

DEFINITION UNDER THE FSMA

FSMA, section 327 provides that the prohibition against carrying on regu- **4.2** lated activities contained in section 19(1) (see above para. 1.2) does not apply to the carrying on of a regulated activity by a member of a profession if certain conditions apply:

(a) the person must be a member of a profession or controlled or managed by one or more such members;

(b) the person must not receive from anyone other than his client any pecuniary reward or other advantage, for which he does not account to his client, arising out of his carrying on of any of the activities;

(c) the manner of the provision of any service in the course of carrying on the activities must be incidental to the provision by him of professional services;

(d) only regulated activities permitted by the DPB's rules may be carried out;

(e) the activities must not be of a description, or relate to an investment of a description specified in an order made by the Treasury;

(f) the activities must be the only regulated activities carried on by that person.

FSMA, Part XX is a major means by which solicitors can avoid the need for authorisation. Consequently care must be taken to ensure that all the conditions in Part XX are complied with. There are six conditions, and each is dealt with in turn in the following paragraphs.

(1) The person must be a member of a profession or controlled or managed by one or more such members

4.3   As noted above, the Law Society is one of the DPBs. *Members* for these purposes is defined in FSMA, section 325(2). They include persons who are entitled to practise the profession in question and, in doing so, are subject to the DPB's rules whether or not they are members of the DPB. Consequently it does not matter if a solicitor is not technically a member of the Law Society; solicitors are subject to Law Society regulation whether or not they are members of the Law Society. Further, the wording of the condition in section 327 ensures that any member of staff (even if a non solicitor) can benefit from the exemption since members of staff will be controlled or managed by members of the DPB.

(2) The person must not receive from anyone other than his client any pecuniary reward or other advantage, for which he does not account to his client, arising out of his carrying on of any of the activities

4.4   This is a similar condition to the one noted above (see para. 3.9) in relation to the exclusions covering dealing as agent and arranging deals. The FSA Guidance, noted above and repeated here, is highly relevant. This provides, in paragraph 1.9.1 G:

> 'The FSA considers that, in order for a professional firm to be accounting to his client for the purposes of section 327(3) of the Act, the firm must treat any com-

mission or other pecuniary benefit received from third parties and which results from regulated activities carried on by the firm, as held to the order of the client. A professional firm will not be accounting to his client simply by telling the client that the firm will receive commission. Unless the client agrees to the firm keeping the commission it belongs to the client and must be paid to the client. There is no de minimis below which the professional firm may retain the sum. In the FSA's opinion, the condition would be satisfied by the professional firm paying over to the client any third party payment it receives. Otherwise, it would be satisfied by the professional firm informing the client of the sum and that he has the right to require the firm to pay the sum concerned to the client, thus allowing the sum to be used to offset fees due from the client in respect of professional services. However it does not permit a professional firm to retain third party payments by seeking its client's agreement through standard terms and conditions. Similarly mere notification to the client that a particular sum has been received coupled with the professional firm's request to retain it does not satisfy the condition.'

The requirement to account to the client for any pecuniary reward or other advantage is also contained in the Law Society's Scope Rules (Solicitors' Financial Services (Scope) Rules 2001) which are covered in detail below (see para. 4.9).

(3) The manner of the provision of any service in the course of carrying on the activities must be incidental to the provision by him of professional services

This condition is the key to the exemption. Part XX can only apply if the **4.5** regulated activity is incidental to the professional services provided by the solicitor. *Professional services* for these purposes are defined in FSMA, section 327(8) as meaning services:

'(a) which do not constitute carrying on a regulated activity, and
(b) the provision of which is supervised and regulated by a designated professional body'.

Further guidance on this condition has been given by FSA. Paragraph 1.10 of their Guidance provides:

'1.10.1 G   The FSA considers that to satisfy the condition in section 327(4) of the Act regulated activities cannot be a major part of the practice of the firm. The FSA also considers the following further factors to be among those that are relevant:

(1) the scale of regulated activities in proportion to other professional services provided;
(2) whether and to what extent services that are regulated activities are held out as separate services; and

(3) the impression given of how the firm provides regulated activities, for example, through its advertising or other promotions or its services.

1.10.2 G In the FSA's opinion, one consequence of this is that the professional firm cannot provide services which are regulated activities if they amount to a separate business conducted in isolation from the provision of professional services. This does not, however, preclude the firm operating its professional business in a way which involves separate teams or departments, one of which handles the regulated activities.'

A number of practical points arise from this guidance. First, exempt regulated activities cannot represent more than 50 per cent of the firm's business. The guidance provides that they cannot be 'a major part of the practice'.

Secondly, in considering the scale of the regulated activities in proportion to other services, the time spent on the regulated activities and the value are likely to be taken into account. For the regulated activities to be incidental to the other services (and thus exempt), it is likely that the time spent on such business will be less than the time spent on the other services. It is also likely that any value placed on the regulated activities by the firm will be less than that placed upon the other services provided.

Thirdly, the Guidance refers to holding out as *separate services*. Whilst firms cannot have a separate business providing regulated activities, it is accepted that a separate department (servicing the other departments of the firm) would be permitted within the scope of this condition.

Finally, reference is made in the Guidance to the manner in which the firm advertises or promotes its services. In considering this aspect of the Guidance, solicitors must also consider the impact of the Financial Promotions Order 2001 (for details of this, see below, Chapter 7).

(4) Only regulated activities permitted by the DPB's rules may be carried out

4.6 The Law Society, as a designated professional body, has been required to make rules which are binding upon solicitors who wish to benefit from the ability to provide exempt regulated activities under FSMA, Part XX. Section 332(3)–(5) of the Act provides:

'(3) A designated professional body must make rules –

(a) applicable to members of the profession in relation to which it is established who are not authorised persons; and

(b) governing the carrying on by those members of regulated activities (other than regulated activities in relation to which they are exempt persons).

(4) Rules made in compliance with subsection (3) must be designed to secure that, in providing a particular professional service to a particular client, the member carries on only regulated activities which arise out of, or are complementary to, the provision by him of that service to that client.

(5) Rules made by a designated professional body under subsection (3) require the approval of the Authority.'

The rules made by the Law Society are the Solicitors' Financial Services (Scope) Rules 2001 (which deal with the activities capable of falling within Part XX – see below, para. 4.9) and the Solicitors' Financial Services (Conduct of Business) Rules 2001 (which deal with compliance requirements – see below, Chapter 6).

(5) The activities must not be of a description, or relate to an investment of a description specified in an order made by the Treasury

The Financial Services and Markets Act 2000 (Professions) (Non-Exempt **4.7** Activities) Order 2001, SI 2001/1227 (NEA Order) identifies those activities excluded from the provisions of Part XX. The activities which are not capable of benefiting from the exemption under Part XX are as follows:

(a) accepting deposits;
(b) effecting and carrying out contracts of insurance;
(c) dealing in investments as principal;
(d) establishing, operating and winding up a collective investment scheme, including acting as a trustee of an authorised unit trust scheme or sole director of an open-ended investment company;
(e) establishing, operating and winding up a stakeholder pension scheme;
(f) managing the underwriting capacity of a Lloyd's syndicate;
(g) entering as provider into funeral plan contracts;
(h) (with effect from the commencement date – expected in 2004) entering into as lender and administering regulated mortgage contracts. However this does not apply to an activity carried on by a trustee or PR in his capacity as such where the borrower under the regulated mortgage contract in question is a beneficiary under the trust, will or intestacy. A further condition is that the trustee/PR is not remunerated for what he does in addition to any remuneration he receives as trustee or PR. For these purposes the trustee/PR is not to be regarded as receiving additional remuneration merely because his remuneration is calculated by reference to time spent. (Amendment to the NEA Order inserted by the Financial Services and Markets Act 2000 (Professions) (Non-Exempt Activities) (Amendment) Order 2001.)
(i) managing, insofar as it consists of buying/subscribing for specified investments unless routine day to day decisions are taken by an

authorised or exempt person or the specific activity is undertaken in accordance with the advice of an authorised or exempt person;

(j) advice, where the advice:

 1. is given to an individual (or his agent);
 2. is a recommendation to buy or subscribe for a particular security or contractually based investment; and
 3. relates to a transaction which would be made –

   (i)   with a person in the course of his carrying on a business of dealing in investments; or
   (ii) on an investment exchange or market; or
   (iii) in response to an invitation to subscribe for investments which are, or are to be, admitted for dealing on an investment exchange or market.

Advice is also excluded from Part XX where it is a recommendation to a member of a personal pension scheme (or his agent) to dispose of any rights or interests which he has under the scheme.

These restrictions are also contained in the Law Society's Scope Rules (with additional restrictions applicable to solicitors). Consequently, for a detailed commentary on these restrictions, see below, para. 4.11.

(6) The activities must be the only regulated activities carried on by that person

4.8 The final condition set out in FSMA, section 327 makes it clear that Part XX cannot apply to firms which are authorised by FSA. Such firms cannot use Part XX for their regulated activities which are non mainstream. Non mainstream regulated activities are defined in the Professional Firms Sourcebook (rule 5.2). The definition replicates the requirements of FSMA, section 327 and ensures that such non mainstream activities are subject to limited compliance requirements. For details of the obligations applicable to FSA authorised firms in respect of their non mainstream activities, see below, para. 6.10.

SOLICITORS' FINANCIAL SERVICES (SCOPE) RULES 2001

4.9 A firm of solicitors wishing to undertake regulated activities which are incapable of benefiting from FSMA, Part XX as a result of the NEA Order will require authorisation from the FSA (assuming that none of the exclusions referred to in Chapter 3 above apply). Solicitors carrying on regulated activities which are not excluded as a result of the NEA Order and which are incidental to their professional services will still need to consider whether their activities are permitted under the Law Society's Solicitors' Financial Services (Scope) Rules 2001 (the Scope Rules).

The full text of the Scope Rules can be found in Appendix B1.

These rules further limit the scope of solicitors benefiting from FSMA, Part XX (in much the same way as solicitors were limited under the Solicitors' Investment Business Rules 1995 (SIBR)). The contents of these rules are as follows.

Application (rule 2)

The rules only apply to firms of solicitors which are not regulated by the FSA. **4.10**

Prohibited activities (rule 3)

A firm must not carry on or agree to carry on any of the following activities: **4.11**

(a) market making in investments;

(b) buying, selling, subscribing or underwriting as principal where the firm holds itself out as engaging in the business of underwriting or buying investments with a view to selling them or regularly solicits the public with the purpose of inducing them to enter into transactions;

(c) buying or selling investments with a view to stabilisation;

(d) acting as a stakeholder pension scheme manager;

(e) entering into broker funds arrangements;

(f) effecting and carrying out contracts of insurance as principal;

(g) establishing, operating or winding up a collective investment scheme;

(h) establishing, operating or winding up a stakeholder pension scheme;

(i) managing underwriting capacity of a Lloyd's syndicate as a managing agent at Lloyd's;

(j) advising a person to become a member of a particular Lloyd's syndicate;

(k) entering as provider into a funeral plan contract;

(l) entering into a regulated mortgage contract as lender or administering a regulated mortgage contract.

Concern has been expressed over problems for professional trustees who enter into regulated mortgage contracts as lenders and who might also be administering regulated mortgage contracts. Amendments were therefore made to the NEA Order (see above para. 4.7). General regulation of regulated mortgage contracts has been delayed (see para. 2.39). In due course appropriate amendments will be made to the Law Society's Scope Rules.

Other basic conditions (Rule 4)

Once a firm has satisfied itself that its intended regulated activities do not fall **4.12** within those prohibited by rule 3, it must then ensure that it complies with the basic conditions set out in rule 4. Only if these conditions are met can a firm claim the benefit of FSMA, Part XX. The Law Society has issued guidance on compliance with these conditions. This is contained in the information pack issued by Professional Ethics and entitled *Financial Services and Solicitors* (August 2001). An extract from the information pack's 'Guidance on the Basic Conditions' is contained in Appendix C2. The conditions in rule 4 are as follows:

The activities must arise out of, or be complementary to, the provision of a particular professional service to a particular client (rule 4(a))

4.13   This condition (which is similar to the *incidental* exception to discrete investment business in SIBR) means that the regulated activity cannot be undertaken in isolation for a client – it must always be shown to be complementary to other professional services provided to a particular client. The Law Society's guidance states:

'To satisfy this basic condition, the firm must be able to identify the relevant professional services.'

Further, the Guidance gives examples of the type of services which the regulated activities might be complementary to or arise out of. Details of the practical application of these rules in relation to the types of services can be found in the appropriate chapters of this handbook referred to below:

Conveyancing (Chapter 12)
Corporate (Chapter 13)
Matrimonial (Chapter 14)
Trusts (Chapter 9)
Probate (Chapter 8)
Acting as attorney (Chapter 10) or
Receiver appointed by the Court of Protection (Chapter 11).

The manner of the provision by the firm of any service in the course of carrying on the activities must be incidental to the provision by the firm of professional services (Rule 4(b))

4.14   The FSA has given guidance on the meaning of *incidental* for these purposes (see above para 4.5). It should be appreciated that the two conditions in rule 4(a) and (b) are different. Rule 4(a) requires solicitors to ensure that the regulated activity is complementary to or arises from a professional service. This can be done by showing that the regulated activity is subordinate to the main purpose for which the professional services are provided.

Rule 4(b) has been inserted as a result of the Investment Services Directive (ISD). The ISD and the Capital Adequacy Directive have an impact on the way in which firms choose to hold out their financial services departments. The ISD provides:

'persons providing an investment service where the service is provided in an incidental manner in the course of a professional activity'

will not be subject to the Directive and therefore will not be subject to capital adequacy requirements. The incidental exemption in the Directive depends upon a qualitative judgement about the way in which the services are provided. Because of this, the way the firm holds itself out as being capable of offering financial services is important as is the way it advertises its investment services. Firms must ensure that any advertisement or promotion does not have the effect of holding out the regulated activity as a separate business.

The firm must account to the client for any pecuniary reward or other advantage which the firm receives from a third party (Rule 4(c))

The FSA Guidance on pecuniary rewards is dealt with above (para. 4.4). The **4.15** Law Society has also given guidance on this condition. Section 4 clause 3 of its Guidance deals with the question of commissions as follows:

'3.1 . . . if a firm receives commission (or any financial benefit) from a third party because of acting for or giving advice to a client, the firm must account for the commission (or other financial benefit) to the client. Accounting to the client does not mean simply telling the client that the firm will receive commission. It means that the commission or reward must be held to the order of the client. This is similar to the requirement under rule 10 of the Solicitors' Practice Rules 1990 . . . The Society believes that solicitors will still account to the client if they have the client's **informed consent** to keep the commission.

3.2 If a firm is charging the client on a fee basis, the firm can off-set the commission against the firm's fees. The firm must send the client a bill or some other written notification of costs to comply with the Solicitors' Accounts Rules 1998.

3.3 The requirement for informed consent would not be met if a firm were to

- seek blanket consent in terms of business to the keeping of all unspecified commissions, or
- seek negative consent.

3.4 There is one important difference between Practice Rule 10 and the condition [in rule 4(c) of the Scope Rules] in that Practice Rule 10 includes a de minimis provision whereby firms are allowed to keep commission of £20 or less. **This £20 de minimis provision does not apply in relation to [rule 4(c)].** Therefore commissions of £20 or less, which arise out of regulated activities, must be treated in the same way as commissions of more than £20.'

The activities must not be of a description, nor must they relate to an investment of a description, specified in any order made by the Treasury under section 327(6) of the Act (rule 4(d))

4.16 Since the provisions of the NEA Order (see above para. 4.7) have been incorporated into the Law Society's Scope rules, compliance with the Scope rules will also be compliance with the NEA Order.

The firm must not carry on or hold itself out as carrying on any regulated activity other than one which is allowed by the Scope Rules or one in relation to which the firm is an exempt person (Rule 4(e))

4.17 The effect of this condition is that firms which are authorised can not take the benefit of FSMA, Part XX. The reference to *exempt persons* allows insolvency practitioners who undertake certain regulated activities as exempt persons (see above para. 1.4) to benefit nonetheless from Part XX.

There must not be in force any order or direction of the FSA under section 328 or section 329 of the Act which prevents the firm from carrying on the activities (Rule 4(f))

4.18 These sections allow the FSA to disapply Part XX from a class of persons or an individual person.

The activities must not otherwise be prohibited by these rules (rule 4(g))

4.19 This condition refers to the further restrictions contained in rule 5 of the Scope Rules (see below para. 4.20 *et seq*).

Packaged products (except personal pension schemes) (rule 5(1))

4.20 Rule 5(1) provides that a firm must not recommend or make arrangements for a client to buy a packaged product except where:

(a) the recommendation, or arrangement for a client to buy a packaged product is by means of an assignment;

(b) the arrangements are made as a result of the firm managing assets within the exception to rule 5(4); or

(c) the arrangement is made for a client where the firm assumes on reasonable grounds that the client is not relying on the firm as to the merits or suitability of the transaction.

Packaged products are defined (in rule 8) as

'long term insurance contracts (including pension products), units or shares in regulated collective investment schemes or an investment trust savings scheme whether or not held within an ISA or PEP or a stakeholder pension scheme'.

Rule 5(1) does not, however apply to personal pension schemes. The restrictions in relation to these investments are dealt with in rule 5(2) (below, para. 4.21).

Note that the restriction applies to recommending a client to *buy* a packaged product or making arrangements for a client to *buy* a packaged product. The following activities are permitted under the Scope Rules (subject to a solicitor's competency) and are therefore capable of taking the benefit of FSMA, Part XX providing all the other conditions are satisfied.

(a) A solicitor may advise a client on the *purchase* of a packaged product provided the advice does not amount to a recommendation. Thus the solicitor may explain the transaction or advise the client to seek further information or clarification in relation to a packaged product.
(b) A solicitor may recommend a client not to buy a particular packaged product, i.e. give negative advice.
(c) A solicitor may recommend a client to *sell or dispose* of a particular packaged product.
(d) A solicitor may recommend or arrange for a client to buy or sell a packaged product by means of an *assignment*.
(e) A solicitor may obtain advice from and/or endorse a recommendation given by an authorised or exempt person. Further, in relation to this activity, the FSA Guidance provides (paragraph 1.11.12 G)

'For the avoidance of doubt, it is not necessary for a professional firm to endorse a recommendation for the same reasons as given by the authorised person.'

(f) A solicitor may also make arrangements arising from management of client assets (see below para. 4.23) and arrangements which are execution only arrangements. (For further comment on execution only transactions, see below, para. 6.8.)

In addition to those activities noted above, remember that although a solicitor cannot arrange the purchase of a packaged product within FSMA, Part XX, in almost all cases the solicitor should be able to ensure that such arrangements are excluded in any event as a result of RAO, article 29 (arrangements made through an authorised person – see above para. 3.12).

Personal pension schemes (rule 5(2))

Rule 5(2) provides that a firm must not recommend a client to *buy* or *dispose* **4.21** of any rights or interests in a personal pension scheme. Further the rule provides that a firm must not make arrangements for a client to *buy* any rights or interests in a personal pension scheme except where the transaction is effectively an execution only transaction. Note, however, the execution only exception does not apply if the transaction involves a pension transfer or an opt out.

For these purposes the following definitions should be noted (rule 8):

personal pension scheme means a scheme of investment in accordance with the Income and Corporation Taxes Act 1988, s.630;

pension transfer means a transaction resulting from a decision by an individual to transfer deferred benefits from a final salary occupational pension scheme, or from a money-purchase occupational pension scheme, in favour of an individual pension contract or contracts; and

opt out means a transaction resulting from a decision by an individual to opt out of or decline to join a final salary or money-purchase occupational pension scheme of which he or she is a current member, or which he or she is, or at the end of a waiting period will become, eligible to join, in favour of an individual pension contract or contracts.

Securities and contractually based contracts (except packaged products) (rule 5(3))

4.22   A firm must not recommend a client to buy or subscribe for securities or contractually based investments (which are not packaged products) where the transactions would be made:

(a)   with a person acting in the course of carrying on the business of buying, selling, subscribing or underwriting the investment, whether as principal or agent;

(b)   on an investment exchange or any other market to which that investment is admitted for dealing; or

(c)   in response to an invitation to subscribe for an investment which is, or is to be, admitted for dealing on an investment exchange or any other market.

This requirement mirrors the restriction contained in the NEA Order (see above para. 4.7). Examples of prohibited acts would include:

(a)   a solicitor could not recommend a client to purchase listed company shares from a stockbroker (clause (a) above);

(b)   a solicitor could not recommend a client to purchase listed securities on the London Stock Exchange (clause (b) above); or

(c)   a solicitor could not recommend a client to subscribe for shares following a public offer or flotation in respect of which an application for listing has been made (clause (c) above).

However, as with the restrictions relating to packaged products, there are still a number of transactions that can be undertaken by solicitors within the terms of the Scope Rules and therefore, subject to the other conditions applying, within FSMA, Part XX. Examples of these transactions include:

(a) a solicitor could make arrangements for the client to buy, sell, subscribe or underwrite these categories of investments. Such arrangements can be made using a stockbroker, or where the transaction is carried out on an investment exchange or following a public offer or flotation where the investment is listed. Rule 5(3) does not restrict arranging (or dealing as agent) provided the basic conditions apply (in particular the need for the activity to be *incidental* and the accounting for any pecuniary award or advantage – see above para. 4.12 *et seq.*);

(b) a solicitor could recommend a client to purchase or subscribe for securities in a private company (where no stockbroker is involved);

(c) a solicitor could advise a client on the merits of the purchase or subscription of these categories of investments provided the advice does not amount to a recommendation;

(d) a solicitor could recommend a client not to buy a particular security or contractually based investment, i.e. give negative advice;

(e) a solicitor could recommend a client to sell investments of this type;

(f) a solicitor could obtain advice from and/or endorse a recommendation given by an authorised or exempt person.

Further, as a result of rule 5(3)(b), the basic restriction in rule 5(3) does not apply where the client is not an individual; where the client is acting in his capacity as a trustee of an occupational pension scheme; or where the client is an individual carrying on a business of which he is or is to be a controller. A controller for these purposes is defined in FSMA, section 422 as meaning, in broad terms, a person who has a 10 per cent or greater shareholding in a business undertaking or one who is able to exercise a significant influence over its management.

Consequently, rule 5(3)(b) would allow a solicitor to recommend to a corporate client the acquisition of shares or other securities in a listed company. A recommendation could also be made to an individual if the individual was intending to acquire a 10 per cent holding in the listed company or otherwise become a controller, as defined.

Discretionary management (rule 5(4))

A firm must not manage assets belonging to another involving the exercise of **4.23** discretion except where the firm/partner/employee is a trustee, PR, donee of a power of attorney or receiver appointed by the Court of Protection and either:

(a) all routine or day to day decisions are taken by an authorised or exempt person; or

(b) any decision to enter into a transaction involving buying or subscribing is undertaken in accordance with the advice of an authorised person with permission to give advice in relation to such an activity, or an exempt person.

Discretionary management is only permitted under the terms of the Scope Rules (and therefore an exempt regulated activity under FSMA, Part XX) if it is undertaken in the capacity of a trustee, PR, donee under a power of attorney or receiver appointed by the Court of Protection. Note that discretionary management undertaken by trustees or PRs may be excluded entirely from the definition of regulated activities as a result of RAO, article 66 (see above, para. 3.23). Discretionary management undertaken under a power of attorney may be excluded as a result of RAO, article 38 (see above, para. 3.16). Consequently it is only necessary for solicitors to consider the restrictions in rule 5(4) of the Scope Rules if they have been unable to bring themselves within the exclusions in RAO, article 66 or 38.

If discretionary management is to be undertaken as an exempt regulated activity, then solicitors must decide which of the two alternative conditions they will utilise. Either they must show that all routine day to day decisions are taken by an authorised person or that any decision which involves buying or subscribing for investments is taken on the advice of an authorised person. As noted above, the FSA has given guidance on the meaning of *all routine or day to day decisions*. The guidance is given in relation to attorneys but there is no reason why it should not apply equally to trustees, PRs and Court of Protection receivers. It is reproduced in para. 3.16 above and repeated here for convenience:

'(1) a "routine" decision is any decision other than one which may properly be regarded as exceptional. In determining whether or not decisions are routine, due account would need to be taken of the usual types of decision which the attorney takes or expects to be taking. Examples of possible non-routine decisions which an attorney might take include where the appointed fund manager has a conflict of interest or decisions relating to certain specified situations (for example, where the appointed fund manager proposes to invest in a particular type of investment such as a company associated with the tobacco or arms supply industries);

(2) a "day-to-day" decision is a decision which relates to the everyday management of the assets in question. It will not include strategic decisions such as decisions on the proportion of the assets which should be invested in equities as compared to fixed interest securities, or decisions on which investment manager(s) to appoint or to whom to apportion cash for investment purposes from time to time;

(3) the exclusion requires that the attorney takes only decisions which are neither "routine" nor "day-to-day" in nature.'

If the solicitor trustee, PR, attorney or receiver chooses not to delegate all routine or day to day decisions to an authorised person, then all decisions involving buying or subscribing for an investment must be taken in accordance with the advice of an authorised person. Note that decisions relating to the sale of investments can be taken by the solicitor in any of these capacities without the involvement of an authorised person. The restriction in rule 5(4) only applies to the purchase of or subscription for investments. Of course, the solicitor must ensure that he is competent to make such a decision. Where an authorised person is used, solicitors should record the fact that advice has been received and followed.

Corporate finance (rule 5(5))

Rule 5(5) prohibits a firm from acting: **4.24**

(a) as a sponsor to an issue in respect of securities to be admitted for dealing on the London Stock Exchange; or
(b) as a nominated adviser to an issue in respect of securities to be admitted for dealing on the Alternative Investment Market of the London Stock Exchange.

Effect of breach of the rules (Rule 6)

Breach of these Scope Rules can give rise to disciplinary proceedings being **4.25**
instigated against the solicitor on the basis of the Law Society's statutory powers of discipline. Further, if solicitors breach the rules, the protection of FSMA, Part XX will not apply. In these circumstances, the solicitor is likely to be committing a criminal offence under FSMA, section 23 (contravention of the general prohibition – see above para. 1.6). The FSA could also make an order against the solicitor under FSMA, section 329, preventing the firm from undertaking any regulated activities.

In determining whether there has been a breach of the rules, the Law Society will take into account whether due regard has been given to the Law Society's guidance on how to determine whether regulated activities are carried on in accordance with the rules.

CONCLUSION

The régime contained in FSMA, Part XX is very valuable for solicitors **4.26**
wishing to avoid authorisation under the Act. Although solicitors may be able to use the exclusions contained in RAO (see above, Chapter 3) not all

activities are capable of being excluded in this way. It is inevitable that in most practices, some activities will have to be treated as exempt regulated activities in order to avoid authorisation. Consequently it is vital that firms have in place appropriate systems to ensure that all fee earners understand:

(a) which activities amount to regulated activities;
(b) which exclusions can take these activities outside the definition of regulated activities; and
(c) which activities remain regulated but can be treated as exempt.

Once these three categories of activities have been identified, the firm's systems should then be such that fee earners can follow the appropriate conditions to ensure that the Law Society's Scope Rules permit the activities in category (c) above to be properly treated as exempt.

It must always be remembered that getting the system wrong may involve the firm in criminal and civil liabilities.

PART II

Compliance

CHAPTER 5

Compliance requirements

INTRODUCTION

Solicitors who undertake activities which could amount to regulated activities but which do not give rise to the requirement for authorisation (either because they are excluded or exempt activities) are still subject to certain compliance requirements. Such activities (generally referred to as financial services) give rise to two types of compliance obligations. First, those applicable to practice as a solicitor generally. These obligations are contained in the Practice Rules; Codes made under the Practice Rules; and other rules. They will apply to solicitors whether they are able to benefit from an exclusion in the RAO or whether they rely upon the exempt regulated activities regime in FSMA, Part XX. These are referred to in outline in this handbook. For further details reference should be made to appropriate Law Society publications. Secondly, those solicitors who rely upon the exempt regulated activities régime will have to comply with the Solicitors' Financial Services (Conduct of Business) Rules 2001. These are dealt with in detail in Chapter 6. **5.1**

COMPLIANCE APPLICABLE TO ALL SOLICITORS INVOLVED IN FINANCIAL SERVICES

Solicitors' Practice Rules 1990 (as amended)

The Solicitors' Practice Rules 1990 together with the Publicity Code 2001 and the Introduction and Referral Code 1990 all apply to the conduct of investment business by a solicitor. Whilst these Rules and Codes are of general application to a solicitor's practice, certain of their provisions are of particular importance to the conduct of investment business. **5.2**

The most relevant of the Practice Rules to apply to solicitors providing financial services are as follows:

Rule 1 (basic principles)

5.3   'A solicitor shall not do anything in the course of practising as a solicitor, or permit another person to do anything on his or her behalf, which compromises or impairs or is likely to compromise or impair any of the following:

(a)   the solicitor's independence or integrity;
(b)   a person's freedom to instruct a solicitor of his or her choice;
(c)   the solicitor's duty to act in the best interests of the client;
(d)   the good repute of the solicitor or of the solicitor's profession;
(e)   the solicitor's proper standard of work;
(f)   the solicitor's duty to the court.'

The importance of this particular rule is that it applies at any stage during the course of a solicitor's practice and, in relation to financial services, ensures that the solicitor is independent and acts in the best interests of his client.

Rule 2 (publicity)

5.4   'Solicitors may at their discretion publicise their practices, or permit other persons to do so, or publicise the businesses or activities of other persons, provided there is no breach of these Rules and provided there is compliance with a solicitor's publicity code promulgated from time to time by the Council of the Law Society with the concurrence of the Master of the Rolls.'

The current Publicity Code is the 2001, which came into effect in November 2001. The Publicity Code must be carefully studied when any aspect of publicity is being considered by a solicitor. In addition, if a solicitor intends to advertise his ability to provide financial services to clients and others, he must have regard to the provisions of the Financial Promotion Order 2001. Details of these requirements are to be found below, Chapter 7.

Rule 3 (introductions and referrals)

5.5   'Solicitors may accept introductions and referrals of business from other persons and may make introductions and refer business to other persons, provided there is no breach of these rules and provided there is compliance with a Solicitors' Introduction and Referral Code promulgated from time to time by the Council of the Law Society with the concurrence of the Master of the Rolls.'

The current Introduction and Referral Code is the 1990 version as amended. Subject to the provisions of the Code a solicitor may enter into an agreement with a third party under the terms of which the third party will introduce clients to the solicitor. This may include clients introduced to the solicitor by third parties for financial services. It must be noted that Clause 2(8) requires a solicitor to communicate directly with the client to obtain or confirm instructions at all appropriate stages of the transaction.

Amendments were made to the Introduction and Referral Code which became effective on 1 January 1992. These permit, in certain defined circumstances, a solicitor to agree to be paid by the introducer to provide conveyancing services for the introducer's customers.

Clause (3) in section 2 of the Code provides:

'Solicitors must not reward introducers by the payment of commission or otherwise. However this does not prevent normal hospitality. A solicitor may refer clients to an introducer provided the solicitor complies with section 4 below.'

Whilst it is normal in the financial services industry for commissions to be paid by the providers of financial services to introducers it must be noted that as a result of the Introduction and Referral Code solicitors are not permitted to make such payments.

The Code also deals with circumstances where the solicitor is the introducer. It is common practice for solicitors to introduce clients to other providers of financial services. This is permitted subject to compliance with section 4 of the Introduction and Referral Code. The relevant paragraphs in this section provide as follows:

'1. If a solicitor recommends that a client use a particular firm, agency or business, the solicitor must do so in good faith, judging what is in the client's best interests. A solicitor should not enter into any agreement or association which would restrict the solicitor's freedom to recommend any particular firm, agency or business.

2. The referral to a tied agent of a client requiring life insurance would not discharge the solicitor's duty to give his client independent advice. In such circumstances, any referral should be to an independent intermediary.

3. If the best interests of the client require it, a solicitor may refer a client requiring a mortgage to a tied agent, provided that the client is informed that the agent offers products from only one company.'

It is therefore important that solicitors (whether authorised or not) who refer clients to advisers only make such referrals to independent financial advisers and not to tied agents.

Rule 5 (offering services other than as solicitor)

Practice Rule 5 reads as follows:

'Solicitors must comply with the Solicitors' Separate Business Code in controlling, **5.6** actively participating in or operating (in each case alone, or by or with others) a business which:

(a) provides any service which may properly be provided by a solicitor's practice, and

(b) is not itself a solicitor's practice or multinational partnership.'

The Solicitors' Separate Business Code 1994 contains prohibitions against solicitors having separate businesses in respect of:

(a) the conduct of matters proceeding before any court, tribunal or inquiry;
(b) advocacy;
(c) instructing counsel;
(d) acting as executor, trustee or nominee company;
(e) drafting wills or trust deeds;
(f) giving legal advice;
(g) reserved activities;
(h) document drafting.

However, the Code permits separate businesses in respect of:

(a) investment business;
(b) estate agency;
(c) trade mark and patent agencies.

For these purposes *investment business* means any *regulated activity* as defined in FSMA (an amendment to the Code made by the Solicitors' Financial Services (Amendment) Rules 2001).

Thus solicitors may provide financial services through a separate business (controlled and owned by solicitors solely or in conjunction with others). In such circumstances the Practice Rules and other solicitor regulations will not apply to the separate business (which will not be a firm of solicitors). In particular the Introductions and Referral Code's prohibition on rewarding introducers will not apply. Nor will Practice Rule 10 on accounting for commissions. However, because the separate business is not that of a firm of solicitors, the Part XX régime for professionals would not apply and almost inevitably the separate business would have to seek authorisation from FSA. Further the indemnity fund and the compensation fund would no longer protect clients of the separate business.

Although the separate business is not regulated by the Law Society, solicitors involved in such businesses will continue to be subject to Law Society regulation and the Code contains detailed safeguards which must be complied with where a separate business is formed unless the Law Society has granted a waiver of any requirement. The safeguards include:

(a) the fact that the name of the separate business must have no substantial element in common with the name of any practice of the solicitor;
(b) any practice and the separate business must operate separate paperwork and accounts;
(c) the non use of the words *solicitors, attorneys or lawyers* in connection with the solicitor's involvement in the separate business;

(d) clients of the separate business referred by any practice of the solicitor must be informed of the solicitor's interest in that business and that they will not enjoy the statutory protections attaching to clients of a solicitor. This information must be given in a personal interview or telephone call and in writing confirming the contents of that interview or call;

(e) there must be a physical division between the accommodation used by the solicitor's practice and that used by the separate business;

(f) there must be compliance with Solicitors' Practice Rules 1990, Rule 12(1)(b) and (2) (for details of this rule, see para. 5.9 below).

Practice Rule 5 continues to contain a prohibition against offering services as executor or trustee other than as a solicitor. Some solicitors operate executor and trustee companies for the benefit of clients as part of their financial services department. As a result of Practice Rule 5, such companies must be an incorporated practice under the Solicitors' Incorporated Practice Rules 2001.

Rule 7 (fee sharing)

'A solicitor shall not share or agree to share his or her professional fees with any person except: **5.7**

(a) a practising solicitor [. . .];

(b) [. . .]

(c) the solicitor's bona fide employee, which provision shall not permit a partnership with a non solicitor under the cloak of employment [. . .]'.

Consequently it is possible for solicitors to employ staff and providing those staff are bona fide employees, to remunerate them by share of profit or commission or otherwise.

Rule 10 (receipt of commissions from third parties)

'(1) Solicitors shall account to their clients for any commission received of more than £20 unless, having disclosed to the client in writing the amount or basis of calculation of the commission or (if the precise amount or basis cannot be ascertained) an approximation thereof, they have the client's agreement to retain it. **5.8**

(2) Where the commission actually received is materially in excess of the amount or basis or approximation disclosed to the client the solicitor shall account to the client for the excess.

(3) This Rule does not apply where a member of the public deposits money with a solicitor who is acting as agent for a building society or other financial institution and the solicitor has not advised that person as a client as to the disposition of the money.'

This practice rule is of vital importance to solicitors who provide financial services. Many commissions are generated as a result of financial services. It is, however, important to recognise the fact that this practice rule applies to all commissions, not just to those commissions received as a result of investment business.

Solicitors must consider at the outset of any retainer involving financial services how those services are to be charged to the client. If the solicitor merely wishes to retain any commission received from a third party he should disclose in writing the amount or basis of calculation or approximation to the client and seek his client's consent (preferably in writing) to the retention of the commission in accordance with Rule 10. By complying with Rule 10, solicitors should be able to show that they have accounted to the client for any pecuniary reward or other advantage so as to allow them to benefit from the exclusions in the RAO, articles 22 (para. 3.5 above) and 26 (para. 3.12 above). Compliance will also indicate that the appropriate basic condition 4(c) in the Scope Rules has been followed (see para. 4.15 above). However, note that in all these cases the £20 *de minimis* provision does not apply. To satisfy the requirements of articles 22 and 26 and basic condition 4(c) in the Scope Rules, all commission must be accounted for.

If, on the other hand, the solicitor wishes to submit a bill then any commission received belongs to the client but may be used to discharge the solicitor's bill. (For further details of the advantages and disadvantages of charging by way of commission or fees, see below, para. 15.3 et seq.)

It should also be noted that Rule 10 applies to renewal commission and where solicitors are disclosing the amount of commission and seeking their client's consent to retain it they should also disclose the amount of the renewal commission and seek consent to the retention of that at the same time. In the absence of consent any renewal commission must be fully accounted to the client. A failure to do so could lead to the potential exclusions to regulated activities being lost or the inability to use the Part XX régime for exempt regulated activities. In turn, the solicitor might find himself subject to criminal and civil liabilities as a result of failure to account.

The Inland Revenue has issued a Statement of Practice on the taxation of commission (SP 4/97). The position is that solicitors receiving commission will have to treat the commission as a receipt of their business, although commission passed on to the client will be deductible for the purposes of Schedule D, Cases I and II provided it is laid out wholly and exclusively for the purpose of their profession (e.g. where a solicitor is obliged to pass on the commission to his or her client).

Rule 12 (investment business)

5.9   '(1) Without prejudice to the generality of the principles embodied in Rule 1 of these rules, solicitors shall not in connection with investment business:

(a) be appointed representatives; or

(b) have any arrangements with other persons under which the solicitor could be constrained to recommend to clients or effect for them (or refrain from doing so) transactions in some investments but not others, with some persons but not others, or through the agency of some persons but not others; or to introduce or refer clients or other persons with whom the solicitor deals to some persons but not others.

(2) Notwithstanding any proviso to Rule 5 of these rules, solicitors shall not by themselves or with any other person set up, operate, actively participate in or control any separate business which is an appointed representative, unless it is the appointed representative of an independent financial adviser . . ..

(5) In this rule "investment business" means any "regulated activity" as defined in the Financial Services and Markets Act 2000; and "appointed representative" and "investment" have the meanings given in that Act.'

(Amended by the Solicitors' Financial Services (Amendment) Rules 2001.)

This practice rule applies to all solicitors undertaking regulated activities (including exempt regulated activities within FSMA, Part XX). The rule is not restricted to those solicitors who are authorised by FSA.

An appointed representative (or tied agent) is only able to promote the products of one company or group and acts as agent for that company. Consequently he does not owe a duty of best advice to the customer beyond choosing the best product for the customer from the company's own range. An independent intermediary acts as agent for the customer and has a duty to find for the customer the best product for his needs from a whole range of companies. Because of the rule 1 requirement for a solicitor to act independently and in the best interests of the client, it is clearly necessary for there to be a prohibition upon solicitors becoming appointed representatives. Further, solicitors who have hived off their financial services departments to separate companies in accordance with Practice Rule 5 (see above, para. 5.6) may not be involved in such companies if they (i.e. the companies) are appointed representatives unless the company is an appointed representative of an independent financial adviser.

The reference in rule 12(1)(b) to arrangements with other parties ensures that a solicitor cannot enter into an exclusive arrangement whereby the solicitor may only use an identified third party for the provision of financial services to his client (for example, the arrangement with an authorised person). This is so even if the identified third party is independent. However, this rule does not in practice prevent a solicitor from regularly using the same third party provided that it is in the client's best interest for the solicitor to do so. It is an agreement with that third party which constrains a solicitor from using other third parties which is prohibited.

Rule 15 (client care)

5.10   'Solicitors shall:

(a) give information about costs and other matters, and

(b) operate a complaints handling procedure

in accordance with a Solicitors' Costs Information and Client Care Code made from time to time by the Council of the Law Society with the concurrence of the Master of the Rolls.'

This particular rule, and the Solicitors' Costs Information and Client Care Code 1999 (which came into effect on 3 September 1999), apply to all retainers including those where financial services are involved.

Solicitors' Accounts Rules 1998

5.11   These rules contain detailed provisions relating to the receipt and payment of client money and the accounting record which must be kept by solicitors. There is no distinction made between monies received and paid out in relation to financial and other services. Details of the Accounts Rules are to be found in appropriate Law Society publications.

The Solicitors' Accounts Rules 1998, Part C, has direct application to solicitors who undertake financial services on behalf of their clients. Part C requires solicitors to account to a client for interest on sums held by solicitors either by placing the client's money in a separate designated account and accounting for the actual interest earned on it or by paying a sum in lieu of interest to the client where the money is not held in a separate designated account.

Where a sum is not held in a separate designated account, payment of interest depends upon the sum involved and the length of time the money is held. It is mandatory for solicitors to pay interest in the following circumstances where:

(a) £1,000 or more is held for eight weeks or more; or

(b) £2,000 or more is held for four weeks or more; or

(c) £10,000 or more is held for two weeks or more; or

(d) £20,000 or more is held for one week or more.

Where a sum in excess of £20,000 is held for less than a week interest must be paid to the client where it is fair and reasonable to do so having regard to all the circumstances.

The 1998 Rules also provide that solicitors need not pay a sum in lieu of interest if the amount calculated is £20 or less.

The Rules give details of the amount of interest payable. The rate of interest to be applied is the rate (whichever is the higher) that would have been paid if:

(a) the money had been kept in a separate designated account; or

(b) the money had been placed on deposit by a member of the business community;

in both cases at the bank or building society where the money was held.

Interest is also payable on money where the solicitor is a trustee, holding money in his capacity as a solicitor but not as a controlled trustee. (A controlled trustee is defined as meaning a solicitor who is a sole trustee or co trustee only with one or more of his partners or employees.) If the solicitor is a controlled trustee the deposit interest rules do not apply. However in these circumstances, the general provisions of trust law will apply and the solicitor must ensure that he does not benefit from the trust. Any interest accruing from the controlled trust money must be fully accounted for to the controlled trust.

Money Laundering Regulations 1993

These Regulations came into effect on 1 April 1994 and are designed to **5.12** ensure that professionals (including solicitors) report to the appropriate authorities any suspicions or knowledge they may have of money laundering activities.

The regulations apply to *relevant financial business*. This term is defined in Regulation 4(1) and the definition includes regulated activities. It should be noted that the scope of these rules extends to exempt regulated activities. Consequently solicitors using the FSMA, Part XX régime (see above Chapter 4) are bound by the Regulations in relation to such activities. At the time of writing, new money laundering regulations are expected as a result of the new EU Directive on Money Laundering. The new regulations are likely to extend the scope to include property transactions and transactions involving the holding of client money.

The Regulations apply to regulated activities where there is a *business relationship* or where there is a *one-off transaction*. *Business relationship* means any arrangement between two or more persons:

(a) where at least one is acting in the course of a business;

(b) where the purpose is to facilitate the carrying out of transactions between the persons on a frequent, habitual or regular basis; and

(c) where the total amount of any payment to be made is not known or capable of being ascertained at the time when the arrangement is made.

However, if the relationship cannot be described as a *business relationship* it is still likely to be caught by the Regulations since a *one-off transaction* is defined as any transaction other than one carried out in the course of an established *business relationship*.

Where the Regulations apply, solicitors must ensure that procedures are put in place covering compliance with four main requirements.

(1) Identification procedures

5.13 Regulation 5(1) provides:

'No person shall, in the course of relevant financial business carried on by him in the UK, form a business relationship, or carry out a one-off transaction, with or for another unless that person –

    (a) maintains the following procedures established in relation to that business –

        (i) identification procedures in accordance with regulations 7 and 9.'

Regulation 7 requires the identification procedures to be adopted as soon as is reasonably practicable after contact is first made between the business and a customer where there is to be a business relationship. Further, the identification procedures will also apply to one-off transactions in the following circumstances:

(a) where there is knowledge or suspicion of money laundering; or
(b) where payment is to be made by or to the client of an amount of 15,000 euros or more.

Where applicable, the procedures require the production by the client of satisfactory evidence of his identity or the taking of other measures which will produce satisfactory evidence of identity. Without such evidence, the regulations state that the business relationship or the one-off transaction shall not proceed further.

Regulation 11 gives further guidance. It states that evidence of identity is satisfactory if it is reasonably capable of establishing that the client is the person he claims to be and that the solicitor is satisfied that it does establish that fact.

Positive identity of the client should be obtained and where possible copies of the evidence should be retained. The best evidence of identity are those articles which are signed by the client and which bear a photograph and address.

In cases of doubt a client's name and address can be verified by checking the electoral roll, making a credit reference agency search, checking the telephone directory or requesting sight of a utility or a local tax bill.

The Regulations contain a number of possible exceptions and exclusions when no evidence or further evidence of identity will be necessary. Most of these are of no great benefit to firms of solicitors involved in investment business. However, two of the exclusions may have limited relevance.

(a) Reinvestments (regulation 10(1)(d)). If the proceeds of a one-off transaction are payable to the client but no repayment is made because the proceeds are reinvested on his behalf in another transaction, no evidence of identity is required. However a record must be kept of this transaction.

(b) Insurance business (regulation 10(1)(f) and (g)). No evidence of identity is required in relation to insurance business where a premium is payable in one instalment of an amount not exceeding 2,500 euros or where periodic premiums are payable and the total payable in any calendar year does not exceed 1,000 euros.

(2) Record-keeping requirements

Regulation 5(1) provides: **5.14**

'No person shall, in the course of relevant financial business carried on by him in the UK, form a business relationship, or carry out a one-off transaction, with or for another unless that person –

(a) maintains the following procedures established in relation to that business –

(ii) record keeping procedures in accordance with regulation 12.'

Regulation 12 requires a record to be kept:

(a) of the evidence of identity obtained in accordance with the Regulations; and

(b) of details relating to all transactions carried out in the course of relevant financial business.

The record of the evidence of identity may either be a copy of the evidence itself or information which would enable the details to be obtained (or re-obtained where necessary). Given the record keeping requirements of the Solicitors' Financial Services (Conduct of Business) Rules (see Chapter 6) and the fact that a solicitor will maintain a file record, it is unlikely that the requirements of Regulation 12 relating to transaction records will add any additional burden to solicitors.

The records must be retained for a period of at least five years beginning from the date on which the business was completed. Since under the Conduct of Business Rules records must be kept for at least six years, this obligation under the regulations should pose no difficulties.

(3) Internal reporting procedures

Regulation 5(1) provides: **5.15**

'No person shall, in the course of relevant financial business carried on by him in the UK, form a business relationship, or carry out a one-off transaction, with or for another unless that person –

(a) maintains the following procedures established in relation to that business –

(iii) except where the person concerned is an individual who in the course of relevant financial business does not employ or act in association with any other person, internal reporting procedures in accordance with reg. 14.'

The internal reporting procedures required by Regulation 14 are as follows. A person must be identified to whom any report is made where partners or employees know or suspect that a client is engaged in money laundering. That person or other designated person, must consider any reports received (together with other relevant information) for the purpose of determining whether there are grounds giving rise to the knowledge or suspicion. He must also have reasonable access to other information which may assist him. Finally, if having considered the report he knows or suspects that a client is engaged in money laundering he must ensure that the information contained in the report is disclosed to a constable. (*Constable* in this context generally means the National Criminal Intelligence Service, the authority responsible for investigating money laundering.)

(4) Training

5.16   Regulation 5(1) provides:

'No person shall, in the course of relevant financial business carried on by him in the UK, form a business relationship, or carry out a one-off transaction, with or for another unless that person –

(a) [. . .]
(b) takes appropriate measures from time to time for the purposes of making employees whose duties include the handling of relevant financial business aware of:

(i) the [established] procedures [. . .] which are maintained by him and which relate to the relevant financial business in question, and
(ii) the enactments relating to money laundering; and

(c) provides such employees from time to time with training in the recognition and handling of transactions carried out by, or on behalf of, any person who is, or appears to be, engaged in money laundering.'

Penalties

5.17   The penalties for contravening the Regulations are:

(a) on conviction on indictment, to imprisonment not exceeding a term of two years or a fine or both;
(b) on summary conviction, to a fine not exceeding the statutory maximum.

Solicitors' Investment Business Rules 1995

The Solicitors' Investment Business Rules 1995 (SIBR) were repealed with **5.18** effect from 1 December 2001. However the requirements to retain records under the SIBR for a period of 6 years from the date on which the record was made means that solicitors must retain their SIBR records until at least 30 November 2007. Further, the Law Society will continue to be responsible for the monitoring and enforcement of compliance with SIBR in respect of any investment business undertaken before 1 December 2001.

Solicitors' Financial Services (Conduct of Business) Rules 2001

These are the primary rules applicable to solicitors who undertake exempt **5.19** regulated activities within FSMA, Part XX. These rules are considered in detail in the following chapter. (For the full text of the rules, see Appendix B2.)

CHAPTER 6

Solicitors' Financial Services (Conduct of Business) Rules 2001

INTRODUCTION

6.1   The full text of these rules can be found in Appendix B2. The rules contain guidance notes. The Law Society has also issued additional guidance on the operation of these rules. This additional guidance is contained in the guidance issued by Professional Ethics and entitled Financial Services and Solicitors (August 2001). The appropriate extracts can be found in Appendix B1.

The rules apply to all solicitors who undertake exempt regulated activities within FSMA, Part XX where the Law Society acts in its role as a DPB (see above Chapter 4). The rules do not apply to solicitors who take the benefit of the statutory exclusions contained in the RAO (see Chapter 3). However the Law Society's guidance states:

> '. . . there may be a fine line between operating under an exclusion and providing services within the DPB régime. It may therefore be easier for firms to apply these rules to all such activities'.

It would certainly be easier for firms to adopt systems applicable to all categories of financial services rather than expecting fee earners to make subtle distinctions between those activities where an exclusion might apply and those activities where the DPB régime is being used.

When considering what rules should apply to solicitors operating under the DPB régime, the Law Society concluded that the number of rules applicable should be kept to a minimum as solicitors undertaking exempt regulated activities should be covered by the same rules as solicitors providing other legal services (see Chapter 5 above). Consequently the Solicitors' Financial Services (Conduct of Business) Rules 2001 (Conduct of Business Rules) are drafted in simple terms and, in many cases, are not as prescriptive as their equivalent provisions in the SIBR.

SOLICITORS' FINANCIAL SERVICES (CONDUCT OF BUSINESS) RULES 2001

These rules are applicable to solicitors carrying out regulated activities in, into, or from the UK where such solicitors are not regulated by the FSA (rule 2(a)). The rules (save for rule 3) also apply to solicitors who are authorised by FSA in respect of their non mainstream activities (see below, para. 6.10).

6.2

Regulated activities under the rules

Status disclosure (rule 3)

Rule 3(2) provides as follows:

6.3

'A firm shall give the client the following information in writing before the firm provides a service which includes the carrying on of a regulated activity:

(a) a statement that the firm is not authorised by the FSA;
(b) the nature of the regulated activities carried on by the firm, and the fact that they are limited in scope;
(c) a statement that the firm is regulated by the Law Society; and
(d) a statement explaining that complaints and redress mechanisms are provided through Law Society regulation.'

There is no prescribed form which must be used for the giving of this information. The information may be included in the firm's engagement letter, client care brochure or in a separate letter.

The reason for this disclosure obligation can be found in the FSA's Professional Firm's Sourcebook. This provides that a DPB firm must avoid making any representation to a client that:

(a) it is authorised under the Act or regulated by the FSA, or
(b) the regulatory protections provided by or under the Act to a person using the services of an authorised person are available.

Firms not authorised by the FSA must remove any statement on letterheads that the firm is authorised for the conduct of investment business by the Law Society. The FSA have indicated that firms may use up old stocks of preprinted stationery provided that the statement is crossed through.

The Professional Firm's Sourcebook also requires firms in the DPB régime, before providing a regulated activity, to disclose in writing to a client that it is not authorised under the Act. The guidance makes it clear that this information does not have to be contained on stationery and the Law Society considers that such a statement on stationery would not be helpful. Rather, the information should be contained in client care/terms of business/retainer letters.

The Law Society has given guidance on how solicitors can comply with these requirements. The Solicitors' Publicity Code 2001 provides that the stationery of a firm of solicitors must include a statement that the firm is regulated by the Law Society (although this statement does not become compulsory until 31 December 2002). This statement will clearly assist firms in complying with rule 3(2)(c). The Law Society has suggested three alternative draft paragraphs that could be included in terms of business to deal with rule 3(2)(a) and (b). These are as follows:

'Sometimes conveyancing/family/probate/company work involves investments. We are not authorised by the Financial Services Authority and so may refer you to someone who is authorised to provide any necessary advice. However we can provide certain limited services in relation to investments, provided they are closely linked with the legal services we are providing to you, as we are regulated by the Law Society.'

'If during this transaction you need advice on investments, we may have to refer you to someone who is authorised by the Financial Services Authority, as we are not. However, as we are regulated by the Law Society, we may be able to provide certain limited investment services where these are closely linked to the legal work we are doing for you.'

'Sometimes family etc. work involves investments. We are able to provide a limited range of advice and arrangements for which we are regulated by the Law Society. For more complicated matters we may refer you to someone who is authorised by the Financial Services Authority, as we are not so authorised.'

Rule 3(2)(d) adds further requirements to those contained in the Solicitors' Costs Information and Client Care Code 1999 relating to the information that should be given to clients on complaints handling. The Code requires every principal in private practice to:

'(i) ensure the client is told the name of the person in the firm to contact about any problem with the service provided;
(ii) have a written complaints procedure and ensure that complaints are handled in accordance with it; and
(iii) ensure that the client is given a copy of the complaints procedure on request' (clause 7(b)).

The Conduct of Business Rules require

'a statement explaining that complaints and redress mechanisms are provided through Law Society regulation.'

The Law Society has stated that firms can ensure compliance with this rule by expanding the paragraph in all client care letters on complaints handling. Alternatively, firms will have to identify those clients who are most likely to receive exempt regulated activities and give a special retainer letter to those clients. The Society's suggested paragraph to be included in such letters is:

'If you have any problem with the service we have provided for you then please let us know. We would have to resolve any problem quickly and do operate an internal complaints handling system to help us to resolve the problems between ourselves. If for any reason we are unable to resolve the problem between us, then we are regulated by the Law Society which also provides a complaints and redress scheme.'

Execution of transactions (rule 4)

Rule 4 provides: **6.4**

'A firm shall ensure that where it has agreed or decided in its discretion to effect a transaction, it shall do so as soon as possible, unless it reasonably believes that it is in the client's best interests not to do so.'

This rule repeats the obligations which were contained in the Solicitors' Investment Business Rules 1995.

As a result of both this obligation and the requirement to act in the client's best interest (Solicitors' Practice Rules 1990, Rule 1) a solicitor should ensure that transactions are effected on the best terms reasonably available. The Law Society, in its guidance on this rule, also reminds firms that rule 15 of the Practice Rules requires clients to be kept fully informed of transactions effected on their behalf, unless those clients have indicated to the contrary. The rule also applies where a firm has discretion to act without the client's specific instructions.

Records of transactions (rule 5)

Rule 5 provides: **6.5**

'(1) Where a *firm* receives instructions from a *client* to effect a *transaction*, or makes a decision to effect a *transaction* in its discretion, it shall keep a record of:

(a) the name of the *client*; and
(b) the terms of the instructions or decision; and
(c) in the case of instructions, the date when they were received.

(2) Where a *firm* gives instructions to another person to effect a *transaction*, it shall keep a record of:

(a) the name of the *client*;
(b) the terms of the instructions;
(c) the date when the instructions were given; and
(d) the name of the other person instructed.'

This rule, again, repeats a requirement of the Solicitors' Investment Business Rules 1995 with subtle changes. It is no longer an obligation to record the time when instructions were received or given.

The following points should be noted regarding this record keeping obligation:

(a) a *transaction* for these purposes means the *purchase, sale, subscription or underwriting of a particular investment* (a definition contained in rule 7(1) of the Scope Rules extended to the Conduct of Business Rules by rule 12). Consequently there are no specific record keeping requirements arising from advising a client; only dealing as agent or arranging transactions will give rise to the record keeping obligation;

(b) the Law Society has given guidance on this obligation in the following terms:

'It is not necessary for the firm to make a separate record. Normal file notes or letters on the file will meet the requirements of this rule provided that they include the appropriate information. If instructions are given or received over the telephone, an appropriate attendance note would satisfy this rule';

(c) *terms of the instructions or decision* means that the record must set out the identity of the investment, the number of units and/or cash value and the nature of the transaction (e.g. sale/purchase);

(d) where the rule refers to making *a decision to effect a transaction in its discretion* this will include a decision by trustees, all of whom are members (partners or employees) of the firm. However, it does not include a decision taken by trustees where the solicitor is a trustee but jointly with lay co trustees. In the latter situation if the trustees (i.e. solicitor and lay co trustees) instruct the firm to effect a transaction, such instructions will give rise to records under rule 5(1) and (2);

(e) the firm must retain records kept under this requirement for at least six years from the date on which the record was made (rule 9).

Record of commissions (rule 6)

6.6　Rule 6 states:

'Where a *firm* receives commission which is attributable to *regulated activities* carried on by the *firm*, it shall keep a record of:

(a) the amount of the commission; and
(b) how the *firm* has accounted to the *client*.'

Where a firm uses the DPB régime, FSMA, section 327 imposes a condition that the firm 'must not receive from anyone other than his client any pecuniary reward or other advantage, for which he does not account to his client, arising out of his carrying on of any of the activities'

(see above para. 4.15). As noted above, this means that all commission arising from exempt regulated activities must be accounted to the client and this includes sums of £20 or less which otherwise would fall within the *de minimis* limits of Practice Rule 10. Consequently rule 6 of the Conduct of Business Rules requires solicitors to record not just the amount of any commission received from regulated activities but also how such sum has been accounted to the client.

The condition to account fully for commission also is a requirement of some of the exclusions contained in RAO (for example see above Chapter 3). Technically such commission does not have to be recorded in accordance with rule 6 since such commission does not arise from regulated activities (the very nature of the exclusions in RAO mean that the activity is not regulated). However because of the fine line distinguishing the exclusions from the DPB régime, firms may find it easier to apply these record keeping requirements to all such activities. In addition, compliance with this rule should assist firms in demonstrating compliance with the conditions in RAO.

The Law Society has given guidance on the nature of the record which must be kept in accordance with rule 6. The guidance states:

'The rule is not prescriptive as to how the record should be kept and it is likely that the normal information on the file, e.g. letters to the client, would provide the relevant record. Where the firm has accounted to the client by setting off the commission against the bill, the bill itself may amount to a record for the purposes of this rule.'

As with other records kept under the Conduct of Business Rules, the commission record must be retained for a period of six years from the date the record was made (rule 9).

Safekeeping of client's investments (rule 7)

Rule 7 provides: 6.7

'(1) Where a firm undertakes the regulated activity of safeguarding and administering investments, the firm must operate appropriate systems, including the keeping of appropriate records, which provide for the safekeeping of assets entrusted to the firm by clients and others.

(2) Where such assets are passed to a third party:

(a) an acknowledgement of receipt of the property should be obtained; and

(b) if they have been passed to a third party on the client's instructions, such instructions should be obtained in writing.'

For the definition of safeguarding and administration, see above, para. 2.32. SIBR contained detailed obligations arising from the safeguarding activity. The Conduct of Business Rules 2001 have greatly simplified the requirements. All that is required is for appropriate systems to be operated. These systems may cover the matters contained in SIBR but without the prescriptive obligations. Firms may therefore wish to consider systems in the following areas:

(a) *Registration of title to clients' investments.* Investments must be properly registered in the client's name or, with the client's consent, in the name of a nominee. Such nominee must either be the firm's own nominee or, where it is in the client's best interests and the client instructs the firm in writing, a third party nominee.

(b) *Safekeeping of clients' assets.* Firms should not release the client's assets without the client's written authority. Firms must have adequate security arrangements to safeguard clients' title documents.

(c) *The use of nominees.* Where a firm uses its own nominee it should ensure that the nominee acts only in accordance with the firm's instructions. Where the firm appoints a third party nominee it should use skill and care in its choice.

(d) *Firm's responsibilities in relation to custodian services.* Where the firm provides custody services (whether or not nominees are used) it should specify details of the custody services. Examples of areas that should be considered include:

  (i) arrangements for recording, registering and separately identifying title to the client's investments;

  (ii) procedures for giving and receiving instructions;

  (iii) provision for possible regular statements to clients indicating the documents held.

(e) *Records of title documents.* The firm should keep a record of all title documents held by the firm or its own nominee. The record must be *appropriate* and firms should consider recording some or all of the following:

  (i) the client's name;

  (ii) the nature, amount and, where appropriate, nominal value of the title documents;

  (iii) where the title documents are kept;

  (iv) the date on which each title document came into or left the custody of the firm or its nominee; and

  (v) whether title documents have been lent or held as collateral.

Such records (being part of required records under the Conduct of Business Rules) must be kept for at least six years from the date the record is made. It is good practice to regularly reconcile the records with the title documents held by the firm, or its nominee.

(f) *Reporting to clients.* Firms should consider whether it is appropriate for a regular statement to be sent to clients, specifying documents of title held by the firm or its nominee.

Packaged products – execution only business (rule 8)

Rule 8 provides: **6.8**

'If a firm arranges for a client on an execution only basis any transaction involving a packaged product, the firm shall send the client written confirmation to the effect that:

(a) the client had not sought and was not given any advice from the firm in connection with the transaction; or

(b) the client was given advice from the firm in connection with that transaction but nevertheless persisted in wishing the transaction to be effected;

and in either case the transaction is effected on the client's explicit instructions.'

A packaged product is defined in rule 8 of the Scope Rules (see above para. 4.20). Under the Scope Rules a solicitor must not make arrangements for a client to buy a packaged product except (*inter alia*) where the arrangement is made and

'the firm assumes on reasonable grounds that the client is not relying on the firm as to the merits or suitability of the transaction'

(Rule 5(1)(c) – see above para. 4.20). If this exceptional set of circumstances applies, the firm will have provided services on an execution only basis and consequently must comply with rule 8 of the Conduct of Business Rules, as noted above. However, although the Scope Rules only refer to *buying* an investment on an execution only basis, rule 8 will equally apply where a solicitor sells investments on an execution only basis. Further, a number of RAO exclusions rely upon the use of the execution only basis (see for example, para. 3.12 above). Compliance with Rule 8 in these circumstances, although strictly not necessary, will assist firms in demonstrating that the conditions in the exclusions have been complied with.

An *execution only (transaction)* is defined in the Scope Rules (Rule 12) as

'a transaction which is effected by a firm for a client where the firm assumes on reasonable grounds that the client is not relying on the firm as to the merits or suitability of that transaction'.

It should be noted that the definition is not simply that the firm has not advised the client. The requirement is that the firm assumes on reasonable grounds that the client is not relying on the firm as to merits or suitability.

This may be difficult to show in the light of Practice Rule 1 which requires the solicitor to act in the best interests of the client. The Law Society has given guidance on the meaning of the term as follows:

'1. Whether a transaction is "execution only" will depend on the existing relationship between the client and the firm and the circumstances surrounding that transaction. Generally, a transaction will be "execution only" if the client instructs the firm to effect it without having received advice from the firm. Even though this is the case, however, the transaction may still not qualify as "execution only" because, in view of the relationship, the client may reasonably expect the firm to indicate if the transaction is inappropriate. In any event, a firm may be negligent (and possibly in breach of rule 1 of the Solicitors' Practice Rules 1990) if it fails to advise on the appropriateness or otherwise.

2. A transaction will also be "execution only" if the firm has advised the client that the transaction is unsuitable, but the client persists in wishing the transaction to be carried out. In those circumstances it is good practice (and in some cases a requirement) for the firm to confirm in writing that its advice has not been accepted, and that the transaction is being effected on an "execution only" basis.'

Where applicable, rule 8 requires firms to send to the client written confirmation to the effect that the client has not sought and was not given advice by the firm, or that the client was given negative advice from the firm, but nevertheless wishes to persist in effecting the transaction. The letter should clarify the fact that the transaction is effected on the client's explicit instructions.

Waivers (rule 10)

6.9 Rule 10 allows the Council of the Law Society to grant waivers in respect of the Conduct of Business Rules in the following terms:

'(1) In any particular case or cases the Council shall have power to waive in writing any of the provisions of these rules, but shall not do so unless it appears that:

(a) compliance with them would be unduly burdensome having regard to the benefit which compliance would confer on investors; and

(b) the exercise of the power would not result in any undue risk to investors.

(2) The Council shall have power to revoke any waiver.'

Because the Conduct of Business Rules have been kept to a minimum and do not impose onerous obligations upon firms, it is unlikely that many applications for waivers will be made or granted in practice.

SOLICITORS AUTHORISED BY THE FSA – NON-MAINSTREAM ACTIVITIES

Firms authorised by FSA will be subject to the FSA's Conduct of Business **6.10**
Sourcebook (COBS) in respect of their mainstream regulated activities.
However such firms will also be carrying on their normal legal activities and,
as such, will be undertaking potential regulated activities in much the same
way as unauthorised firms of solicitors.

Such firms can take the benefit of the statutory exclusions contained in
RAO as noted above (see Chapter 3). Where these exclusions apply the
activities will not amount to regulated activities and will therefore be
outside the scope of FSA regulation. However, for those activities which do
not fall within the statutory exclusions it must be noted that FSMA, Part XX
(exempt regulated activities) does not apply to firms authorised by FSA.

However, COBS 1.2.1 states that the Conduct of Business Rules do not
apply to an authorised professional firm with respect to its non-mainstream
regulated activities, except for:

(a) COB 2.1 (Clear fair and not misleading communications to customers);
(b) COB 3 (Financial promotions);
(c) COB 4.2 (Terms of business and client agreements – in particular
     4.2.1–4.2.6; 4.2.9–4.2.11; and 4.2.15).

(This publication does not purport to cover the contents of the FSA's
Conduct of Business Sourcebook. Details of the rules applicable to a firm's
non-mainstream regulated activities are to be found on the FSA's website
(www.fsa.gov.uk).)

Non-mainstream regulated activities are defined in the Professional Firms
Sourcebook (rule 5.2). The definition replicates the requirements of FSMA,
section 327. Thus the conditions for non-mainstream activities are:

(a) The person must be a member of a profession which is a DPB or
     controlled or managed by one or more such members;
(b) The person must not receive from anyone other than his client any pecu-
     niary reward or other advantage, for which he does not account to his
     client, arising out of his carrying on of any of the activities;
(c) The manner of the provision of any service in the course of carrying on
     the activities must be incidental to the provision by him of professional
     services;
(d) The activities must not be of a description specified in an order made by
     the Treasury.

The same comments apply to the interpretation of the above conditions as
noted above (see the detailed commentary in Chapter 4, para. 4.21).

Authorised firms who undertake non-mainstream regulated activities will
not be subject to the Law Society's Scope Rules. Rule 2 of the Scope Rules
provides:

'These rules apply only to firms which are not regulated by the FSA.'

However, because the conditions for non-mainstream activities include reference to the order made by the Treasury, the restrictions contained in the Non Exempt Activities Order will apply (see para. 4.7). These are very similar to the restrictions contained in the Scope Rules. Those firms undertaking non-mainstream regulated activities will be subject to the Law Society's Conduct of Business Rules. Rule 2 provides

'Apart from rule 3 (status disclosure), these rules apply to:

(a) firms which are not regulated by the FSA; and
(b) firms which are regulated by the FSA but these rules only apply to such firms in respect of their non-mainstream regulated activities.'

Consequently firms authorised by FSA must consider the Conduct of Business Rules in respect of their non-mainstream activities and ensure that they have appropriate systems in place to comply with those rules. Those paragraphs of this chapter from 6.2 onwards will be relevant.

MONITORING AND COMPLAINTS

6.11 There is no specific provision for the monitoring by the Law Society of firms relying upon FSMA, Part XX. Consequently there will be no formal monitoring visits checking on compliance with the Scope Rules or the Conduct of Business Rules. However, as noted above, breach of the rules could amount to (in the case of the Scope Rules) a criminal offence under FSMA, section 23 and an order by the FSA preventing the firm from carrying on any regulated activities. Breach of the Conduct of Business Rules whilst not amounting to a criminal offence could lead to disciplinary action.

The Society will continue to be responsible for the monitoring and enforcement of compliance with SIBR in respect of investment business which was undertaken by firms before 1 December 2001. In particular, solicitors must ensure that any records that they were required to keep under the SIBR must be retained for at least six years from the date on which the record was made. The Office for the Supervision of Solicitors will deal with any complaints concerning these activities in the usual manner.

The Council has issued a number of statements dealing with investment business related matters such as the review of pension transfers and opt outs. Some of these statements continue to be relevant as they relate to acts or omissions occurring before 1 December 2001. Therefore, the Council has decided that the following Council statements will remain in being:

(a) Guidance – preservation of pension records (dated 2 March 1994);
(b) Council statement – Document C (review of pension transfers and opt outs) (dated 7 June 1995);

(c) Council statement – Document D (phase 2 of review of pension transfers and opt outs) (dated 16 October 1998); and

(d) Council statement on review of free standing additional voluntary contributions (dated 12 July 2000).

The above statements are published in *The Guide to the Professional Conduct of Solicitors* (8th edition) and copies are available from Professional Ethics (telephone number 0870 606 2577).

The Law Society will also be responsible for complaints concerning non-mainstream regulated activities undertaken by solicitors' firms which are authorised by the FSA.

CHAPTER 7

Financial promotions

INTRODUCTION

7.1 Solicitors who avoid the need for authorisation from the FSA as a result of excluded activities or exempt regulated activities must still consider whether authorisation is necessary as a result of the financial promotion regime. As noted above (para. 1.5) FSMA, section 21 restricts certain communications in relation to investment activities unless the communication is made by an authorised person or the content of the communication is approved by an authorised person. Section 21 states:

'(1) A person ('A') must not, in the course of business, communicate an invitation or inducement to engage in investment activity.

(2) But subsection (1) does not apply if:

(a) A is an authorised person; or

(b) the content of the communication is approved for the purposes of this section by an authorised person.'

Communication for these purposes is restricted to communications made in the course of a business. *Engaging in investment activity* is defined in section 21(8) as meaning:

'(a) entering or offering to enter into an agreement the making or performance of which by either party constitutes a controlled activity; or

(b) exercising any rights conferred by a controlled investment to acquire, dispose of, underwrite or convert a controlled investment.'

Controlled activities and controlled investments are defined in Schedules 1 and 2 to FPO. The definition of controlled activities follows very closely the definition of regulated activities contained in RAO (see above paras. 2.25 *et seq.*). Thus the activities which could be relevant to solicitors include:

(a) dealing in securities and contractually based investments;

(b) arranging deals in investments;

(c) managing investments involving the exercise of discretion;

(d) safeguarding and administration of investments;

(e) advising on investments;
(f) providing qualifying credit (i.e. credit which is provided pursuant to an agreement under which –

    (i) the lender is a person who carries on the regulated activity of entering into or administering a regulated mortgage contract; and
    (ii) the obligation of the borrower to repay is secured on land. *Note:* this activity is unlikely to give rise to financial promotions until the provisions relating to regulating to regulated mortgage activities come into force, probably sometime in 2004.)

However there is a very important distinction to be drawn between the definition of regulated activities under the RAO and controlled activities under the FPO. The RAO contains a number of important exclusions (for example the authorised person exclusion (para. 3.5 above); the introductions exclusion (para. 3.14 above); the exclusion for trustees and personal representatives (para. 3.23 above); the exclusion for *necessary* activities (para. 3.32 above); the corporate activities exclusion (para. 3.33 above). These exclusions **do not** apply to the definition of controlled activities under the FPO. Consequently solicitors who avoid undertaking regulated activities as a result of any of these statutory exclusions must look elsewhere for an exemption relating to any financial promotion arising as a result of these activities. Further the FSMA, Part XX régime for exempt regulated activities does not apply specifically to financial promotions. Again it will be necessary to look elsewhere to find an appropriate exemption for any financial promotion.

Controlled investments within the meaning of the FPO follow the same basic definition of investments for the purposes of the RAO (for the full list, see above paras. 2.3 *et seq.*). Consequently controlled activities in relation to the following investments are likely to be most relevant for solicitors:

(a) shares or stock in the share capital of a body corporate (subject to the same exclusions for open-ended investment company shares and the shares of building societies incorporated in the UK);
(b) instruments acknowledging indebtedness, including debentures, loan stock, bonds and certificates of deposits (again subject to the same exclusions in respect of loans for consideration payable under contracts for the sale of goods or services; cheques, banker's drafts etc.; banknotes; contracts of insurance);
(c) government and public securities;
(d) units in collective investment schemes;
(e) rights under an agreement for qualifying credit (see above for the definition of qualifying credit and note the delayed implementation date).

The result of these provisions is that solicitors must ensure that they and their staff understand what amounts to a financial promotion and ensure that an appropriate exemption under the FPO applies. Failure to do this could lead to criminal liability. FSMA, section 25 creates an offence which is committed when a person contravenes section 21. The punishment is, on summary conviction, imprisonment for a term not exceeding six months or a fine not exceeding the statutory maximum, or both; on conviction on indictment, imprisonment for a term not exceeding two years or a fine, or both. There is a defence to show that the accused believed on reasonable grounds that the content of the communication was prepared, or approved for the purposes of section 21, by an authorised person; or that he took all reasonable precautions and exercised all due diligence to avoid committing the offence.

TYPES OF FINANCIAL PROMOTION

7.2   Financial promotions caught by the restriction in FSMA, section 21 include both *real time* and *non-real time* promotions. A real time promotion is defined in FPO, art. 7(1) by reference to

> 'any communication made in the course of a personal visit, telephone conversation or other interactive dialogue'.

Article 7(2) defines a non-real time promotion as

> 'a communication not falling within paragraph (1)'.

Consequently all oral and written communications with clients and others are capable of falling within the FPO if they communicate an invitation or inducement to enter into investment activity. It is important to distinguish real time from non-real time promotions since the exemptions contained in the FPO depend, in many cases, on the type of promotion.

FPO, article 7(5) provides further indicators which are useful in determining whether a communication is non-real time. The following factors indicate that it is a non-real time communication:

(a)   the communication is made to or directed at more than one recipient in identical terms (save for details of the recipient's identity);

(b)   the communication is made or directed by way of a system which in the normal course constitutes or creates a record of the communication which is available to the recipient to refer to at a later time;

(c)   the communication is made or directed by way of a system which in the normal course does not enable or require the recipient to respond immediately to it.

Solicitors who communicate to clients by telephone or meetings could be involved in real time promotions; their brochures, letters, faxes, e-mails and websites might be non-real time promotions.

Real time promotions are further categorised as *solicited* or *non-solicited*. Again it is vital to make this distinction since many of the exemptions in the

FPO depend upon this categorisation. FPO, article 8(1) defines a solicited real time promotion where it is made in the course of a personal visit, telephone call or other interactive dialogue and the call, visit or dialogue:

'(a) was initiated by the recipient of the communication; or
(b) takes place in response to an express request from the recipient of the communication'.

A real time communication is unsolicited where it is made otherwise than as described in article 8(1).

Article 8(3) provides further guidance on the definition of solicited real time communications. It provides for the purposes of paragraph (1):

'(a) a person is not to be treated as expressly requesting a call, visit or dialogue –

(i) because he omits to indicate that he does not wish to receive any or any further visits or calls or to engage in any or any further dialogue;
(ii) because he agrees to standard terms that state that such visits, calls or dialogue will take place, unless he has signified clearly that, in addition to agreeing to the terms, he is willing for them to take place;

(b) a communication is solicited only if it is clear from all the circumstances when the call, visit or dialogue is initiated or requested that during the course of the visit, call or dialogue communications will be made concerning the kind of controlled activities or investments to which the communications in fact made relate'.

Not surprisingly, the more beneficial exemptions in the FPO apply to solicited communications. As noted in article 8(3), solicitors cannot rely upon standard terms in their engagement letters to indicate that a client is *expressly requesting a call, visit or dialogue*. However, the FSA has included guidance on financial promotions in its published guidance for professional firms. Paragraph 1.26.29 G provides:

'Professional firms, in issuing terms of engagement letters to clients may consider it prudent to draw specific attention, where relevant, to the possibility of the firm making unsolicited real time financial promotions and seek the client's specific acceptance of this as well as acceptance of other terms. This could be achieved, for example, by the client providing a separate signature by the side of the relevant term.'

By approaching their terms of business in this way it should be possible for solicitors to show that any future promotion takes place in response to an express request and is, in consequence a solicited communication.

If a solicitor makes a real time financial promotion to a client who has expressly requested it, but at the same time it is also made to other persons present, then it will be an unsolicited promotion to those other persons unless they are either a close relative of the requesting client or it is to someone who would be expected to engage in any activity jointly with the requesting client (FPO, article 8(4)). *Close relative* means for these purposes, a person's:

(a) spouse;
(b) children and stepchildren; parents and stepparents; brothers and sisters; and stepbrothers and stepsisters; and
(c) the spouse of any person within (b) above.

EXEMPTIONS UNDER THE FPO

7.3 Failure of an unauthorised firm of solicitors to identify an appropriate exemption under the FPO could lead to criminal liability and could lead to contracts being unenforceable (see above para. 7.1). It is therefore vital for unauthorised solicitors to ensure that any communication with a client or potential client or other person which amounts to a financial promotion is only made in circumstances covered by the exemptions. There are two exemptions which are of particular importance to professional firms (and thus solicitors) together with a number of further exemptions which might be relevant in specific situations.

Some of the exemptions apply only to real time promotions; others to non-real time promotions. Some exemptions are dependent upon whether a real time promotion is solicited or unsolicited. These concepts are dealt with above (para. 7.2 *et seq.*) and their definitions are not repeated in this section of the chapter.

Communications by members of professions

Article 55

7.4 Article 55(1) provides:

'The financial promotion restriction does not apply to a real time communication (whether solicited or unsolicited) which –

(a) is made by a person ('P') who carries on a regulated activity to which the general prohibition does not apply by virtue of section 327 of the Act; and
(b) is made to a recipient who has, prior to the communication being made, engaged P to provide professional services,

where the controlled activity to which the communication relates is an excluded activity which would be undertaken by P for the purposes of, and incidental to, the provision by him of professional services to or at the request of the recipient.'

This article requires some commentary which appears in the following paragraphs.

REAL TIME COMMUNICATIONS (WHETHER SOLICITED OR UNSOLICITED)

7.5 The exemption in article 55 is only available to real time communications, i.e. those of an oral rather than written nature. However, the exemption is available whether those real time promotions are solicited or unsolicited.

SECTION 327 OF THE ACT

7.6 The exemption is only available to those solicitors who carry on exempt regulated activities within FSMA, Part XX, section 327 and who are therefore subject to regulation by the Law Society as a DPB. Consequently the exclusion is not available to those firms who are authorised by FSA.

A RECIPIENT WHO HAS, PRIOR TO THE COMMUNICATION BEING MADE, ENGAGED THE SOLICITOR TO PROVIDE PROFESSIONAL SERVICES

7.7 The exclusion is only available to existing clients of the firm. It would not, therefore be available for real time communications made to potential clients of the firm, or to third parties on behalf of potential clients.

RELATES TO AN EXCLUDED ACTIVITY WHICH WOULD BE UNDERTAKEN BY THE SOLICITOR

7.8 An excluded activity for these purposes is defined in article 55(3) as being an activity to which the general prohibition would apply (i.e. the prohibition in FSMA s.19, see above para. 1.2) but for the application of FSMA s.327 (the Part XX régime – see above Chapter 4) or RAO, art. 67 (the *necessary* exclusion' – see above para. 3.32).

INCIDENTAL TO THE PROVISION OF PROFESSIONAL SERVICES TO OR AT THE REQUEST OF THE RECIPIENT

7.9 The effect of this condition is that the financial promotion must relate to an activity which is incidental to other professional services. Given the condition noted in para. 7.8 above, this should always be the case.

Consequently solicitors can only use article 55 where oral communications are made to existing clients in respect of potential activities which would either be excluded because of RAO, article 67 or fall within the definition of exempt regulated activities under FSMA, Part XX. The article 55 exemption would not be available for oral communications made in respect of potential regulated activities where the activities would be excluded as a result of another exclusion in RAO, for example the authorised person exclusion for dealing or arranging deals, the article 66 exclusion for trustees or PRs or the corporate exclusion in RAO, article 70. Article 55 also would not be available for any non-real time communications (i.e. marketing material in brochures, or websites), even if that marketing material related to exempt or necessary activities. (However, note para. 7.10 below which deals with the exemption for non-real time activities contained in FPO, article 55A.) Firms should therefore identify those circumstances where article 55 will provide an exemption and those where article 55 will not assist; these circumstances should then be stated in the firm's compliance manual and clearly communicated to relevant fee earners.

Article 55A

7.10 As noted above, article 55 does not apply to non-real time (i.e. written) communications. Article 55A was added to the FPO by the Financial Services and Markets Act 2001 (Financial Promotion) (Amendment) Order 2001, SI 2001/2633. It applies to non-real time promotions and therefore extends the exemptions in the FPO for professionals to brochures, letters, e-mails and websites. Article 55A provides:

'(1) The financial promotion restriction does not apply to a non-real time communication which is –

(a) made by a person ("P") who carries on Part XX activities; and

(b) limited to what is required or permitted by paragraphs (2) and (3).

(2) The communication must be in the following terms –

"This [firm/company] is not authorised under the Financial Services and Markets Act 2000 but we are able in certain circumstances to offer a limited range of investment services to clients because we are members of [relevant designated professional body]. We can provide these investment services if they are an incidental part of the professional services we have been engaged to provide."

(3) The communication may in addition set out the Part XX activities which P is able to offer to his clients, provided it is clear that these are the investment services to which the statement in paragraph (2) relates.'

This is a very valuable amendment for unauthorised solicitors allowing them to communicate to clients, potential clients and other third parties by way of non-real time promotions provided the communication does not contain an invitation or inducement relating to activities not covered by FSMA, Part XX (exempt regulated activities). However, it should be noted that, unlike article 55 (real time exclusion), the article 55A exemption does not apply where the communication relates to a regulated activity covered by RAO, article 67 (the *necessary* exclusion).

Solicitors should consider very carefully whether the content of their written publicity requires the benefit of this exclusion. Where appropriate they should err on the side of caution and include the statement referred to in article 55A(2). The FSA has given guidance on the operation of the article 55A exclusion. Paragraph 1.26.12 G states:

'(1) it is not necessary for the details concerning the Part XX activities to be set out in one place or adjacent to the statement. A brochure or website, for example, may contain details of Part XX activities in various places so long as it is made clear that they will be incidental investment activities as referred to in the statement (which, as a result, needs to be set out only once in the brochure or website).'

One problem which has been considered arises from the fact that in some cases, the written publicity attracting a potential client might, in order to benefit from article 55A, refer to Part XX activities, but when the solicitor undertakes the actual work, the activity is excluded as a result of one of the RAO exclusions. Does this affect the exemption in article 55A? Again there is useful FSA guidance on this point in their guidance, paragraph 1.26.12 G (3):

'the mere fact that a financial promotion made under article 55A may be likely, on occasion, to result in the carrying on by the professional firm of activities which are excluded under the RAO does not mean that the financial promotion must fail to satisfy the terms of article 55A. There will be occasions where a professional firm will, of necessity, offer to provide services which may or may not involve Part XX activities or excluded activities. In the area of corporate finance, for example, a professional firm may offer its services in relation to the sale of an incorporated business or a substantial shareholding in such a business. It will not be apparent whether the professional firm's services will be Part XX activities or excluded activities until details of a proposed deal are known [. . .]. In practice, it will often be impossible for the professional firm to distinguish between Part XX activities and excluded activities at the preliminary stage of a brochure or website offering its services. In the FSA's view, the article 55A exemption will apply provided the only regulated activities held out in the brochure, website or other non-real time financial promotion are Part XX activities'.

It is therefore important that in drafting brochures, websites etc., solicitors only refer to Part XX activities. Thereafter, if it appears that an exclusion contained in the RAO is available in respect of the solicitor's retainer, that exclusion can be used by the solicitor without risking the loss of the article 55A exemption.

Whilst many communications made by solicitors will benefit from either article 55 or article 55A of FPO, there are still likely to be circumstances where communications will not fall within these articles. In such cases other possible exemptions might be available. Most solicitors who, for any reason, cannot use articles 55 and 55A should be able to identify other exemptions and therefore avoid the need for authorisation or the need to have their promotions approved by an authorised person.

One-off financial promotions

Article 28

7.11 FPO, article 28 provides an exemption for one-off non-real time communications and solicited real time communications. For the purposes of article 28, it is necessary to distinguish between solicited and unsolicited real time promotions. The article only applies to solicited real time promotions (although, note below article 28A, dealt with in para. 7.12, which provides an exemption for unsolicited real time promotions).

Article 28 states:

'(1) The financial promotion restriction does not apply to a one-off communication which is either a non-real time communication or a solicited real time communication.

(2) If all the conditions set out in paragraph (3) are met in relation to a communication it is to be regarded as a one-off communication. In any other case in which one or more of those conditions are met, that fact is to be taken into account in determining whether the communication is a one-off communication (but a communication may still be regarded as a one-off communication even if none of the conditions in paragraph (3) is met).

(3) The conditions are that –

(a) the communication is made only to one recipient or only to one group of recipients in the expectation that they would engage in any investment activity jointly;

(b) the identity of the product or service to which the communication relates has been determined having regard to the particular circumstances of the recipient;

(c) the communication is not part of an organised marketing campaign.'

One-off financial promotions are promotions which are personal to the recipient (or group of recipients) and therefore not part of a marketing campaign. The essence of this exemption is that the solicitor has applied his mind to the individual circumstances of the client and tailors the promotion accordingly. It is unlikely, therefore, that article 28 could apply to brochures or websites. This exemption could, however, apply to non-real time (i.e. written) communications made to clients, potential clients or third parties (whether solicited or non solicited) provided such communications are not part of a marketing strategy. Further, it should be noted that this particular exemption is not dependent upon any type of regulated activity. In other words, it is capable of applying where the solicitor intends to use any of the RAO exclusions or where the solicitor intends providing exempt regulated activities within FSMA, Part XX. Although brochures and websites will not benefit from this exemption, other written material may benefit. For example, a letter, e-mail or fax which is addressed to a specific recipient may contain an inducement or invitation to the recipient to engage in investment activities. Providing this is not part of an organised marketing campaign, article 28 should assist. Real time promotions (i.e. oral) made to clients, potential clients or others must be solicited to benefit from this exclusion. This would cover solicited communications made in meetings or by way of telephone calls.

The FSA guidance states the following in respect of article 28:

'1.26.15 G   In the FSA's view, financial promotions which are part of a series of communications made to a particular client are capable of remaining one-off financial promotions.

I1.26.16 G   It is appreciated that there will be times when a financial promotion is made by a professional firm to a client and, at the same time, to another person who is present (for example a friend or relative or other supporter or an ex-spouse and their adviser in the case of a matrimonial dispute). Provided the financial promotion made in such circumstances remains personal to the client it is the FSA's view that it would continue to be regarded as 'one-off' in nature.'

If the conditions laid down in article 28(3) apply to the promotion, it will be regarded as a one-off communication. However, as noted in article 28(2), if not all the conditions apply, the conditions are still to be taken into account in determining whether there is a one-off promotion. The article states specifically that a communication may still be regarded as one-off even if none of the conditions apply. Consequently, in cases of doubt, reference should be made to the FSA's guidance and in particular their definition of 'one-off' being personal to the recipient.

Article 28A

Article 28 does not exempt unsolicited real time promotions. An additional **7.12** exemption for such promotions was added by Financial Services and Markets Act 2001 (Financial Promotion) (Amendment) Order 2001, SI 2001/2633. This article provides:

'(1) The financial promotion restriction does not apply to an unsolicited real time communication if the conditions in paragraph (2) are met.

(2) The conditions in this paragraph are that –

    (a) the communication is a one-off communication;

    (b) the communicator believes on reasonable grounds that the recipient understands the risks associated with engaging in the investment activity to which the communication relates;

    (c) at the time that the communication is made, the communicator believes on reasonable grounds that the recipient would expect to be contacted by him in relation to the investment activity to which the communication relates.

(3) Paragraphs (2) and (3) of article 28 apply in determining whether a communication is a one-off communication for the purposes of this article as they apply for the purposes of article 28.'

Because the same definition of *one-off* is used in article 28A as appears in article 28, this exemption cannot be used as part of an organised marketing campaign. Subject to the definition of *one-off* applying and to the specific conditions in article 28A, the exemption should provide scope for solicitors. The FSA has provided guidance on both the circumstances where such exemption might be available to professional firms and to the interpretation of the requirement relating to risk, contained in the article.

With regard to the circumstances where the exemption might apply, the FSA has stated (paragraph 1.26.19 G of their guidance):

'The article 28A exemption should provide scope for professional firms to make unsolicited real time financial promotions in various situations, for example, when approaching persons with whom their clients are proposing to do business or those persons' professional advisers. The exemption will not apply where the financial promotions are part of an organised marketing campaign. So in cases where a professional firm is to contact a number of persons on a matter which involves each of them (for instance, where they are significant shareholders in a company for which an offer has been made) it will be necessary for the firm to consider whether the approaches would be an organised marketing campaign. In the FSA's view, provided the professional firm applies its mind to the circumstances of each recipient and tailors the financial promotion accordingly it should be possible for the financial promotion to be regarded as one-off in nature.'

The second condition necessary before article 28A can apply is that the solicitor must believe on reasonable grounds that the recipient understands the risks associated with engaging in the investment activity to which the promotion relates. Here, the FSA believes that the question of reasonableness will have to be judged on particular circumstances. However the FSA states (paragraph 1.26.20 G):

'In the FSA's opinion, it would be reasonable to believe that a person understands the risk involved if he is understood to be a professional or to be professionally advised, in relation to the investment activity to which the financial promotion relates. A person may also reasonably be regarded as understanding the risks involved if, for example, he occupies a position in a company which it is reasonable to suppose would require him to have such an understanding (such as a finance director for example).'

Follow-up communications (article 14)

7.13 Article 14 applies to non-real time communications and solicited real time communications. The article states:

'(1) Where a person makes or directs a communication ('the first communication') which is exempt from the financial promotion restriction because, in compliance with the requirements of another provision of this Order, it is accompanied by certain indications or contains certain information, then the financial promotion restriction does not apply to any subsequent communication which complies with the requirements of paragraph (2).

(2) The requirements of this paragraph are that the subsequent communication –

(a) is a non-real time communication or a solicited real time communication;

(b) is made by the same person who made the first communication;

(c) is made to a recipient of the first communication;

(d) relates to the same controlled activity and the same controlled investment as the first communication; and

(e) is made within 12 months of the recipient receiving the first communication.'

This exemption only applies where the communication follows an earlier communication which was accompanied by certain indications or contains certain information. Therefore the only circumstances where this follow-up communication will be exempt under article 14 is where the earlier communication is exempt as a result of article 55A (see para. 7.10) above or where the earlier communication is exempt because of the exemptions relating to *high net worth investors* (see para. 7.15 and 7.16 below). Since the latter exemptions will apply to only a few solicitors it is likely that follow-up communications will be more commonly available where the original communication is made in a brochure or website containing the appropriate statement as required by article 55A. Following the communication by brochure or website any follow-up communication satisfying the details of article 14(2) will itself be exempt.

Introductions (article 15)

Article 15 states: **7.14**

'(1) If the requirements of paragraph (2) are met, the financial promotion restriction does not apply to any real time communication which is made with a view to or for the purposes of introducing the recipient to –

(a) an authorised person who carries on the controlled activity to which the communication relates; or

(b) an exempt person where the communication relates to a controlled activity which is also a regulated activity in relation to which he is an exempt person.

(2) The requirements of this paragraph are that –

(a) the maker of the communication ('A') is not a close relative of, nor a member of the same group as, the person to whom the introduction is, or is to be, made;

(b) A does not receive from any person other than the recipient any pecuniary reward or other advantage arising out of his making the introduction; and

(c) it is clear in all the circumstances that the recipient, in his capacity as an investor, is not seeking and has not sought advice from A as to the merits of the recipient engaging in investment activity (or, if the client has sought such advice, A has declined to give it, but has recommended that the recipient seek such advice from an authorised person).'

Article 15 is potentially a useful exemption for solicitors. As noted above, RAO, article 33 allows solicitors to make introductions to third parties with a view to the provision of independent advice without undertaking an arranging activity and thereby without the need for authorisation. This exemption allows solicitors to promote the fact that they can make such an introduction. Two points must, however, be noted. First, under article 33 an introduction can be made without undertaking a regulated activity even if the solicitor receives commission or other pecuniary reward (for example receives a commission of £20 or less; Practice Rule 10 allows the solicitor to retain this sum without the client's consent). Where the solicitor is relying on FPO, article 15 in respect of any promotion relating to the introduction, he must not receive any commission arising out of making the introduction. The FSA has given guidance on this. Paragraph 1.26.23 provides:

'It is the FSA's view that a professional firm may be regarded as not receiving payment other than from his client in circumstances where there is a clear pre-existing understanding between the firm and its client that the firm would account to the client for any payment he may receive from a third party.'

Secondly where a firm has hived off its financial services activities into a separate business (authorised by FSA), introductions to this separate business will not benefit from article 15 since, with common ownership, the hived off business will be a member of the same group as the solicitor's firm. In these circumstances other exemptions will still be available, subject to appropriate conditions being met.

Certified high net worth individual (article 48)

7.15 Article 48 contains an exemption where a non-real time or solicited real time communication is made to a certified high net worth individual. The communication can only be made in respect of certain investments (generally unlisted company shares or debentures or collective investment schemes investing wholly or predominantly in such investments). A certified net worth individual must have a current certificate of high net worth signed by the individual's accountant or employer showing annual income of not less than £100,000 or net assets of not less than £250,000 (excluding the value of his primary residence or loan secured on that residence). The individual must sign a statement (within 12 months ending with the day on which the communication was made) in the following terms:

> 'I make this statement so that I am able to receive promotions which are exempt from the restriction on financial promotion in section 21 of the Financial Services and Markets Act 2000. The exemption relates to certified high net worth individuals and I declare that I qualify as such. I accept that the content of promotions and other material that I receive may not have been approved by a person who has been authorised under that Act and that their content may not therefore be subject to controls which would apply if the promotion were made or approved by an authorised person. I am aware that it is open to me to seek advice from someone who is authorised under the Act and who specialises in advising on this kind of investment.'

Any communication relying upon this exemption must be accompanied by an indication as required by article 48(4):

> '(a) that it is exempt from the general restriction (in section 21 of the Financial Services and Markets Act 2000) on the communication of invitations or inducements to engage in investment activity on the grounds that it is made to a certified high net worth individual;
>
> (b) of the requirements that must be met for a person to qualify as a certified high net worth individual;
>
> (c) that the content of the communication has not been approved by an authorised person and that such approval is, unless this exemption or any other exemption applies, required by section 21 of the Act;
>
> (d) that reliance on the communication for the purpose of engaging in any investment activity may expose the individual to a significant risk of losing all of the property invested;
>
> (e) that any person who is in any doubt about the investment to which the communication relates should consult an authorised person specialising in advising on investments of the kind in question.'

Any further communications are capable of benefiting from the follow-up exemption in article 14 (see above para. 7.13).

High net worth companies, unincorporated associations etc. (article 49)

Article 49 provides an exemption for any communication made to persons who are: **7.16**

(a) a body corporate with called up share capital or net assets of not less than £500,000 (where the body or its parent undertaking has 20 or more members) or not less than £5 million (in all other cases);

(b) an unincorporated association or partnership with net assets of not less than £5 million;

(c) the trustee of a high value trust (i.e. where the net aggregate value of the cash and investments is £10 million or more).

Where article 49 is relied upon certain further conditions laid down in article 49(4) must be met. These are:

'(a) the communication includes an indication of the description of persons to whom it is directed and an indication of the fact that the controlled investment or controlled activity to which it relates is available only to such persons;

(b) the communication includes an indication that persons of any other description should not act upon it;

(c) there are in place proper systems and procedures to prevent recipients other than persons to whom paragraph (2) applies engaging in the investment activity to which the communication relates with the person directing the communication, a close relative of his or a member of the same group.'

It should be noted that article 49, unlike article 48 (net worth individuals) is not subject to restrictions relating to the type of financial promotion or the category of investment. Follow-up communications are capable of benefiting from article 14.

Settlors, trustees and PRs (article 53)

7.17   Article 53 provides:

'The financial promotion restriction does not apply to any communication which is made between –

(a) a person when acting as a settlor or grantor of a trust, a trustee or a personal representative; and

(b) a trustee of the trust, a fellow trustee or a fellow personal representative (as the case may be),

if the communication is made for the purposes of the trust or estate.'

Whilst this article will not benefit those solicitors who are acting for outside trustees or PRs, it may assist those who are trustees or PRs in respect of communications made to fellow trustees or representatives for the purposes of the trust fund or estate. It should be linked with RAO, article 66 and the excluded activities arising under that article (see Chapter 3).

Beneficiaries of trust, will or intestacy (article 54)

7.18   Article 54 states:

'The financial promotion restriction does not apply to any communication which is made –

(a) between a person when acting as a settlor or grantor of a trust, trustee or personal representative and a beneficiary under the trust, will or intestacy; or

(b) between a beneficiary under a trust, will or intestacy and another beneficiary under the same trust, will or intestacy,

if the communication relates to the management or distribution of that trust fund or estate.'

Again, this is only available to those solicitors who are trustees or PRs; it is not available to those simply acting for external trustees or PRs. However, it will allow communications to be made to beneficiaries in connection with the management of the trust fund or estate.

MARKETING A SOLICITOR'S PRACTICE

The Financial Promotions Order is clearly important when solicitors are considering a marketing strategy in respect of controlled activities. The following chapters of this handbook cover the practical application of the financial services regulations to different sectors of a solicitor's practice. In each chapter there is specific reference to any suitable exclusion contained in the FPO. What follows here are some general points relating to marketing strategy. **7.19**

Brochures and websites

Solicitors who use brochures and websites as part of their marketing strategy must consider carefully whether such publications contain communications which might induce or invite potential or existing clients to engage in investment activities. Brochures and websites will be non-real time promotions. As such they can benefit from the exemption in article 55A provided solicitors ensure that the appropriate statement is included in the publication (see above para. 7.10) and that the only regulated activities referred to are those capable of being exempt within the meaning of FSMA, Part XX (see Chapter 4). **7.20**

The brochure or website may refer to activities such as management, and safeguarding and administration (i.e. as trustee or PR). These activities are capable of falling within Part XX and therefore such communications can benefit from the exemption in article 55A. However when the solicitor accepts instructions to act, he may decide that the exclusions in RAO, article 66 may be available (see above para. 3.23). FSA takes the view that the benefit of article 55A is still available in these circumstances (see para. 7.10 above). However solicitors should take care not to lose the benefit of article 66 by holding out themselves as providing these services (see para. 3.23 above).

Cross-selling to existing clients

7.21 A solicitor may wish to notify existing clients of the fact that the firm can offer other services. This could be undertaken at meetings with the client or in writing by letter, e-mail etc. The oral statements may amount to a real time communication if they contain an inducement or invitation to engage in investment activities; these could be solicited or unsolicited depending upon the circumstances. Any written statements of a similar nature will be non-real time communications. Provided the non-real time communications satisfy the requirements of article 55 (i.e. they are made to an existing client and relate to either activities which are exempt under FSMA, Part XX or excluded under RAO, article 67) it should provide an appropriate exemption under the FPO. Alternatively, where the communications are solicited, the one-off exemption in article 28 may apply.

The written statements (including letters and e-mails) should contain the appropriate article 55A statement to ensure that these documents can benefit from article 55A. Alternatively, if the appropriate conditions apply, firms might be able to use article 28 (one-off communications) for non-real time communications.

Oral communications made to non-clients

7.22 Oral communications made to non-clients are not capable of benefiting from article 55. If these communications are solicited, article 28 (one-off promotions) might assist. If they are unsolicited article 28A might apply. However, this must not be part of a marketing campaign (i.e. a series of lectures given by a member of the firm where the intent is to market the firm's services). If the solicited real time communication is made following the use of a firm's brochure (which itself is exempt as a result of article 55A) it may amount to a follow-up communication within FPO, article 14.

Solicitors may simply introduce a client to an authorised person and thereby benefit from the *introductions* exemption in FPO, article 15.

CHAPTER 8

Probate and administration

INTRODUCTION

Regulated activities and the estate

Potentially the probate department of any firm is likely to give rise to a **8.1** substantial amount of regulated activities as defined by the RAO. Obviously the starting point is to ascertain whether the retainer involves specified investments. An estate which merely consists of real property and cash is unlikely to give rise to any compliance problems insofar as the administration is concerned. (There may be compliance problems if the real property is sold and the beneficiary seeks investment advice from the solicitor.)

Assuming the estate does include specified investments (e.g. shares and other securities and unit trusts) the administration could give rise to the following examples of regulated activities.

Management

If a partner or employee is an administrator or PR, he or she will be 'man- **8.2** aging assets belonging to another'. If those assets include investments as defined, this management will potentially amount to a regulated activity if it involves the exercise of discretion (RAO, article 37 – see above para. 3.16).

If a partner or employee is the sole PR or is a joint PR with another partner or employee of the firm, the management is likely to be discretionary (and thus potentially caught as a regulated activity). If, however, a partner or employee is a PR jointly with an outsider, then management is vested in all the PRs and it cannot be said that the firm has discretion unless discretion has been expressly delegated to the firm. In this situation, if there is no delegation, the non discretionary management does not give rise to a regulated activity.

Advice

8.3   It is likely that during the course of the administration of an estate members of the firm may be called upon to make recommendations in relation to certain investments. This may be so whether or not partners or employees of the firm are the PRs or administrators. The firm may be asked to advise on the disposal of certain investments or the retention of other investments. In these circumstances, the firm will be giving advice on the merits of buying or selling investments and will potentially be undertaking a regulated activity.

Firms may also be asked to advise beneficiaries on the merits of investing their inheritance or on whether to take an investment *in specie* or to sell and take the cash.

Dealing and arranging deals

8.4   Solicitors involved in probate and administration work will often be asked to make arrangements for the disposal of investments held in the estate. Whether these investments are disposed of by the solicitor or through a third party such arrangements are likely to amount to a regulated activity.

Safeguarding and administration services

8.5   It is likely that probate practitioners will be providing safeguarding and administration services as defined in the RAO on the basis that they will be safeguarding and administering assets belonging to another – see Chapter 2.

Sending dematerialised instructions

8.6   Where securities are held in an uncertificated form, probate practitioners may be involved in sending instructions relating to, for example the disposal of the securities. This activity may amount to sending dematerialised instructions and as such will potentially amount to a regulated activity within RAO, art. 45 – see Chapter 2.

STATUTORY EXCLUSIONS

8.7   Acknowledging that many probates will potentially give rise to regulated activities, it is necessary to identify how probate practitioners can properly avoid the need for authorisation. For this purpose it is helpful to distinguish between those circumstances where a principal or employee of the firm acts as PR (whether or not there are any outside PRs) and those circumstances where the firm is simply acting for outside PRs.

Acting as a PR

Management

If a partner or employee of the firm is a PR or administrator then any dis-   **8.8**
cretionary management undertaken by such a partner or employee in his
capacity as such is capable of falling within the statutory exclusion in RAO,
art. 66. This exclusion is subject to the two important conditions contained
in article 66:

(a) that the firm does not hold itself out as providing discretionary management services; and
(b) that the person carrying on the management activity is not remunerated
for what he does in addition to any remuneration he receives as PR (for
details of this exclusion, see Chapter 3).

Care must be taken to ensure that the firm's publicity material does not hold
out the firm as providing discretionary management services.

Advice

Generic advice will not be caught as a regulated activity under the RAO (see   **8.9**
Chapter 2). However it might be difficult to show that any advice is generic if
the advice can be shown to relate to the specific investments held in the estate.
Specific advice (whether it is advice to sell or buy investments) given by a
partner or employee of the firm in his capacity as a PR will be excluded by
RAO, art. 66 where the advice is given to a fellow PR for the purpose of the
estate or to a beneficiary under the will or intestacy concerning his interest in
the estate. The only condition applicable to this exclusion is the 'no additional
remuneration' condition referred to above in para. 3.29. It should, however, be
noted that this exclusion will only apply to advice given to beneficiaries where
the advice concerns their interests in the estate. If a solicitor has paid a
pecuniary legacy to a beneficiary in accordance with the terms of the will or
intestacy and the beneficiary then approaches the solicitor for advice as to
how to invest such sum, the advice would not concern the beneficiary's
interest in the estate and would not, therefore, be excluded by article 66.

It might also be possible to use the 'necessary' exclusion in article 67 of the
RAO if it can be shown that the advice could reasonably be regarded as a
necessary part of other professional services (see Chapter 3 for details of this
exclusion). This would be particularly helpful if the solicitor PR has to advise
fellow external PRs that all the assets of the estate have to be sold in order to
pay debts or beneficiaries. It is less likely to be available where only some of
the investment assets have to be sold and therefore a choice has to be made
as to which assets are to be sold. Article 67 is subject to a condition that there
is no separate remuneration for carrying out the necessary activities.

Dealing and arranging deals

8.10   A sole PR or one who is a joint PR with partners or employees might be dealing as principal where investments are held in the name of the PR(s) and are sold during the winding up of the estate. Providing the PRs are not holding themselves or the firm out as providing stockbroking services they will not be undertaking a regulated activity when dealing as principal (see the details for this exclusion to apply in Chapter 3).

Arrangements made by partner or employee of the firm in his capacity as a PR will be excluded by RAO, article 66 where the arrangement is made on behalf of himself and fellow PR(s) acting in their capacity as such or where the arrangement is made for a beneficiary under the will or intestacy. Again, the only condition applicable to this exclusion is the 'no additional remuneration' condition referred to above in para. 3.25.

The 'necessary' exclusion in RAO, article 67 may also be available for arrangements made. As noted above this is only likely to be relevant where all the assets are being sold.

Safeguarding, administration and sending dematerialised instructions

8.11   Where a partner or employee is acting as a PR and is involved in safeguarding and administration and/or sending dematerialised instructions, article 66 may again provide an exclusion. In both cases where PRs undertake these activities, they will be excluded from being regulated activities if the appropriate conditions are met. For the exclusion to apply to safeguarding and administration services, both the conditions noted above in para. 3.27 (no additional remuneration and no holding out) must be satisfied.

It might also be possible to use the 'necessary' exclusion in article 67.

Activities undertaken by other members of the firm

8.12   In many cases, although a partner or employee is appointed as the PR, the actual activities (which potentially could bring the firm within the scope of regulated activities) might be undertaken by other members of staff. Support staff may research and advise the internal PRs; support staff may make arrangements for the disposal of investments on behalf of internal and external PRs; and support staff may be involved in safeguarding and administration and/or sending dematerialised instructions. In each of these cases, providing the other appropriate conditions are met, the firm should be able to benefit from the exclusions in RAO, article 66 as noted above. The FSA guidance makes it clear that the exclusion will apply to other members of staff who carry out the activities on behalf of the PRs. Details of the guidance can be found in para. 3.31 above and in Appendix C1.

Acting for external PRs

Where a firm is simply acting for external PRs, the important exclusions **8.13** contained in RAO, article 66 have no application. Article 66 can only apply where a member of the firm is a PR.

Management

If the firm is acting for external PRs there should be no management activity. **8.14** Management is only caught if it is discretionary management. Provided the firm has not had discretionary management delegated to it by the external PRs, no management activity will arise. If there is discretionary management, no statutory exclusion is available and such activity will inevitably lead to a requirement that the firm is authorised by FSA.

Advice

Members of the firm may wish to give advice to external PRs on the merits **8.15** of selling investments held in the estate. Such advice is potentially a regulated activity if it is specific as opposed to generic advice. The 'necessary' exclusion in RAO, art. 67 might be available but as noted above (para. 8.9) this exclusion is only likely to be available where the advice relates to the disposal of all the assets in the estate. The exclusion is subject to the requirement that no separate remuneration is received for carrying out the necessary activity.

Also, as noted above, simply obtaining and passing on the advice of an authorised person is not a regulated activity (see para. 3.7 above). However to avoid a regulated activity, care must be taken not to comment on the advice since such commentary could be interpreted as 'advice on the merits'. If commentary is required (although the advice is not 'necessary' within article 67) solicitors should consider the DPB régime (see below, para. 8.18).

Dealing and arrangements

Firms acting for external PRs will not be dealing as principal. They may, **8.16** however deal as agent for their client or make arrangements on behalf of their clients. Since RAO, article 66 will not apply, firms will have to look elsewhere for exclusions. It may be possible to use the 'necessary' exclusion in article 67 but, as noted above this is likely to be limited to those transactions where all the assets of the estate are being sold. Of more general benefit is the 'authorised person' exclusion contained in both RAO, articles 22 and 29. This exclusion is dealt with in some detail in paras. 3.5 *et seq.* above. It applies where a solicitor enters into a transaction with or through an authorised person and one of two alternative conditions are satisfied together with, in either case, a further condition relating to pecuniary reward. The alternative conditions are:

(a) the transaction is entered into on advice given to the client by an authorised person; or

(b) it is clear in all the circumstances that the client, in his capacity as an investor, is not seeking and has not sought advice from the solicitor as to the merits of the client entering the transaction (or if the client has sought advice the solicitor has declined to give it but has recommended the client to seek advice from an authorised person).

The further condition provides that the exclusion does not apply if the agent receives from any person other than the client any pecuniary reward or advantage, for which he does not account to the client, arising out of his entering into the transaction.

An alternative means of assisting external PRs would be to introduce them to an authorised person for independent advice. This introduction would not be a regulated activity (see above para. 3.14).

Safeguarding and administration and sending dematerialised instructions

8.17 Where firms provide safeguarding and administration services and/or send dematerialised instructions for or on behalf of external PRs they will be undertaking regulated activities. The only possible statutory exclusion available is that contained in article 67 (the 'necessary' exclusion).

FSMA, PART XX RÉGIME

8.18 It may not be possible in all circumstances for probate practitioners to avoid regulated activities through the use of the statutory exclusions. For example, solicitors who are PRs may be undertaking management activities in circumstances where the firm's brochure holds out the fact that management services may be provided. Solicitors who are acting for external PRs may wish to comment on or endorse the advice of authorised persons. Further those solicitors acting for external PRs may provide safeguarding and administration services and/or send dematerialised instructions in circumstances where it is not strictly necessary for them to do so and consequently cannot use the 'necessary' exclusion in article 67. In any of these situations, solicitors who wish to remain unauthorised will have to ensure that they provide exempt regulated activities within FSMA, Part XX. To do so, they will have to bring themselves within the Law Society's Scope Rules, meeting the necessary basic and other conditions laid down by those Scope Rules (for details of the conditions, see Chapter 4).

For the conditions in the Scope Rules to apply it will be necessary for the solicitor to show that the manner in which regulated activities are being provided is such that they are incidental to the provision by the firm of professional services. (In this chapter 'incidental' should be taken to mean that the activities are both incidental and arise out of or are complementary to other professional services.) This should not be difficult in practice. The various regulated activities should be capable of being incidental to the administration of the estate – the administration representing the necessary professional legal services.

Again it is helpful to look at the detailed activities permitted by the Scope Rules, distinguishing between those situations where a member of the firm acts as a PR and as such gives rise potentially to management and dealing as principal activities, from all other situations (whether members of the firm are PRs or simply acting for external PRs).

Acting as a PR

Management

Where there is discretionary management (i.e. a member of the firm is a sole **8.19** PR or one jointly with other members of the firm) the Scope Rules allow for this provided either all routine day to day decisions are taken by an authorised person or any decision which involves buying or subscribing for investments is taken on the advice of an authorised person. Details of these conditions appear above in para. 4.23. The FSA has provided guidance on the interpretation of these conditions (which also appear in the NEA Order). This guidance can be found in Appendix C2 above.

The overall impact of the statutory exclusion from management for PRs (article 66) and the exempt status of management under FSMA, Part XX is as follows. If a PR wants complete discretion to decide which investments to sell, which to buy, etc. then, provided he has the necessary competence, the exclusion in article 66 will permit this. The necessary conditions required for article 66 to apply must be complied with. On the other hand, if a PR is relying upon the fact that discretionary management will be an exempt regulated activity within the terms of FSMA, Part XX, the Law Society Scope Rules will generally require the involvement of an authorised person. Note, however, under the Scope Rules if the second option is adopted by firms (i.e. any decision which involves buying or subscribing for investments is taken on the advice of an authorised person) decisions relating to the sale of investments can be taken without authorised person involvement. One way or the other, firms should be able to ensure that any discretionary management arising from probate work will not give rise to the need for authorisation under the FSMA.

Dealing as principal

8.20 For the reasons given above (para. 8.10) it is highly unlikely that members of the firm who are PRs will be dealing since they will not be holding themselves out as providing stockbroker services.

Acting as or for PRs

Advice

8.21 Members of the firm who are PRs (whether or not there are external PRs) or who act for external PRs or who are support staff may advise PRs on the sale of all types of investments held in the estate in accordance with the terms of the will or intestacy. The Scope Rules do not impose any restrictions (other than the basic conditions) on advice relating to the sale of investments. This advice may amount to a recommendation to sell; advice on the merits of selling; or a commentary on or endorsement of an authorised person's advice. Provided the advice arises from the legal work undertaken as part of the administration of the estate it will satisfy the condition that it is 'incidental'.

Members of a firm who wish to advise PRs on the purchase of specified investments are, however, subject to certain restrictions contained in the Scope Rules. In the vast majority of probate cases there will be no purchase of investments. However on the rare occasion where this is the case, reference must be made to the Scope Rules. For details, see Chapter 4, but in broad terms, the Scope Rules prohibit solicitors from recommending the purchase of securities and contractually based investments (other than packaged products) where the transaction would be carried out through, for example, a stockbroker or other investment professional; on an investment exchange or investment market; or in response to an invitation to subscribe for investments to be admitted for dealing on an investment exchange or market. Further, if the investment is a packaged product (for example unit trusts or shares in an open ended investment company) the Scope Rules prohibit a solicitor from recommending the purchase of such investments.

However, the Scope Rules would not prohibit solicitors from advising PRs on the purchase of these categories of investments where the advice amounted to:

(a) negative advice; i.e. do not buy;
(b) advice falling short of a recommendation; i.e. explaining the transaction; or
(c) an endorsement or commentary on an authorised person's advice.

If a member of the firm is a PR, solicitors should consider RAO, article 66 regarding any advice to fellow PRs or to beneficiaries. The article 66 exclusion (see Chapter 3) is not limited to advice on the sale of an investment.

Dealing and arranging deals

Where a member of a firm deals as agent for PRs or makes arrangements for **8.22**
PRs (whether internal or external), provided the transaction relates to the
sale of investments such activities will be capable of falling within the Scope
Rules and thus be treated as exempt regulated activities. All investments can
benefit from this provision.

In the rare cases where the dealing or arrangement activity relates to the
purchase of investments, solicitors may undertake such transactions on
behalf of PRs within the Scope Rules provided the investments are not packaged products (for details of these provisions, see above para. 4.20). Under
the Scope Rules solicitors may not make arrangements for the purchase of
packaged products except where such arrangements are made as a result of
the firm managing assets within the Scope Rules (see Chapter 4 above) or
where the arrangements are effectively 'execution only'. However, in the rare
cases where dealing or arrangements need to be made on behalf of PRs the
'authorised person' exclusion (noted above, Chapter 4) should be an easier
means of avoiding the need for authorisation.

Safeguarding and administration and sending dematerialised instructions

Safeguarding and administration services and the sending of dematerialised **8.23**
instructions are both activities capable of being treated as exempt regulated
activities. Apart from the basic conditions in the Scope Rules, no additional
requirements need be considered in order to bring these activities within
FSMA, Part XX.

WILL TRUSTS

The rules relating to trusts are very similar to the rules relating to probate **8.24**
(Chapter 9 deals with trusts). There are, however, some minor differences and
it is important to recognise when an administration of an estate comes to an
end and the will trust administration commences. Although it is not as
important as it used to be under SIBR to determine the precise moment of
change, it is useful for practitioners to consider when the estate administration has completed and the trust administration has commenced. Matters
which are clearly relevant in identifying when the administration has come to
an end include:

(a) the distribution of any assets to beneficiaries;
(b) the agreement of and payment of inheritance tax;
(c) the completion of (or the capability of completing) the estate accounts;
     and
(d) the purchase of investments for the continuing trust.

BENEFICIARIES

8.25 Care must be taken in giving advice to and making arrangements for beneficiaries. The incidental condition required for Part XX will only apply to the administration of the estate. Where the administrator and beneficiary are one and the same person, it may be possible to argue that advice given to or arrangements made for the administrator/beneficiary to sell is incidental to the administration of the estate. It is unlikely that advice to purchase could be incidental. However, where a beneficiary who is not an administrator seeks the solicitor's advice on investments, it is highly unlikely that such advice will be incidental to the administration of the estate. Further, even if the solicitor is an administrator in these circumstances, article 66 will not assist since the advice or arrangement would not be made in his capacity as such. Should the solicitor wish to assist the client and avoid the need for authorisation it would be necessary for alternative steps to be taken. In most cases this means using the services of an authorised person in such a way that the solicitor avoids undertaking regulated activities.

COMPLIANCE

8.26 Where a firm provides probate services which do not amount to regulated activities as a result of any of the statutory exclusions no specific compliance will be necessary under the Conduct of Business Rules. It will of course still be necessary for solicitors to comply with the Solicitors' Practice Rules and other conduct obligations.

Where the firm provides probate services which are exempt regulated activities within FSMA, Part XX, in addition to ensuring that the Scope Rules have been complied with, the Law Society's Conduct of Business Rules will also have to be considered. Details can be found in Chapter 6 and include the requirements relating to:

(a) status disclosure;
(b) execution of transactions;
(c) records of transactions;
(d) record of commissions;
(e) safekeeping of client's investments; and
(f) confirmation of execution only business where the investment is a packaged product.

FINANCIAL PROMOTIONS

Where a solicitor is a PR, he may benefit from FPO, article 53 (trustees and **8.27** personal representative) and/or article 54 (beneficiaries) in respect of any communication amounting to a financial promotion. In both cases the promotion must be made for the purposes of the estate. In other cases (i.e. general marketing of the probate department and matters where the firm is acting for outside PRs) any communication amounting to an inducement or invitation to engage in investment activities must be given in accordance with appropriate exemptions in the FPO, for example: articles 55 and 55A, communications by members of professions; articles 28 and 28A, one-off communications; article 14, follow up communications; or article 15, introductions (for details see Chapter 7).

CHAPTER 9

Trusts

INTRODUCTION

Regulated activities and trust funds

9.1   For many solicitors trust work poses the greatest risk when it comes to considering compliance under the terms of the FSMA. Solicitors can avoid consideration of compliance matters in very few trust files.

As with probate, it is necessary first to identify the investment. A trust fund which consists of assets invested solely in, for example, real property and National Saving products will not be subject to regulation under the financial services legislation. However, where a trust fund includes, e.g. shares, unit trusts, and other securities, this will give rise to the possibility of regulation. It is necessary, by way of introduction, to consider the various activities in relation to a trust fund which could give rise to regulated activities under the Act.

Dealing

9.2   Solicitors who are trustees and who buy or sell investments which are held in their own name are potentially dealing in investments as principal under the provisions of RAO, article 14. Dealing as principal will only affect those solicitors who are sole trustees or trustees jointly with a partner or employee. It will not apply to those firms of solicitors who merely act for outside trustees. Solicitors who act for outside trustees may be dealing as agent within the provisions of RAO, article 21.

Management

9.3   Only discretionary management is potentially a regulated activity. If a partner or employee is a sole trustee or is a joint trustee with another partner or employee of the firm, the management is likely to be discretionary (and thus potentially caught). If, however, a partner or employee is a trustee jointly with an outsider or the firm is simply acting for outside trustees, then management is vested in all the trustees and it cannot be said that the firm has discretion. In this situation (assuming there has been no delegation of discretion) the management cannot give rise to a regulated activity.

Advice

Whilst it is not possible for trustees to give investment advice to themselves, **9.4** they can advise their fellow trustees and it is also very common for a firm to give investment advice to trustees. This can occur where a partner is a trustee and receives advice from fee earners in his trust department, or where the trustees are outsiders and receive advice from the firm. In either case if the advice is on the merits of buying or selling investments it will be caught by RAO, article 53.

Arranging deals in investments

Trustees cannot make arrangements for themselves to deal in investments; **9.5** where the investments are in the trustees' own names they will be dealing as principal. However, the firm may make arrangements for the acquisition or disposal of investments on behalf of either trustees who are, for example, partners in the firm or for trustees who are lay persons outside the firm. Such arrangements will be caught by RAO, article 25.

Safeguarding and administration

Trust administration could also give rise to the provision of safeguarding and **9.6** administration services to a client as defined by RAO, article 40.

Sending dematerialised instructions

Trust administration could also give rise to sending dematerialised instructions **9.7** where trust assets are held in a non certificated form.

Regulated mortgage activities

Occasionally solicitors, as trustees, may enter into regulated mortgage **9.8** contracts as lenders as part of a tax planning or other device. Members of the firm may administer such mortgage contracts on behalf of the trustees. (Note that administration of a mortgage where outside trustees are the lenders is unlikely to give rise to regulated activities. For administration, the mortgage contract must have been entered into in the course of business (see Chapter 2). Provided the outside trustees are lay trustees rather than professional trustees, they will not have entered into a contract in the course of business.) Note also the delay in the implementation of mortgage regulation – see above para 2.39.

STATUTORY EXCLUSIONS

9.9 Acknowledging that many trust funds will potentially give rise to regulated activities, it is necessary to identify how trust practitioners can properly avoid the need for authorisation. For this purpose it is helpful to distinguish between those circumstances where a principal or employee of the firm acts as a trustee (whether or not there are any outside trustees) and those circumstances where the firm is simply acting for outside trustees.

Acting as trustee

Management

9.10 If a partner or employee of the firm is a trustee then any discretionary management undertaken by such a partner or employee in his capacity as such is capable of falling within the statutory exclusion in RAO, article 66. This exclusion is subject to the two important conditions contained in article 66:

(a) that the firm does not hold itself out as providing discretionary management services; and

(b) that the person carrying on the management activity is not remunerated for what he does in addition to any remuneration he receives for acting as trustee (for details of this exclusion, see Chapter 3).

Care must be taken to ensure that the firm's publicity material does not hold out the firm as providing discretionary management services.

Advice

9.11 Generic advice will not be caught as a regulated activity under the RAO. However it might be difficult to show that any advice is generic if the advice can be shown to relate to the specific investments held in the trust fund. Specific advice (whether it is advice to sell or buy investments) given by a partner or employee of the firm in his capacity as a trustee will be excluded by RAO, article 66 where the advice is given to a fellow trustee for the purpose of the trust or to a beneficiary under the trust concerning his interest in the trust. The only condition applicable to this exclusion is the 'no additional remuneration' condition referred to above in 3.31.

It might also be possible to use the 'necessary' exclusion in RAO, article 67 if it can be shown that the advice could reasonably be regarded as a necessary part of other professional services (see Chapter 3 for details of this exclusion). This would be particularly helpful if the solicitor trustee had to advise that all the assets of the trust fund had to be sold in order to pay for example, a tax bill. It is less likely to be available where only some of the investment assets have to be sold and therefore a choice has to be made as to which assets were to be sold. Article 67 is subject to a condition that there is no separate remuneration for carrying out the necessary activities.

Dealing and arrangements

A sole trustee or one who is a joint trustee with partners or employees might **9.12** be dealing as principal where investments held in the name of the trustees are bought or sold. Providing the trustee(s) are not holding themselves or the firm out as providing stockbroking services they will not be undertaking a regulated activity when dealing as principal (see the details for this exclusion to apply in Chapter 3).

Arrangements made by partner or employee of the firm in his capacity as a trustee will be excluded by RAO, article 66 where the arrangements are made on behalf of himself and a fellow trustee acting in their capacity as such or where the arrangements are made for a beneficiary under the trust. Again, the only condition applicable to this exclusion is the 'no additional remuneration' condition referred to above in para. 3.31.

The 'necessary' exclusion in RAO, article 67 may also be available for arrangements made. As noted in para. 9.11, this is only likely to be relevant where all the assets are being sold.

Safeguarding and administration and sending dematerialised instructions

Where a partner or employee is acting as a trustee and is involved in safe- **9.13** guarding and administration and/or sending dematerialised instructions, article 66 may again provide an exclusion. In both cases where trustees undertake these activities, they will be excluded from being regulated activities if the appropriate conditions are met. For the exclusion to apply, both the conditions noted above in para. 3.30 and 3.31 (no additional remuneration and no holding out) must be satisfied.

It might also be possible to use the 'necessary' exclusion in article 67.

Activities undertaken by other members of the firm

In many cases, although a partner or employee is appointed as a trustee, the **9.14** actual activities (which potentially could bring the firm within the scope of regulated activities) might be undertaken by other members of staff. Support staff may research and advise the internal trustees; support staff may make arrangements for the disposal of investments on behalf of internal and external trustees; and support staff may be involved in safeguarding and administration and/or sending dematerialised instructions. In each of these cases, providing the other appropriate conditions are met, the firm should be able to benefit from the exclusions in RAO, article 66 as noted above. The FSA guidance makes it clear that the exclusion will apply to other members of staff who carry out the activities on behalf of the trustees. Details of the guidance can be found in Appendix C1.

Acting for external trustees

9.15   Where a firm is simply acting for external trustees, the important exclusions contained in RAO, article 66 have no application. Article 66 can only apply where a member of the firm is a trustee.

Management

9.16   If the firm is acting for external trustees there should be no management activity. Management is only caught if it is discretionary management. Provided the firm has not had discretionary management delegated to it by the external trustees, no management activity will arise. If there is discretionary management, no statutory exclusion is available and such activity will inevitably lead to a requirement that the firm is authorised by FSA.

Advice

9.17   Members of the firm may wish to give advice to external trustees on the merits of selling investments held in the estate. Such advice is potentially a regulated activity if it is specific as opposed to generic advice. The 'necessary' exclusion in RAO, article 67 might be available but as noted above, this exclusion is only likely to be available where the advice relates to the disposal of all the assets in the trust fund. The exclusion is subject to the requirement that no separate remuneration is received for carrying out the necessary activity.

As noted above, simply obtaining and passing on the advice of an authorised person is not a regulated activity (see para. 3.7 above). However to avoid a regulated activity, care must be taken not to comment on the advice since such commentary could be interpreted as 'advice on the merits'. If commentary is required (although the advice is not 'necessary' within article 67) solicitors should consider the DPB régime (see below, para. 9.21).

Dealing and arrangements

9.18   Firms acting for external trustees will not be dealing as principal. They may, however deal as agent for their client or make arrangements on behalf of their clients. Since RAO, article 66 will not apply, firms will have to look elsewhere for exclusions. It may be possible to use the 'necessary' exclusion in article 67 but, as noted above this is likely to be limited to those transactions where all the assets of the trust fund are being sold. Of more general benefit is the 'authorised person' exclusion contained in both articles 22 and 29 of RAO. This exclusion is dealt with in some detail above. It applies where a solicitor enters into a transaction with or through an authorised person and one of two alternative conditions are satisfied together with, in either case, a further condition relating to pecuniary reward. The alternative conditions are:

(a) the transaction is entered into on advice given to the client by an authorised person; or

(b) it is clear in all the circumstances that the client, in his capacity as an investor, is not seeking and has not sought advice from the solicitor as to the merits of the client entering the transaction (or if the client has sought advice the solicitor has declined to give it but has recommended the client to seek advice from an authorised person).

The further condition provides that the exclusion does not apply if the agent receives from any person other than the client any pecuniary reward or advantage, for which he does not account to the client, arising out of his entering into the transaction.

An alternative means of assisting external trustees would be to introduce them to an authorised person for independent advice. This introduction would not be a regulated activity (see above para. 3.14).

Safeguarding and administration and sending dematerialised instructions

Where firms provide safeguarding and administration services and/or send **9.19** dematerialised instructions for or on behalf of external trustees they will be undertaking regulated activities. The only possible exclusion available is that contained in article 67 (the 'necessary' exclusions).

NOMINEE COMPANIES

A number of firms providing services as or to trustees operate a nominee **9.20** company for the purposes of holding the investments subject to the trust. Nominee companies, being separate legal entities, would require authorisation in their own name if they were undertaking regulated activities. The relevant activity appears to be that of undertaking or arranging the safeguarding and administration of investments in the course of a business.

The FSA has given guidance on the treatment of nominee companies. It appears as paragraph 1.19.3 G of their guidance and states as follows:

'Where a nominee company exists purely to hold investments and other assets and has no staff or resources it is likely that it will be only safeguarding the assets and that it is the person who controls the nominee company who has undertaken to provide the service of safeguarding and administration and who undertakes the actual administration. Furthermore, it is unlikely that such a nominee company would be regarded as carrying on business of any kind.'

Providing this is the case, nominee companies should not give rise to any additional compliance obligation.

FSMA, PART XX RÉGIME

Introduction

9.21 It may not be possible in all circumstances for trust practitioners to avoid regulated activities through the use of the statutory exclusions. For example, solicitors who are trustees may be undertaking management activities in circumstances where the firm's brochure holds out the fact that management services may be provided. Solicitors who are acting for external trustees may wish to comment on or endorse the advice of authorised persons. Further, those solicitors acting for external trustees may provide safeguarding and administration services and/or send dematerialised instructions in circumstances where it is not strictly necessary for them to do so and consequently cannot use the 'necessary' exclusion in article 67. In any of these situations, solicitors who wish to remain unauthorised will have to ensure that they provide exempt regulated activities within FSMA, Part XX. To do so, they will have to bring themselves within the Law Society's Scope Rules, meeting the necessary conditions laid down by those Scope Rules (for details of the conditions, see Chapter 4).

For the conditions in the Scope Rules to apply it will be necessary for the solicitor to show that the manner in which regulated activities are being provided is such that activities are incidental to the provision by the firm of professional services. (In this chapter 'incidental' should be taken to mean that the activities are both incidental and arise out of or are complementary to other professional services.) This should not be difficult in practice. The various regulated activities should be capable of being incidental to the administration of the trust fund – the administration representing the necessary professional legal services.

Again it is helpful to look at the detailed activities permitted by the Scope Rules, distinguishing between those situations where a member of the firm acts as a trustee and, as such, gives rise potentially to management and dealing as principal activities from all other situations (whether members of the firm are trustees jointly with external trustees or simply acting for external trustees).

Acting as trustee

Management

9.22 Where there is discretionary management (i.e. a member of the firm is a sole trustee or one jointly with other members of the firm) the Scope Rules allow for this provided either all routine day to day decisions are taken by an authorised person or any decision which involves buying or subscribing for investments is taken on the advice of an authorised person. Details of these conditions appear above in para. 4.23. The FSA have provided guidance on the interpretation of these conditions (which also appear in the NEA Order). This guidance can be found in Appendix C2.

The overall effect of the statutory exclusion from management for trustees (article 66) and the exempt status of management under FSMA, Part XX is as follows. If a trustee wants complete discretion to decide which investments to sell, which to buy, etc. then, provided he has the necessary competence, the exclusion in article 66 will permit this. The necessary conditions required for article 66 to apply must be complied with. On the other hand, if a trustee is relying upon the fact that discretionary management will be an exempt regulated activity within the terms of FSMA, Part XX, the Law Society Scope Rules generally require the involvement of an authorised person. Note, however, under the Scope Rules if the second option is adopted by firms (i.e. any decision which involves buying or subscribing for investments is taken on the advice of an authorised person) decisions relating to the sale of investments can be taken without authorised person involvement. One way or the other, firms should be able to ensure that any discretionary management arising from trust work will not give rise to the need for authorisation under the FSMA.

Dealing as principal

For the reasons given above (see para. 8.10) it is highly unlikely that members **9.23** of the firm who are trustees will be dealing since they will not be holding themselves out as providing stockbroker services.

Acting as, or for, trustees

Advice

Members of the firm who are trustees (whether or not there are external **9.24** trustees) or who act for external trustees or who are support staff may wish to advise trustees on the purchase or sale of all types of investment held in the trust in accordance with the terms of the trust deed. The Scope Rules do not impose any restrictions (other than the basic conditions) on advice relating to the sale of investments. This advice may amount to a recommendation to sell; advice on the merits of selling; or a commentary on or endorsement of an authorised person's advice. Provided the advice arises from the legal work undertaken as part of the administration of the trust fund it will satisfy the condition that it is 'incidental'.

Members of a firm who wish to advise trustees on the purchase of regulated investments are, however, subject to certain restrictions contained in the

Scope Rules. Where this is the case, reference must be made to the Scope Rules. For details, see Chapter 4, but in broad terms, the Scope Rules prohibit solicitors from recommending the purchase of securities and contractually based investments (other than packaged products) where the transaction would be carried out: through, for example, a stockbroker or other investment professional; on an investment exchange or investment market; or in response to an invitation to subscribe for investments to be admitted for dealing on an investment exchange or market. Further, if the investment is a packaged product (for example unit trusts or shares in an open ended investment company) the Scope Rules prohibit a solicitor from recommending the purchase of such investments.

However, the Scope Rules do not prohibit solicitors from advising trustees on the purchase of these categories of investments where the advice amounts to:

(a) negative advice; i.e. do not buy;
(b) advice falling short of a recommendation; i.e. explaining the transaction; or
(c) an endorsement or commentary on an authorised person's advice.

If a member of the firm is a trustee, solicitors should consider RAO, article 66 regarding any advice to fellow trustees. The article 66 exclusion (see Chapter 3) is not limited to advice on the sale of an investment.

Dealing and arranging deals

9.25 Where a member of a firm deals as agent for trustees or makes arrangements for trustees (whether internal or external), provided the transaction relates to the sale of investments such activities will be capable of falling within the Scope Rules and thus be treated as exempt regulated activities. All investments can benefit from this provision.

In the circumstances where the dealing or arrangement activity relates to the purchase of investments, solicitors may undertake such transactions on behalf of trustees within the Scope Rules provided the investments are not packaged products (for details of these provisions, see Chapter 4). Under the Scope Rules solicitors may not make arrangements for the purchase of packaged products except where such arrangements are made as a result of the firm managing assets within the Scope Rules or where the arrangements are effectively 'execution only'. However, in the circumstances where dealing activities or arrangements need to be made on behalf of trustees the 'authorised person' exclusion (noted above, para. 3.12) should be an easier means of avoiding the need for authorisation.

Safeguarding and administration and sending dematerialised instructions

Safeguarding and administration services and the sending of dematerialised **9.26** instructions are both activities capable of being treated as exempt regulated activities. Apart from the basic conditions in the Scope Rules, no additional requirements need be considered in order to bring these activities within FSMA, Part XX.

Regulated mortgage contracts

Activities in relation to regulated mortgage contracts are unlikely to become **9.27** subject to regulation until sometime in 2004. The NEA Order as originally drafted provided that regulated mortgage activities could not fall within FSMA, Part XX. This is reflected in the Law Society's Scope Rules which provide that the prohibited activities for solicitors include

'entering into a regulated mortgage contract as lender or administering a regulated mortgage contract'.

The NEA Order was, however amended allowing for the Part XX régime to apply to an activity carried on by a trustee in his capacity as such where the borrower under the regulated mortgage contract in question is a beneficiary under the trust. A further condition is that trustee is not remunerated for what he does in addition to any remuneration he receives as trustee. For these purposes the trustee is not to be regarded as receiving additional remuneration merely because his remuneration is calculated by reference to time spent (amendment to NEA Order inserted by the Financial Services and Markets Act 2000 (Professions) (Non-Exempt Activities) (Amendment) Order 2001). In due course appropriate amendments will be made to the Law Society's Scope Rules.

COMPLIANCE

Where a firm provides trust services which do not amount to regulated activi- **9.28** ties as a result of any of the statutory exclusions, no specific compliance will be necessary under the Conduct of Business Rules. It will of course still be necessary for solicitors to comply with the Solicitors' Practice Rules and other conduct obligations.

Where the firm provides trust services which are exempt regulated activities within FSMA, Part XX, in addition to ensuring that the Scope Rules have been complied with, the Law Society's Conduct of Business Rules will also have to be considered. Details can be found in Chapter 6 and include the requirements relating to:

(a)   status disclosure;
(b)   execution of transactions;
(c)   records of transactions;
(d)   record of commissions;
(e)   safekeeping of client's investments; and
(f)   confirmation of execution only business where the investment is a packaged product.

FINANCIAL PROMOTIONS

9.29   Where a solicitor is a trustee, he may benefit from FPO, article 53 (trustees and PR) and/or article 54 (beneficiaries) in respect of any communication amounting to a financial promotion. In both cases the promotion must be made for the purposes of the trust fund. In other cases (i.e. general marketing of the trust department and matters where the firm is acting for outside trustees) any communication amounting to an inducement or invitation to engage in investment activities must be given in accordance with appropriate exemptions in the FPO (for example: articles 55 and 55A, communications by members of professions; articles 28 and 28A, one-off communications; article 14, follow-up communications; or article 15, introductions (for details see Chapter 7).

CHAPTER 10

Powers of attorney

INTRODUCTION

A solicitor who is a donee under a power of attorney, in certain circumstances, will be involved in regulated activities. In general the appointment of a solicitor as a donee will give rise to the possibility of management by the solicitor of assets belonging to the donor. A solicitor donee could also be involved in dealing as principal or arranging deals, advising, safeguarding and administration services and/or sending dematerialised instructions.

10.1

It is necessary to identify whether any specified investments are involved in the transaction involving the power of attorney. Clearly if a solicitor is given a specific power of attorney which permits him at his discretion to buy or sell shares in the name of his client, this will amount to discretionary management and consequently a regulated activity. On the other hand if a solicitor is given a specific power of attorney which is restricted to selling, for example real property, this will not amount to a regulated activity.

The problem in practice is that most powers of attorney are of a general nature and do not specify exactly which assets are under the control of the donee. In these circumstances it is necessary to look at the precise definition of management as contained in RAO, article 37.

Managing investments is defined as:

'Managing assets belonging to another person, in circumstances involving the exercise discretion [. . .] if:

(a) the assets consist of or include any investment which is a security or contractually based investment; or

(b) the arrangements for their management are such that the assets may consist of or include such investments, and either the assets have at any time since 29 April 1988 done so, or the arrangements have at any time (whether before or after that date) been held out as arrangements under which the assets would do so.'

In terms of general powers of attorney, article 37(b) is important. On the assumption that at the time when the power is granted the assets do not include investments it is first necessary to ascertain whether the power is sufficiently wide to give discretion to the solicitor to acquire regulated investments. If it is, it is then necessary to consider whether at any time since 29 April 1988 investments have been included as part of the assets the subject of the power. If not, it must be further ascertained whether the transaction is such that the parties intended that the assets would include investments.

Solicitors should carefully consider when drafting powers of attorney in their own favour whether the power should be restricted to exclude investments. If it is, this will avoid any regulated activity being undertaken by the solicitor. If the power is not restricted so as to exclude investments, and it appears from the facts that there is discretionary management within article 37(a) or (b), it is then necessary to consider whether the regulated activity is excluded or exempt.

It should be noted that enduring powers of attorney (registered or unregistered) and trustee powers of attorney are capable of giving rise to a regulated activity in the manner referred to above.

STATUTORY EXCLUSIONS

Management

10.2 Article 38 provides for a specific exclusion for persons appointed to manage under a power of attorney where:

> 'all routine or day-to-day decisions, so far as relating to investments of a kind mentioned in article 37, are taken on behalf of that person by –
>
> (i) an authorised person with permission to carry on activities of the kind specified by article 37;
> (ii) a person who is an exempt person in relation to activities of that kind or
> (iii) an overseas person'.

As noted above, para. 3.16, the FSA Guidance assists in the definition of the words *routine* and *day-to-day* for these purposes. Paragraph 1.18.2 G of that guidance is reproduced below:

> '(1) a "routine" decision is any decision other than one which may properly be regarded as exceptional. In determining whether or not decisions are routine, due account would need to be taken of the usual types of decision which the attorney takes or expects to be taking. Examples of possible non-routine decisions which an attorney might take include where the appointed fund manager has a conflict of interest or decisions relating to certain specified situations (for example, where the appointed fund manager proposes to invest in a particular type of investment such as a company associated with the tobacco or arms supply industries);

(2) a "day-to-day" decision is a decision which relates to the everyday management of the assets in question. It will not include strategic decisions such as decisions on the proportion of the assets which should be invested in equities as compared to fixed interest securities, or decisions on which investment manager(s) to appoint or to whom to apportion cash for investment purposes from time to time;

(3) the exclusion requires that the attorney takes only decisions which are neither "routine" nor "day-to-day" in nature.'

Consequently providing the attorney restricts his decisions to those which are non-routine and not day to day, the discretionary management arising from such decisions will not be a regulated activity. However, one further question arises: is it the firm or the attorney who benefits from this exclusion. It might be argued that the strict wording of article 38 excludes the attorney only. If the attorney is acting as a partner or member of the firm, then the firm too, could be said to be undertaking discretionary management and therefore require authorisation.

Paragraph 1.18.3 G of the FSA Guidance assists again. It provides:

'It is usually the case that where a professional firm provides attorney services it will be an individual partner or employee of the firm who becomes the attorney. The question then arises as to whether it is the firm or the actual attorney who is potentially covered by the exclusion. It is the FSA's view that, provided it is the case that the firm has offered to provide the services of a partner or employee to act as attorney and that the client accounts to the firm for fees payable for the services of the attorney, it will be the firm which has and needs the benefit of the exclusion. This is because the attorney will be carrying on the firm's business and not his own business. It follows that if the attorney, in implementing a decision which is not a routine or day-to-day decision uses other employees, offices or partners of the firm to execute or arrange the transaction, the firm would be entitled to make use of any exclusion which may be available to a person acting as attorney.'

This guidance now makes it clear that anyone in the firm who undertakes discretionary management on behalf of an attorney will be capable of benefiting from the exclusion, if the management was undertaken in such a way that, if undertaken by the attorney it would have been excluded by article 38.

Dealing as principal

For the reason given above (see para. 2.28), attorneys, when buying or selling investments, are unlikely to be dealing as principal since they will not hold themselves out as providing stockbroking services. **10.3**

Advice

10.4 Donees of a power of attorney might give investment advice to the donor of the power or to an external co-attorney. In these circumstances such advice is likely to be caught by RAO, article 53 unless it is generic. Note the exclusion in RAO, article 66 for trustees and PRs does not apply to attorneys. The only statutory exclusion which appears relevant is the *necessary* exclusion in RAO, article 67 (see above para. 3.32). Given that it is generally possible for attorneys to seek advice from an authorised person, this exclusion is unlikely to be of any great benefit.

Arranging deals in investments

10.5 Where a solicitor is a co-attorney with an outsider, it is possible for the solicitor to make arrangements on behalf of himself and his co-attorney. Again, it is not possible to use the article 66 exclusion for trustees or PRs and for the reasons mentioned in para. 3.32 above, the article 67 exclusion may not be available. The authorised person exclusion in RAO, article 29 (see above para. 3.12) would be available subject to the conditions of the article being complied with.

Safeguarding and administration/sending dematerialised instructions

10.6 An attorney could undertake both these activities. The only possible statutory exclusion (given that article 66 does not apply) would appear to be the *necessary* exclusion in article 67. This should be available if it can be shown that these activities may reasonably be regarded as a necessary part of other professional services (i.e. acting as attorney).

FSMA PART XX RÉGIME

10.7 It may not be possible in all circumstances for attorneys to avoid regulated activities through the use of the statutory exclusions. An alternative means of avoiding authorisation is to provide exempt regulated activities within FSMA, Part XX. To do so, they will have to bring themselves within the Law Society's Scope Rules, meeting the necessary conditions laid down by those Scope Rules (for details of the conditions, see above Chapter 4).

For the conditions in the Scope Rules to apply it will be necessary for the solicitor to show that the manner in which regulated activities are being provided is such that activities are incidental to the provision by the firm of professional services. (In this chapter 'incidental' should be taken to mean that the activities are both incidental and arise out of or are complementary to other professional services.) This should not be difficult in practice. The various regulated activities should be capable of being incidental to the work done as a donee under the power of attorney.

Management

Where there is discretionary management (see above para. 4.23) the Scope **10.8** Rules allow for this provided either all routine day to day decisions are taken by an authorised person or that any decision which involves buying or subscribing for investments is taken on the advice of an authorised person. Details of these conditions appear above in para. 3.16. The FSA has provided guidance on the interpretation of these conditions (which also appear in the NEA Order). This guidance can be found in Appendix C1. Note that the management activity in the Scope Rules provides the attorney with greater flexibility compared with activity permitted by way of statutory exclusion in RAO, article 38. No routine or day to day decisions can be taken by the attorney using article 38. Under the Scope Rule, where the second option is adopted the attorney can take decisions relating to the sale of assets without the involvement of an authorised person.

Dealing as principal

For the reasons given above (see para. 2.28) it is highly unlikely that members **10.9** of the firm who are attorneys will be dealing since they will not be holding themselves out as providing stockbroker services.

Advice

Members of the firm who are donees under a power of attorney may wish to **10.10** advise donors or co-attorneys on the purchase or sale of all types of investment. The Scope Rules do not impose any restrictions (other than the basic conditions) on advice relating to the sale of investments. This advice may amount to a recommendation to sell; advice on the merits of selling; or a commentary on or endorsement of an authorised person's advice. Provided the advice arises from the legal work undertaken as part of the attorneyship it will satisfy the condition that it is *incidental*.

Members of a firm who wish to advise donors or co-attorneys on the purchase of investments are, however, subject to certain restrictions contained in the Scope Rules. Where this is the case, reference must be made to the Scope Rules. For details, see Chapter 4, but in broad terms, the Scope Rules prohibit solicitors from recommending the purchase of securities and contractually based investments (other than packaged products) where the transaction would be carried out: through, for example, a stockbroker or other investment professional; on an investment exchange or investment market; or in response to an invitation to subscribe for investments to be admitted for dealing on an investment exchange or market. Further, if the investment is a packaged product (for example unit trusts or shares in an open ended investment company) the Scope Rules prohibit a solicitor from recommending the purchase of such investments (see Chapter 4 above for details).

However, the Scope Rules do not prohibit solicitors from advising donors or co-attorneys on the purchase of these categories of investments where the advice amounts to:

(a)   negative advice; i.e. do not buy;
(b)   advice falling short of a recommendation; i.e. explaining the transaction; or
(c)   an endorsement or commentary on an authorised person's advice.

Arranging deals

10.11   Where a member of a firm makes arrangements for themselves and co-attorney(s), provided the transaction relates to the sale of investments such activities will be capable of falling within the Scope Rules and thus be treated as exempt regulated activities. (For details, see above Chapter 4.) All investments can benefit from this provision.

In the circumstances where the arrangement activity relates to the purchase of investments, solicitors may undertake such transactions on behalf of themselves and co-attorneys within the Scope Rules provided the investments are not packaged products (for details of these provisions, see above Chapter 4). Under the Scope Rules solicitors may not make arrangements for the purchase of packaged products except where such arrangements are made as a result of the firm managing assets within the Scope Rules or where the arrangements are effectively *execution only*. However, in the circumstances where arrangements need to be made on behalf of themselves and co-attorney the *authorised person* exclusion (noted above, para. 3.12) should be an easier means of avoiding the need for authorisation.

Safeguarding and administration and sending dematerialised instructions

10.12   Safeguarding and administration services and the sending of dematerialised instructions are both activities capable of being treated as exempt regulated activities. Apart from the basic conditions in the Scope Rules, no additional requirements need be considered in order to bring these activities within FSMA, Part XX.

COMPLIANCE

10.13   Where a solicitor is a donee under a power of attorney and provides services which can benefit from any of the statutory exclusions, no specific compliance will be necessary under the Conduct of Business Rules. It will of course still be necessary for solicitors to comply with the Solicitors' Practice Rules and other conduct obligations.

Where the firm provides services which are exempt regulated activities within FSMA, Part XX, in addition to ensuring that the Scope Rules have been complied with, the Law Society's Conduct of Business Rules will also have to be considered. Details can be found in Chapter 6 and include the requirements relating to:

(a) status disclosure;
(b) execution of transactions;
(c) records of transactions;
(d) record of commissions;
(e) safekeeping of client's investments; and
(f) confirmation of execution only business where the investment is a packaged product.

FINANCIAL PROMOTIONS

10.14 Where a solicitor is a donee under a power of attorney, there are no specific exclusions applicable. In all cases (i.e. general marketing of the private client department and matters where a member of the firm is acting under a power of attorney) any communication amounting to an inducement or invitation to engage in investment activities must be given in accordance with appropriate exemptions in the FPO (for example: articles 55 and 55A, communications by members of professions; articles 28 and 28A, one off communications; article 14, follow up communications; or article 15, introductions (for details see Chapter 7).

CHAPTER 11

Receivers

INTRODUCTION

11.1 This chapter is concerned with the compliance requirements where a solicitor is appointed as a receiver by the Court of Protection.

STATUTORY EXCLUSIONS

Management

11.2 If the solicitor is appointed as a receiver by the Court of Protection, and the fund under the control of the receiver includes specified investments as defined, potentially the solicitor is involved in management. The exclusions for attorneys in RAO, article 38 (see above para. 3.16) and for trustees in RAO, article 66 (see above para. 3.23) do not apply to receivers. However the Law Society has given guidance on receivers and potential management activities. Their guidance states:

> 'It is unlikely that a receiver appointed by the Court of Protection would be managing investments in circumstances involving the exercise of discretion as a receiver would need to obtain the authority of the Court of Protection to buy or sell investments.'

Other activities

11.3 The Law Society's guidance on the use of the statutory exclusions for receivers is as follows:

> 'The application of exclusions in the RAO to receivers appointed by the Court of Protection is not entirely clear and it may be advisable for receivers to operate under the Scope Rules.'

FSMA, PART XX RÉGIME

Management

In the light of the comments above, para. 11.2, it is unlikely receivers will be **11.4** managing in circumstances involving discretion. However, for the avoidance of doubt, if there is discretionary management the Scope Rules allow for this provided either all routine day to day decisions are taken by an authorised person or that any decision which involves buying or subscribing for investments is taken on the advice of an authorised person. Details of these conditions appear above in Chapter 4. The FSA has provided guidance on the interpretation of these conditions (which also appear in the NEA Order). This guidance can be found in Appendix C1.

Dealing as principal

For the reasons given above (see para. 2.28) it is highly unlikely that members **11.5** of the firm who are receivers will be dealing since they will not be holding themselves out as providing stockbroker services.

Advice

A receiver appointed by the Court of Protection is unlikely to be giving **11.6** advice. The authority for transactions will come from the Court.

Arranging deals

Where arrangements are made by or on behalf of a receiver appointed by **11.7** the Court of Protection and the transaction relates to the sale of investments such activities will be capable of falling within the Scope Rules and thus be treated as exempt regulated activities. (For details, see Chapter 4.) All investments can benefit from this provision.

In the circumstances where the arrangement activity relates to the purchase of investments, receivers may undertake such transactions within the Scope Rules provided the investments are not packaged products (for details of these provisions, see Chapter 4). Under the Scope Rules solicitors may not make arrangements for the purchase of packaged products except where such arrangements are made as a result of the firm managing assets within the Scope Rules or where the arrangements are effectively *execution only*. Whilst the receiver is unlikely to be managing since the authority for any transaction comes from the Court of Protection, it is possible that the transaction could be treated as execution only. The authorised person exclusion is unlikely to apply since no advice will normally be sought from an authorised person.

Safeguarding and administration and sending dematerialised instructions

11.8 Safeguarding and administration services and the sending of dematerialised instructions are both activities capable of being treated as exempt regulated activities. Apart from the basic conditions in the Scope Rules, no additional requirements need be considered in order to bring these activities within FSMA, Part XX.

COMPLIANCE

11.9 Where a solicitor is a receiver appointed by the Court of Protection and provides services which can benefit from any of the statutory exclusions, no specific compliance will be necessary under the Conduct of Business Rules. It will of course still be necessary for solicitors to comply with the Solicitors' Practice Rules and other conduct obligations.

However, given the Law Society's Guidance on the use of the statutory exclusions, receivers are recommended to use the Part XX exempt activities régime. In such circumstances, in addition to ensuring that the Scope Rules have been complied with, the Law Society's Conduct of Business Rules will also have to be considered. Details can be found in Chapter 6 and include the requirements relating to:

(a) status disclosure;
(b) execution of transactions;
(c) records of transactions;
(d) record of commissions;
(e) safekeeping of client's investments; and
(f) confirmation of execution only business where the investment is a packaged product.

FINANCIAL PROMOTIONS

11.10 Where a solicitor is a receiver appointed by the Court of Protection there are no specific exclusions applicable. In all cases where any communication amounts to an inducement or invitation to engage in investment activities consideration must be given to the appropriate exemptions in the FPO (for example: articles 55 and 55A, communications by members of professions; articles 28 and 28A, one off communications; article 14, follow up communications; or article 15, introductions (for details see Chapter 7).

CHAPTER 12

Property department

INTRODUCTION

Before looking at the various requirements affecting solicitors who act in **12.1**
property matters, it is first necessary to identify the most common regulated
investments likely to be met within this department.

Land

Land is not an investment within the definition contained in the RAO. **12.2**
Consequently any straightforward dealing in land or any advice to invest in
land will not of itself amount to a regulated activity.

Mortgages

Regulated mortgage contracts will be caught by the RAO as an investment. **12.3**
Entering into such a contract as lender or administering a regulated mortgage
contract will be a regulated activity (see above para. 2.21), but it is unlikely
to be caught for regulation until 2004.

Insurance contracts

Compliance in the property department generally arises from advice given **12.4**
and arrangements made in respect of long-term insurance contracts. As
noted above (see para. 2.13) both general and long-term insurance contracts
will be investments as defined by the RAO. However, not all insurance
policies are contractually based investments. It is the contractually based
investment which will be of most concern to solicitors.

Straightforward indemnity policies (e.g. contents insurance or insurance
against the risk of fire or destruction) will not amount to contractually based
investments within the meaning of the RAO.

Further, the RAO expressly excludes from the definition of contractually
based investments those contracts in respect of which the following conditions
are met:

(a)   the benefits under the contract are payable only on death or in respect of incapacity due to injury, sickness or infirmity;

(b)   the contract provides that benefits are payable on death (other than death due to an accident) only where the death occurs within 10 years of the date on which the life of the person in question was first insured under the contract, or where the death occurs before that person attains a specified age not exceeding 70 years;

(c)   the contract has no surrender value, or the consideration consists of a single premium and the surrender value does not exceed that premium; and

(d)   the contract makes no provision for its conversion or extension in a manner which would result in it ceasing to comply with any of the above conditions).

Thus most term assurance will not be long-term insurance contracts and this means that activities relating to many *mortgage protection policies* will not give rise to regulated activities.

Broadly speaking, only those policies which involve an investment element will be caught as contractually based investments. Two common forms of insurance contract caught will be the endowment policy and the pension policy.

Solicitors who advise on or make arrangements in respect of mortgages where an endowment or pension policy is to be used as additional security may well find themselves undertaking regulated activities.

Shares in management companies

12.5   The other area relevant to the property department where regulated activities may be undertaken relates to the acquisition or disposal of shares in a management or service company. As noted above (see para. 2.5) shares and stock in the share capital of a company are investments regardless of the type of company. Technically, therefore, any advice relating to or arrangements made for the acquisition or disposal of such shares will amount to a regulated activity. There should be no problems where the company is limited by guarantee without a share capital.

Conclusion

12.6   It should be clear from above that three areas are of concern for solicitors involved in property transactions:

(a)   regulated activities in relation to regulated mortgage contracts;

(b)   regulated activities in relation to additional securities to be used as part of a client mortgage; and

(c)   regulated activities in relation to shares in management companies.

Each of these points is dealt with separately in the following paragraphs.

REGULATED MORTGAGE CONTRACTS

Introduction

A contract is a regulated mortgage contract if, at the time it is entered into,   **12.7**
the following conditions are met:

(a)   the contract is one under which a person (the lender) provides credit to
an individual or to trustees (the borrower);

(b)   the contract provides for the obligation of the borrower to repay to be
secured by a first legal mortgage on land (other than timeshare
accommodation) in the UK;

(c)   at least 40 per cent of that land is used, or is intended to be used, as or
in connection with a dwelling by the borrower or (in the case of credit
provided to trustees) by an individual who is a beneficiary of the trust,
or by a related person (RAO, article 61(3) as amended).

Under RAO, article 61(1), entering into a regulated mortgage contract as
lender is a regulated activity. Further under article 61(2), administering a regulated mortgage contract is also a regulated activity, but only where the contract is entered into by way of business after the coming into force of this
article. The words *by way of business* were inserted by the Financial Services
and Markets Act 2000 (Regulated Activities) (Amendment) Order 2001,
SI 2001/3544. This amendment ensures that administering *private* mortgages
will be excluded from this article.

Administering a regulated mortgage contract means either or both of:

(a)   notifying the borrower of changes in interest rates or payments due
under the contract, or of other matters of which the contract requires
him to be notified; and

(b)   taking any necessary steps for the purposes of collecting or recovering
payments due under the contract from the borrower.

Unlike most of the provisions contained in FSMA and RAO, this
particular article is unlikely to come into force until sometime in 2004.

Solicitors providing conveyancing services will not be undertaking regulated activities by giving advice on or making arrangements for a client to
acquire or discharge a regulated mortgage contract. These activities are not
currently caught by the RAO (although general regulation of mortgages
expected in 2004, may change this position). However, solicitors who offer
bridging facilities to a client where the loan satisfies the definition of a
regulated mortgage contract will be caught. Further solicitors administering

regulated mortgage contracts (as defined) will potentially be undertaking regulated activities. Solicitors not authorised by the FSA must, in these circumstances, consider if any statutory exclusion applies or whether the activity can be treated as exempt within the terms of FSMA, Part XX.

Statutory exclusions

12.8 There are no statutory exclusions in relation to entering into a regulated mortgage contract. Solicitors doing so as lender will be undertaking regulated activities. There are, however, statutory exclusions in relation to administering a regulated mortgage contract, contained in RAO, article 62. As noted above, as a result of the late amendment, solicitors who, after the commencement date, administer a private mortgage (for example by notifying the borrower of changes in interest or taking steps for the purpose of collecting or recovering payments) will not be undertaking regulated activities.

Further, a person who is not authorised does not administer a regulated mortgage contract in accordance with article 62(2) where he:

(a) arranges for an authorised person with permission to carry on an activity of that kind, to administer the contract; or

(b) administers the contract himself during a period of not more than one month beginning with the day on which any such arrangement comes to an end.

This will allow solicitors to make arrangements for an authorised person to administer regulated mortgages. It will also give solicitors a period of one month's grace, during which they themselves can administer such mortgage contracts, where the original arrangements have come to an end and before new arrangements are put in place.

In addition, a person who is not an authorised person does not carry on an activity of the kind specified by article 61(2) in relation to a regulated mortgage contract where he administers the contract pursuant to an agreement with an authorised person who has permission to carry on an activity of that kind. Solicitors are therefore able to administer regulated mortgages (for example by taking steps for the purpose of collecting or recovering payments) on behalf of commercial mortgage providers (who will have to be authorised by the FSA from the commencement date).

FSMA, Part XX régime

12.9 Currently rule 3 of the Law Society's Scope Rules prohibits solicitors from carrying on, or agreeing to carry on the activity of

> 'entering into a regulated mortgage contract as lender or administering a regulated mortgage contract'.

Although this rule will be amended before the commencement date to take into account the exception for trustees now provided for in the NEA Order (see above para. 4.11), this change is unlikely to assist conveyancing practitioners.

In consequence unless solicitors can bring themselves within any of the statutory exclusions noted above, they will need authorisation from the FSA to undertake regulated activities in relation to regulated mortgage contracts. Unless solicitors are regulated by the FSA they will not be permitted (after the commencement date) to provide clients with bridging facilities where the loan satisfies the definition of a regulated mortgage.

CONTRACTUALLY BASED INVESTMENTS

12.10 Solicitors who advise on and make arrangements for repayment mortgages are unlikely to be involved in regulated activities. Although term assurance policies (mortgage protection products) are specified investments, because they are not contractually based investments, advice and arrangement activities made in respect of such policies are unlikely to involve regulated activities (see above Chapter 2).

Solicitors who advise on or make arrangements in respect of endowment policies, pension policies or ISA products as part of an *interest only* mortgage are, however, likely to be involved in regulated activities. Consequently statutory exclusions or the Part XX régime must be used if the firm is not authorised by FSA. If, following the transaction, solicitors retain the documents of title to such investments by way of safe custody, they are unlikely to be *administering* such investments and therefore will not be involved in safeguarding and administration services.

Statutory exclusions

12.11 Where a solicitor advises on the difference between a repayment mortgage and an interest only mortgage without mentioning any specific products, this will be generic advice and not treated as a regulated activity. Simply obtaining and handing on to the client the recommendation of an authorised person, without comment, will not be a regulated activity (see above para. 3.7 for details).

Where a solicitor wishes to make arrangements for the client to obtain an endowment or pension policy to be used as additional security for an interest only mortgage, there are a number of exclusions available as a result of the RAO:

(a)   A solicitor may introduce clients to an authorised person or exempt person where such introduction is made with a view to the provision of independent advice (RAO, article 33 – see above para. 3.14 and in particular note the restrictions contained in the Solicitors' Introduction and Referral Code 1990).

(b) A solicitor may make the arrangement using an authorised person in accordance with RAO, article 29. This is available if the solicitor makes arrangements with a view to a transaction which is or is to be entered into by a client with or through an authorised person if:

   (i) the transaction is entered into on advice given to the client by an authorised person; or

   (ii) it is clear in all the circumstances that the client, in his capacity as an investor, is not seeking and has not sought advice from the solicitor as to the merits of the client entering the transaction (or if the client has sought advice the solicitor has declined to give it but has recommended the client to seek advice from an authorised person).

The above exclusion does not apply if the agent receives from any person other than the client any pecuniary reward or advantage, for which he does not account to the client, arising out of his entering into the transaction. (For detailed guidance on this exclusion, see Chapter 3 and Appendix C1.)

(c) In limited circumstances, a solicitor may use the *necessary* exclusion in RAO, article 67 (see above para. 3.32). This is unlikely to be of assistance in most cases, since it is possible for solicitors to use the other available exclusions and consequently any advice or arrangement would not be *necessary*. However, where a solicitor is required to advise and/or make arrangements in respect of an assignment of a life policy in connection with a conveyancing or mortgage transaction, it may not be possible to use the services of an authorised person and consequently the article 67 exclusion might apply.

FSMA, Part XX régime

12.12 Conveyancing practitioners should be able to benefit from the Part XX régime in respect of advice and arrangements made for the acquisition or disposal of insurance or pension policies or ISA products used in conjunction with an interest only mortgage. The activities are likely to be treated as incidental and complementary to the conveyancing services and provided the other basic conditions contained in the Scope Rules (see Chapter 4) apply, such activities are capable of being treated as exempt regulated activities.

However, endowment policies and many ISA products fall within the definition of *packaged products*. Pension policies will be *personal pension schemes* within the meaning of the Scope Rules. Both categories of investments are therefore subject to the detailed restrictions contained in the Scope Rules.

Rule 5(1) of the Scope Rules provides that a firm must not recommend or make arrangements for a client to buy a packaged product except where:

(a) recommending, or arranging for, a client to buy a packaged product by means of an assignment;

(b) the arrangements are made as a result of the firm managing assets within the exception to rule 5(4); or

(c) the arrangement is made for a client where the firm assumes on reasonable grounds that the client is not relying on the firm as to the merits or suitability of the transaction.

Packaged products are defined (in rule 8) as

'long term insurance contracts (including pension products), units or shares in regulated collective investment schemes or an investment trust savings scheme whether or not held within an ISA or PEP or a stakeholder pension scheme'.

Thus the definition covers endowment policies. Personal pension schemes are dealt with in rule 5(2) discussed below.

The restriction applies to recommending a client to buy an endowment policy or making arrangements for a client to buy an endowment policy. The following activities are permitted under the Scope Rules (subject to a solicitor's competency) and are therefore capable of taking the benefit of FSMA, Part XX providing all the other conditions are satisfied:

(a) A solicitor may advise a client on the purchase of an endowment policy provided the advice does not amount to a recommendation. Thus the solicitor may explain the transaction or advise the client to seek further information or clarification in relation to a packaged product.

(b) A solicitor may recommend a client not to buy a particular endowment policy, i.e. give negative advice.

(c) A solicitor may recommend a client to dispose of a particular endowment policy. The disposal may be by way of sale, conversion of joint policies into single life, assignment, making the policy paid up or surrendering (although surrendering certain types of policy is rarely the best way of realising the full value of the policy).

(d) A solicitor may obtain advice from and/or endorse a recommendation given by an authorised or exempt person. Further, in relation to this activity, the FSA Guidance provides (clause 1.11.12 G)

'For the avoidance of doubt, it is not necessary for a professional firm to endorse a recommendation for the same reasons as given by the authorised person'.

(e) A solicitor may also make arrangements which are execution only arrangements. (For further comment on execution only transactions, see above, para. 6.8.)

In addition to those activities noted above, remember that although a solicitor cannot arrange the purchase of an endowment policy within FSMA, Part XX, in almost all cases the solicitor should be able to ensure that such arrangements are excluded in any event as a result of RAO, article 29 (arrangements made through an authorised person – see above para. 3.12).

Where the mortgage is being taken out in conjunction with a pension policy, solicitors must refer to rule 5(2) of the Scope Rules. This provides that a firm must not recommend a client to buy or dispose of any rights or interests in a personal pension scheme. Further the rule provides that a firm must not make arrangements for a client to buy any rights or interests in a personal pension scheme except where the transaction is effectively an execution only transaction. Note, however, the execution only exception does not apply if the transaction involves a pension transfer or an opt out (for details of the definitions applicable to rule 5(2), see above para. 4.21).

The restriction in rule 5(2) does not apply to arranging the disposal of rights in a personal pension scheme. However advising in relation to such a disposal is prohibited.

SHARES IN A MANAGEMENT OR SERVICE COMPANY

12.13 As part of a conveyancing transaction, solicitors may have to advise on the acquisition or disposal of shares held in a management or service company. Since RAO, article 76 applies to shares in the share capital of any body corporate, such shares will be specified investments. Solicitors may also deal as agent or make arrangements for the acquisition or disposal of such shares. It is unlikely that solicitors will be involved in safeguarding and administration services relating to such shares. Although a solicitor may hold the shares in safe custody he is unlikely to be involved in administration activities.

To avoid authorisation, solicitors must ensure that their advice, dealing and arranging activities in relation to such shares are either excluded or come within the Part XX régime.

Excluded activities

12.14 RAO, article 67 allows solicitors to deal as agent in, make arrangements for the acquisition or disposal of, advise on (and if appropriate, safeguard and administer) investments where it may reasonably be regarded as a necessary part of other services. It is almost inevitable that such activities relating to management or service companies will be a necessary part of the conveyancing transaction. Note that the exclusion is subject to the condition that there is no separate remuneration for carrying on such activities (for full details of this exclusion, see above para. 3.32).

FSMA, Part XX régime

It will be possible for all the activities noted in paragraph 12.14 above to be **12.15** treated as exempt regulated activities if the basic conditions of the Law Society's Scope Rules apply.

COMPLIANCE

Where a conveyancing practitioner provides services which are excluded from **12.16** the definition of regulated activities as a result of any of the statutory exclusions, no specific compliance will be necessary under the Conduct of Business Rules. It will of course still be necessary for solicitors to comply with the Solicitors' Practice Rules and other conduct obligations.

However where solicitors use the Part XX exempt activities régime in addition to ensuring that the Scope Rules have been complied with, the Law Society's Conduct of Business Rules will also have to be considered. Details can be found in Chapter 6 and include the requirements relating to:

(a) status disclosure;
(b) execution of transactions;
(c) records of transactions;
(d) record of commissions;
(e) safekeeping of client's investments; and
(f) confirmation of execution only business where the investment is a packaged product.

FINANCIAL PROMOTIONS

Where a solicitor is acting in conveyancing matters there are no specific FPO **12.17** exclusions applicable. However, conveyancing practitioners should note that included within the definition of controlled activities for the purposes of the FPO are regulated mortgage activities (after the commencement date, expected to be sometime in 2004) and activities relating to general insurance contracts. Solicitors must take care to ensure that any inducement or invitation to a client to engage in these activities falls within an appropriate exemption in the FPO. Although solicitors may avoid undertaking these activities as regulated activities, any financial promotion in respect of these activities will be caught by the FPO.

In all cases where a communication amounts to an inducement or invitation to engage in investment activities consideration must be given to the appropriate exemptions in the FPO (for example: articles 55 and 55A, communications by members of professions; articles 28 and 28A, one off communications; article 14, follow up communications; or article 15, introductions (for details see Chapter 7).

CHAPTER 13

Corporate department

REGULATED ACTIVITIES

13.1 There are a number of circumstances where regulated activities within the meaning of the RAO may be carried on in the corporate department. For example:

(a) advice on or the arrangement for the acquisition or disposal of shares in a public or private company;

(b) advice on or arrangements made in respect of the subscription for shares following a company formation;

(c) advice on or the arrangement of a debenture when acting for the lender of money to a company (although note the circumstance where debentures are not specified investments – see Chaper 2);

(d) advice on and arrangements made in respect of share options (e.g. as part of a shareholder agreement or otherwise);

(e) advice on or arrangements made for companies in respect of key man insurance where the insurance contract is a contractually based investment;

(f) advice on or arrangements made in respect of pension policies; and

(g) advice on or arrangements made in respect of the underwriting of a share issue.

It should be noted that regulated activities will only arise where advice is given to or an arrangement is made for a client to acquire or dispose or subscribe for or underwrite an investment. RAO, article 3 provides that disposing of an investment for valuable consideration includes 'issuing or creating the investment'. Although a solicitor will not be 'arranging' where a company issues shares or debentures (see the exclusion in article 34, para. 3.15 above) advice given on the issue of shares or debentures could be caught as a regulated activity.

A firm's corporate department may also be involved in regulated activities where it offers safeguarding and administration services (see above, para. 2.32). Shares in the share capital of companies could be caught under this activity. Although it is necessary for the firm to do more than just hold share certificates for safekeeping, administration can be undertaken by carrying out corporate actions such as proxy voting (including exercising rights conferred by an investment on behalf of the beneficial owner).

STATUTORY EXCEPTIONS

Where it appears from the above that a firm is undertaking regulated activi- **13.2** ties as a result of its corporate work, it is then necessary to ascertain whether any of the statutory exceptions contained in the RAO take the activity outside the scope of regulation. There are four exceptions which may benefit corporate lawyers.

Introductions

Solicitors can use RAO, article 33 and make introductions to authorised or **13.3** exempt persons with a view to the provision of independent advice. (For details, see above para. 3.14.)

Sale of body corporate

Dealing as principal or agent, arranging deals and investment advice in **13.4** connection with the sale of a body corporate are all excluded (RAO, article 70) if:

(a) The shares acquired or disposed are not shares in an open-ended investment company;
(b) The following conditions are met:

    (i) The shares consist of or include 50 per cent or more of the voting shares in the company; or
    (ii) the shares together with those already held by the person acquiring them consist of at least 50 per cent or more of the voting shares; and
    (iii) the acquisition or disposal is between parties each of whom is a body corporate, a partnership, a single individual or a group of connected individuals.

A group of connected individuals, for the purposes of article 70 means: in relation to a party disposing of shares in a body corporate, a single group of persons each of whom is –

(a) a director or manager of the body corporate;
(b) a close relative of any such director or manager;
(c) a person acting as trustee for any person falling within paragraph (a) or (b) above.

In relation to a party acquiring shares in a body corporate, a single group of persons each of whom is –

(a) a person who is or is to be a director or manager of the body corporate;
(b) a close relative of any such person; or
(c) a person acting as trustee for any person falling within paragraph (a) or (b) above.

A close relative is defined, for the purpose of para. 3.31 above as meaning:

(a) his spouse;
(b) his children and stepchildren, his parents and stepparents, his brothers and sisters and his stepbrothers and stepsisters; and
(c) the spouse of any person falling within (b) above.

Even if the above conditions are not met the activities will be excluded if the object of the transaction may, nevertheless, be reasonably regarded as the acquisition of day to day control of the affairs of the body corporate. The FSA has provided guidance on this aspect of the exclusion. Paragraph 1.20.13 G states:

'In any case where the conditions referred to in [article 70] are not met, it will be necessary to consider the circumstances in which the transaction takes place in order to determine whether the objective is the acquisition of day to day control. In situations where the 50 per cent holding of voting shares test is not met it remains possible that the objective of a transaction could still be the acquisition of day to day control – for instance, because the remaining shareholders represent a large number of small shareholders who it is reasonable to suppose will not regularly act in concert.'

The Guidance further deals with the position where the test regarding the status of the parties is not met. It states:

'Where the nature of the parties test is not met (typically because there are two or more parties involved as buyer or seller and they do not collectively represent a group of connected individuals as defined) it may still be the case that the objective of the transaction is the acquisition of day to day control when due account is taken of the purpose for which the person concerned holds or proposes to hold the voting shares. This may typically occur, for example, where shares are to be held by:

(1) a person (of either sex) with whom a manager or director cohabits;
(2) a venture capital company which has invested, or proposes to invest, in the company and which provides or is to provide a representative to act as manager or director of the company; or
(3) a private company used as a vehicle to hold shares by a person who is or is to be a manager or director of the company (or a close relative).'

Authorised person

A corporate lawyer may deal as agent or make arrangements using an **13.5** authorised person in accordance with RAO, article 29. This may be relevant where the investment product consists of key man insurance. This is available if the solicitor deals or makes arrangements with a view to a transaction which is or is to be entered into by a client with or through an authorised person if:

(a) the transaction is entered into on advice given to the client by an authorised person; or

(b) it is clear in all the circumstances that the client, in his capacity as an investor, is not seeking and has not sought advice from the solicitor as to the merits of the client entering the transaction (or if the client has sought advice the solicitor has declined to give it but has recommended the client to seek advice from an authorised person).

The above exclusion does not apply if the agent receives from any person other than the client any pecuniary reward or advantage, for which he does not account to the client, arising out of his entering into the transaction.

Necessary exclusion

The necessary exclusion in article 67 may be helpful for corporate activities. **13.6** For example, in acting on the acquisition or disposal of a company it is reasonable to regard as necessary the fact that solicitors will give advice on the merits of buying or selling and that arrangements will be made for the acquisition or disposal of shares. This exclusion is also likely to benefit advice on the issue of shares or debentures. No separate remuneration must be charged for carrying on the activities in question. For details of this exclusion, see above para. 3.30.

FSMA, PART XX RÉGIME

Securities and contractually based investments

Where the regulated investments consist of securities and contractually based **13.7** investments other than packaged products (i.e. shares, debentures, options and contracts for differences), the Law Society's Scope Rules permit solicitors to advise on and to make arrangements for the sale of such investments as part of a corporate transaction. It will, of course, be necessary for the solicitor to comply with all the basic conditions of the Scope Rules (for details, see Chapter 4).

Where the regulated activities relate to the purchase of these investments, the Scope Rules contain restrictions. A firm must not recommend a client to buy or subscribe for securities or contractually based investments (which are not packaged products) where the transactions would be made:

(a) with a person acting in the course of carrying on the business of buying, selling, subscribing or underwriting the investment, whether as principal or agent;

(b) on an investment exchange or any other market to which that investment is admitted for dealing; or

(c) in response to an invitation to subscribe for an investment which is, or is to be, admitted for dealing on an investment exchange or any other market.

Examples of prohibited acts would include:

(a) a solicitor could not recommend a client to purchase listed company shares from a stockbroker (clause (a) above);

(b) a solicitor could not recommend a client to purchase listed securities on the London Stock Exchange (clause (b) above); or

(c) a solicitor could not recommend a client to subscribe for shares following a public offer or flotation in respect of which an application for listing has been made (clause (c) above).

However, there are still a number of transactions that can be undertaken by solicitors within the terms of the Scope Rules. Examples of these permitted transactions include:

(a) a solicitor could make arrangements for the client to buy, sell, subscribe or underwrite these categories of investments. Such arrangements can be made using a stockbroker, or where the transaction is carried out on an investment exchange or following a public offer or flotation where the investment is listed. Rule 5(3) does not restrict arranging (or dealing as agent) provided the basic conditions apply (in particular the need for the activity to be incidental and complementary and the accounting for any pecuniary award or advantage – see above para. 4.22);

(b) a solicitor could recommend a client to purchase or subscribe for securities in a private company (where no stockbroker is involved);

(c) a solicitor could advise a client on the purchase or subscription of these categories of investments provided the advice does not amount to a recommendation;

(d) a solicitor could recommend a client not to buy a particular security or contractually based investment, i.e. give negative advice;

(e) a solicitor could obtain advice from and/or endorse a recommendation given by an authorised or exempt person.

Further, as a result of rule 5(3)(b), the basic restriction in rule 5(3) does not apply where the client is not an individual; where the client is acting in his capacity as a trustee of an occupational pension scheme; or where the client is an individual carrying on a business of which he is or is to be a controller. A controller for these purposes is defined in FSMA, article 422 as meaning, in broad terms, a person who has a 10 per cent or greater shareholding in a business undertaking or one who is able to exercise a significant influence over its management.

Consequently, subject to complying with the basic conditions, rule 5(3)(b) would allow a solicitor to recommend to a corporate client, the acquisition of shares or other securities in a listed company. A recommendation could also be made to an individual if the individual was intending to acquire a 10 per cent holding in the listed company or otherwise become a controller, as defined.

Packaged products (other than pensions)

Corporate lawyers may be asked to advise on and make arrangements for key **13.8** man insurance contracts or other life policies. Where these policies are contractually based investments they will be packaged products and any attempt to use the FSMA, Part XX régime will be subject to the restrictions contained in the Law Society's Scope Rules.

Rule 5(1) of the Scope Rules provides that a firm must not recommend or make arrangements for a client to buy a packaged product except where

(a) recommending, or arranging for, a client to buy a packaged product by means of an assignment;
(b) the arrangements are made as a result of the firm managing assets within the exception to rule 5(4); or
(c) the arrangement is made for a client where the firm assumes on reasonable grounds that the client is not relying on the firm as to the merits or suitability of the transaction.

The following activities are permitted under the Scope Rules (subject to a solicitor's competency) and are therefore capable of taking the benefit of FSMA, Part XX providing all the other conditions are satisfied.

(a) A solicitor may advise a client on the purchase of a packaged product provided the advice does not amount to a recommendation. Thus the solicitor may explain the transaction or advise the client to seek further information or clarification in relation to a packaged product.
(b) A solicitor may recommend a client not to buy a particular packaged product, i.e. give negative advice.
(c) A solicitor may recommend a client to sell or dispose of a particular packaged product.
(d) A solicitor may recommend or arrange for a client to buy or sell a packaged product by means of an assignment.
(e) A solicitor may obtain advice from and/or endorse a recommendation given by an authorised or exempt person. Further, in relation to this activity, the FSA Guidance provides (clause 1.11.12 G)

'For the avoidance of doubt, it is not necessary for a professional firm to endorse a recommendation for the same reasons as given by the authorised person'.

In addition to those activities noted above, remember that although a solicitor cannot arrange the purchase of a packaged product within FSMA, Part XX, in almost all cases the solicitor should be able to ensure that such arrangements are excluded in any event as a result of RAO, article 29 (arrangements made through an authorised person – see above para. 3.12).

Pension policies

13.9   Rule 5(2) of the Scope Rules provides that a firm must not recommend a client to buy or dispose of any rights or interests in a personal pension scheme. Further the rule provides that a firm must not make arrangements for a client to buy any rights or interests in a personal pension scheme except where the transaction is effectively an execution only transaction. Note, however, the execution only exception does not apply if the transaction involves a pension transfer or an opt out.

Corporate finance

13.10   Rule 5(5) of the Scope Rules prohibits a firm from acting:

(a)   as a sponsor to an issue in respect of securities to be admitted for dealing on the London Stock Exchange; or

(b)   as a nominated adviser to an issue in respect of securities to be admitted for dealing on the Alternative Investment Market of the London Stock Exchange.

The Law Society has provided guidance on other corporate finance activities as follows:

'Whether FSA authorisation will be required for other corporate finance activities will depend basically on whether:

- those activities are regulated activities; and
- the activities arise out of or are complementary to particular legal services provided to a particular client.

Most corporate lawyers will be able to meet the "arising out or complementary to" test. However, this may be difficult to establish where the main or only service required by the client is advising on or arranging an investment, particularly where no other authorised adviser is involved. Firms who specialise in corporate finance, particularly if the legal work is provided by another firm of solicitors, may need to consider FSA authorisation.'

Safeguarding and administration

Activities which amount to safeguarding and administration should be **13.11**
capable of benefiting from the Part XX régime provided the basic conditions
apply.

INSOLVENCY PRACTITIONERS

Insolvency practitioners may benefit from the provisions of FSMA, section **13.12**
38 and the Financial Services and Markets Act 2000 (Exemption) Order 2001
which provides exemption for insolvency practitioners from most regulated
activities.

COMPLIANCE

Where in a corporate transaction a solicitor uses any of the statutory exclu- **13.13**
sions, no specific compliance will be necessary under the Conduct of Business
Rules. It will of course still be necessary for solicitors to comply with the
Solicitors' Practice Rules and other conduct obligations.

Where the firm uses the Part XX exempt activities régime, in addition to
ensuring that the Scope Rules have been complied with, the Law Society's
Conduct of Business Rules will also have to be considered. Details can be
found in Chapter 6 and include the requirements relating to:

(a) status disclosure;
(b) execution of transactions;
(c) records of transactions;
(d) record of commissions;
(e) safekeeping of client's investments; and
(f) confirmation of execution only business where the investment is a
     packaged product.

FINANCIAL PROMOTIONS

Where a solicitor is involved in corporate activities there are no specific exclu- **13.14**
sions in the FPO applicable. In all cases where any communication amounts
to an inducement or invitation to engage in investment activities consideration must be given to the appropriate exemptions in the FPO (for example:
articles 55 and 55A, communications by members of professions; articles 28
and 28A, one off communications; article 14, follow-up communications; or
article 15, introductions (for details see Chapter 7).

The Law Society has provided guidance on the financial promotions régime as it affects corporate lawyers. This guidance is reproduced below:

'Solicitors involved in corporate work generally and corporate finance in particular, should make sure that they also understand the régime for the regulation of financial promotions. The definition of financial promotion is very wide and communications which amount to a financial promotion should be made by, or approved by, an authorised person. The Financial Promotions Order (FPO) contains a number of exceptions, some of which will apply to solicitors. The DPB régime as such does not apply to financial promotions and the FPO does not contain an exemption which matches with the DPB régime.

The FSA Perimeter Guidance (section 9) explains the exemptions in the FPO which will be most useful for solicitors.

In larger scale transactions when a merchant bank or other authorised advisers are involved as part of a team of advisers, then communications which are subject to the FPO could be delivered by the authorised person. It is more difficult with smaller companies, particularly those becoming involved in the OFEX market as they may not be able to afford multiple advisers. Solicitors who are not FSA authorised, advising these companies, will not be able to issue or approve investment advertisements. Firms will have to take particular care when communicating in writing or in meetings with individuals who are not clients. Some firms may take the view that, particularly in relation to corporate work, the application of the exemptions in the FPO are so complex that the safer course is for the firm to be authorised by the FSA.'

CHAPTER 14

Litigation department (including matrimonial work)

REGULATED ACTIVITIES

The general litigation department of a firm of solicitors is likely to give the **14.1**
fewest problems in terms of compliance with the financial services legislation
and regulations. In the most part litigators will not be involved in giving
advice on investments or making arrangements in respect of investments.
Matrimonial lawyers will, however, come across a wide range of investments
as part of their work.

Advice may be given to clients or arrangements made in respect
investments for clients involved in litigation. For example:

(a) advice on or arrangements made for the investment of monies received
    by way of damages;
(b) advice on or arrangements made for the transfer of shares in a company
    (private or public) or other investments as a result of a settlement
    agreement in general or matrimonial litigation;
(c) advice on and arrangements made for the sale, surrender or assignment
    of a life policy in matrimonial litigation;
(d) advice on and arrangements made for the transfer of pension rights in
    matrimonial litigation.

STATUTORY EXCEPTIONS

Where it appears from the above that a firm is undertaking regulated activi- **14.2**
ties as a result of its litigation work, it is then necessary to ascertain whether
any of the statutory exceptions contained in the RAO take the activity
outside the scope of regulation. There are three exceptions which may benefit
litigation lawyers.

Introductions

14.3   Solicitors can use RAO, article 33 and make introductions to authorised or exempt persons with a view to the provision of independent advice (for details, see above para. 3.14). This is particularly useful in matrimonial cases where the investments may be of high value and it will be in the best interests of the client to obtain specialist advice from independent authorised persons. The need for specialist advice in relation to pensions is important in matrimonial (and other) matters. In considering whether the use of an introduction would be appropriate, solicitors must consider the needs of their clients. The Law Society has given guidance on this in relation to matrimonial matters and the following facts must be taken into account:

> 'The need for specialist advice is particularly important in relation to pensions and firms must be aware of the need to give proper advice in relation to pension sharing. Solicitors' firms may be exposed to negligence claims if they fail fully to advise clients about the options, and about the effect of taking different options. However, it is equally important that solicitors remain involved in these decisions with their clients as there will be legal and personal matters that will also affect the client's decision in these areas and the solicitors' knowledge of the client generally is an important part of the picture. For example advice from a pensions adviser may lead to a situation where the parties would continue to have contact. You may be aware that this advice does not meet the wishes of your client.'

It must be appreciated that where the 'introductions' exclusion is used, the solicitor must take no further part in any transaction. In the light of the Law Society's guidance it may be necessary to consider the 'authorised person' exclusion.

Authorised person

14.4   A litigation lawyer may deal as agent or make arrangements using an authorised person in accordance with RAO, article 22 or 29. This is available if the solicitor deals or makes arrangements with a view to a transaction which is or is to be entered into by a client with or through an authorised person if:

(a)   the transaction is entered into on advice given to the client by an authorised person; or

(b)   it is clear in all the circumstances that the client, in his capacity as an investor, is not seeking and has not sought advice from the solicitor as to the merits of the client entering the transaction (or if the client has sought advice the solicitor has declined to give it but has recommended the client to seek advice from an authorised person).

The above exclusion does not apply if the agent receives from any person other than the client any pecuniary reward or advantage, for which he does not account to the client, arising out of his entering into the transaction. (For detailed guidance on this exclusion, see above para. 3.12.)

However, in many cases (particularly matrimonial litigation) clients are not acquiring or disposing of investments from or to third parties. Frequently they will be transferring assets between themselves in an equitable or agreed way or by direction of the court. In certain circumstances the *execution only* exclusion noted in either article 22 or 29 might be appropriate.

Necessary exclusion

The necessary exclusion in article 67 may be helpful for litigation activities in **14.5** certain circumstances. No separate remuneration must be charged for carrying on the activities in question. It is not likely to be *necessary* for a solicitor to advise a successful litigation client on how to invest the damages. The FSA has, however, provided specific guidance on the application of this exclusion to matrimonial lawyers. It appears in paragraph 1.20.6 G of their guidance and states:

> 'Much of the work undertaken by lawyers in negotiating and putting into effect matrimonial or structured settlements may reasonably be regarded to be a necessary part of their professional services. For example, following the provision of necessary advice in a matrimonial dispute it may be reasonably regarded to be necessary for the solicitor to instigate the sale of an insurance policy by instructing an authorised intermediary to find a buyer at the best price and then to arrange the deal. It would be unlikely, however, that it would reasonably be regarded as necessary for the solicitor to undertake the role of that authorised intermediary.'

For further details of this exclusion, see above para. 3.32.

FSMA, PART XX RÉGIME

Securities and contractually based investments

Where the regulated investments consist of securities and contractually based **14.6** investments other than packaged products (i.e. shares, debentures, government and public securities), the Law Society's Scope Rules permit solicitors to advise on and to make arrangements for the sale of such investments as part of a general or matrimonial litigation transaction. It will, of course, be necessary for the solicitor to comply with all the basic conditions of the Scope Rules. There is unlikely to be any difficulty in complying with the condition that any exempt regulated activity must arise out of or be complementary to another professional service. The areas where solicitors may not have sufficient competence to advise alone will normally be in relation to the valuation of a variety of investment products and perhaps the method of disposal (for details, see Chapter 4).

Where the regulated activities relate to the purchase of these investments, the Scope Rules contain restrictions. A firm must not recommend a client to buy or subscribe for securities or contractually based investments (which are not packaged products) where the transactions would be made:

(a) with a person acting in the course of carrying on the business of buying, selling, subscribing or underwriting the investment, whether as principal or agent;

(b) on an investment exchange or any other market to which that investment is admitted for dealing; or

(c) in response to an invitation to subscribe for an investment which is, or is to be, admitted for dealing on an investment exchange or any other market.

Examples of prohibited acts would include:

(a) a solicitor could not recommend a client to purchase listed company shares from a stockbroker (clause (a) above);

(b) a solicitor could not recommend a client to purchase listed securities on the London Stock Exchange (clause (b) above); or

(c) a solicitor could not recommend a client to subscribe for shares following a public offer or flotation in respect of which an application for listing has been made (clause (c) above).

However, there are still a number of transactions that can be undertaken by solicitors within the terms of the Scope Rules. Examples of these permitted transactions include:

(a) a solicitor could make arrangements for the client to buy, sell, subscribe or underwrite these categories of investments. Such arrangements can be made using a stockbroker, or where the transaction is carried out on an investment exchange or following a public offer or flotation where the investment is listed. Rule 5(3) does not restrict arranging (or dealing as agent) provided the basic conditions apply (in particular the need for the activity to be incidental and complementary and the accounting for any pecuniary award or advantage – see above para. 4.22);

(b) a solicitor could recommend a client to purchase or subscribe for securities in a private company (where no stockbroker is involved);

(c) a solicitor could advise a client on the purchase or subscription of these categories of investments provided the advice does not amount to a recommendation;

(d) a solicitor could recommend a client not to buy a particular security or contractually based investment, i.e. give negative advice;

(e) a solicitor could obtain advice from and/or endorse a recommendation given by an authorised or exempt person;

Packaged products (other than pensions)

14.7 Litigation and matrimonial lawyers may be asked to advise on and make arrangements for life policies. Where these policies are contractually based investments they will be packaged products and any attempt to use the FSMA, Part XX régime will be subject to the restrictions contained in the Law Society's Scope Rules.

Rule 5(1) of the Scope Rules provides that a firm must not recommend or make arrangements for a client to buy a packaged product except where

(a) recommending, or arranging for, a client to buy a packaged product by means of an assignment;

(b) the arrangements are made as a result of the firm managing assets within the exception to rule 5(4); or

(c) the arrangement is made for a client where the firm assumes on reasonable grounds that the client is not relying on the firm as to the merits or suitability of the transaction.

The following activities are permitted under the Scope Rules (subject to a solicitor's competency) and are therefore capable of taking the benefit of FSMA, Part XX providing all the other conditions are satisfied:

(a) A solicitor may advise a client on the purchase of a packaged product provided the advice does not amount to a recommendation. Thus the solicitor may explain the transaction or advise the client to seek further information or clarification in relation to a packaged product.

(b) A solicitor may recommend a client not to buy a particular packaged product, i.e. give negative advice.

(c) A solicitor may recommend a client to sell or dispose of a particular packaged product.

(d) A solicitor may recommend or arrange for a client to buy or sell a packaged product by means of an assignment.

(e) A solicitor may obtain advice from and/or endorse a recommendation given by an authorised or exempt person. Further, in relation to this activity, the FSA Guidance provides (clause 1.11.12.G):

'For the avoidance of doubt, it is not necessary for a professional firm to endorse a recommendation for the same reasons as given by the authorised person.'

In addition to those activities noted above, remember that although a solicitor cannot arrange the purchase of a packaged product within FSMA, Part XX, in almost all cases the solicitor should be able to ensure that such arrangements are excluded in any event as a result of RAO, article 29 (arrangements made through an authorised person – see above para. 3.12).

Pension policies

14.8   Rule 5(2) of the Scope Rules provides that a firm must not recommend a client to buy or dispose of any rights or interests in a personal pension scheme. Further the rule provides that a firm must not make arrangements for a client to buy any rights or interests in a personal pension scheme except where the transaction is effectively an execution only transaction. Note, however, the execution only exception does not apply if the transaction involves a pension transfer or an opt out.

Safeguarding and administration

14.9   Although this activity is unlikely to be undertaken by litigation or matrimonial solicitors, it is capable of being treated as an exempt regulated activity within FSMA, Part XX.

COMPLIANCE

14.10   Where a litigation practitioner undertakes services which are excluded from the definition of regulated activities as a result of any of the statutory exclusions, no specific compliance will be necessary under the Conduct of Business Rules. It will of course still be necessary for solicitors to comply with the Solicitors' Practice Rules and other conduct obligations.

However where solicitors use the Part XX exempt activities régime in addition to ensuring that the Scope Rules have been complied with, the Law Society's Conduct of Business Rules will also have to be considered. Details can be found in Chapter 6 and include the requirements relating to:

(a)   status disclosure;
(b)   execution of transactions;
(c)   records of transactions;
(d)   record of commissions;
(e)   safekeeping of client's investments; and
(f)   confirmation of execution only business where the investment is a packaged product.

FINANCIAL PROMOTIONS

14.11   Where a solicitor is acting in general or matrimonial litigation matters there are no specific FPO exclusions applicable. In all cases where a communication amounts to an inducement or invitation to engage in investment activities consideration must be given to the appropriate exemptions in the FPO (for example: articles 55 and 55A, communications by members of professions; articles 28 and 28A, one off communications; article 14, follow-up communications; or article 15, introductions (for details see Chapter 7).

CHAPTER 15

Private clients

INTRODUCTION

There are a number of circumstances where private clients may seek advice **15.1**
on financial service products from solicitors sometimes without any associated retainer.

Examples of these include:

(a) advice on and arrangements made for tax matters;
(b) advice on and arrangements made for pensions;
(c) advice on school fees;
(d) advice on and arrangements made for the surrender of a life policy;
(e) general portfolio management.

Whilst some of these activities will undoubtedly be capable of being reasonably regarded as a necessary part of other professional services (and thus
benefit from RAO, article 67 – see above para. 3.32) or complementary to
other professional services (and thus be capable of being treated as exempt
regulated activities under FSMA, Part XX – see Chapter 4), some stand
alone and may give rise to regulated activities.

TAX, PENSIONS AND SCHOOL FEES

Advice given regarding taxation, pensions or school fees will only give rise to **15.2**
problems if investments (as defined) are involved. In many cases tax advice
will involve advice on the acquisition or disposal of an investment. Such
advice will amount to a regulated activity unless the solicitor can show a
statutory exclusion applies or the FSMA, Part XX régime applies (see
Chapter 4 for details of Part XX and note the guidance given by the FSA on
tax advice in para. 3.32 above).

Where the FSMA, Part XX régime is used, care must be taken to show
that all the basic conditions are met along with the specific conditions in relation to packaged products, pension policies, securities and contractually
based investments (see above Chapter 4).

Concern has been expressed in the financial services industry as a whole as a result of advice relating to pension transfers and opt outs. Firms which, in the past, have undertaken this type of work have been required to carry out a detailed review of relevant cases. The Law Society's Council has issued a statement on Past Pension Transfers and Opt outs and this is available from the professional ethics division of the Law Society (telephone 0870 606 2577). As noted above (para. 6.11), these statements continue to be relevant as they relate to acts or omissions pre-1 December 2001. Consequently they remain in force.

With regard to pension transfers and opt outs generally see rule 5(2) of the Scope rules (above para. 4.21).

COSTS VERSUS COMMISSION

15.3 One problem which must be faced by solicitors carrying on investment activities (whether the activities are excluded or exempt regulated activities) is how best to charge for such business.

Solicitors who receive commission from third parties (e.g. life offices, stockbrokers, unit trust operators, etc.) are subject to Rule 10 of the Solicitors' Practice Rules 1990 (see above, para. 5.8). They must either account to the client for the commission or must seek the client's consent to retain any part of or the whole of the commission (after satisfying the detailed provisions contained in Rule 10).

Solicitors using the exclusions in the RAO or the FSMA, Part XX régime must generally account to the client for any pecuniary reward or advantage which the firm receives from a third party. For details of this requirement see Chapters 3 and 4 but note that all commission or other reward must be accounted for. The £20 *de minimis* provision contained in Practice Rule 10 does not apply.

If solicitors rebate the full amount of commission, their fees will be collected by submission of a bill of costs. If they retain commission (with the client's consent) they may forgo other fees or submit a reduced bill of costs. Both methods have their advantages.

Remuneration on a fee-paying basis

15.4 Solicitors who are remunerated on a fee-paying basis for their financial services work are subject to the provisions of the Solicitors' (Non-Contentious Business) Remuneration Order 1994. Financial services will amount to non-contentious work. Consequently any bill submitted must be fair and reasonable having regard to all the circumstances of the case and in particular to:

(a) the complexity of the matter or difficulty or novelty of the question raised;

(b) the skill, labour, specialised knowledge and responsibility involved;

(c) the time spent;

(d) the number and importance of the documents prepared or perused;

(e) the place where and the circumstances in which the business is transacted;

(f) the amount or value of any money or property involved;

(g) whether any land involved is registered land;

(h) the importance of the matter to the client; and

(i) the approval (express or implied) of the client to:

    (i) the solicitor undertaking all or any part of the work giving rise to the costs; or

    (ii) the amount of the costs.

Obviously not all these matters will be of relevance to the provision of financial services. However, points a, b, c, d, f, h and i could be relevant in appropriate circumstances.

Further, clients who are not satisfied with the amount charged by their solicitor can require their solicitor to obtain a remuneration certificate from the Law Society. This certificate may either certify that the bill is fair and reasonable or it will reduce the amount of the bill. Where a reduced sum is certified, it is this reduced amount which becomes payable.

Solicitors who are remunerated on a fee-paying basis will generally pass over any commission received to the client in accordance with Rule 10. In most cases this commission will be paid into client account (for the account of the named client) and may then be used by the solicitor to the discharge of his bill of costs (in accordance with Rule 19 of the Solicitors' Accounts Rules 1998). Solicitors who simply deliver a bill equal to the commission received may find it difficult, in some cases, to persuade the Law Society that the various criteria under the 1994 Order have been met. They risk the possibility of their bill being reduced.

One way to avoid an application for a remuneration certificate is for the solicitor to enter into a non-contentious costs agreement with the client in accordance with the Solicitors Act 1974, section 57. This section allows a solicitor to make a written agreement with his client regarding remuneration. It permits the remuneration to be by way of gross sum, commission or percentage, by salary or otherwise.

The reference to commission is likely to be interpreted as a fee calculated by reference to property dealt with or recovered by the solicitor, rather than commission received from a third party. However, the words *or otherwise* are likely to be sufficiently wide enough to cover the situation where a client agrees with the solicitor that the solicitor should retain a third party's commission by way of remuneration.

Where such an agreement has been entered into, the remuneration certificate procedure is not available under the Solicitors' Remuneration Order. However, section 57(5) provides that the court may set aside such an agreement if it considers it unfair or unreasonable.

In conclusion, therefore, the fee-paying basis has the advantage of not requiring the client's consent to the retention of the commission. The solicitor can package the service to his client by showing that all commissions are rebated to the client (thus satisfying Practice Rule 10, and the requirements relating to accounting for commission contained in both the statutory exclusions and the Law Society's Scope Rules). However, the solicitor does then risk being asked to justify his bill in accordance with the Remuneration Order, unless a section 57 non-contentious costs agreement has been entered into.

Remuneration by retention of commission

15.5   It is open to solicitors to seek their client's agreement enabling them to retain all the commission (and thus discharge or partially discharge the costs of the matter). As has been mentioned earlier (see above, para. 5.8), Rule 10 of the Solicitors' Practice Rules 1990 requires the solicitor to account to clients for any commission received of more than £20 unless the client consents. The £20 *de minimis* does not however apply to the requirement to account for commission contained in the statutory exclusions or the Law Society's Scope Rules.

Such consent must be obtained after the solicitor has disclosed to his client in writing:

(a)   the amount or basis of calculation of the commission; or
(b)   (where the precise amount or basis cannot be ascertained) an approximation of the amount.

If the approximation of the amount is given to the client and the client agrees that the solicitor should retain the commission, but the actual sum received by the solicitor is materially different and in excess of the approximation, the excess must be accounted for to the client.

Solicitors who decide upon this route are advised that the best place to disclose the amount, basis or approximation of the commission is a client agreement. If the client signs the agreement (and the agreement contains a clause that the client agrees to the solicitor retaining the commission) the provisions of Rule 10 should be satisfied. Further, as mentioned above, it is possible that this clause will amount to a section 57 non-contentious costs agreement. As such the Solicitors' Remuneration Order will be excluded. Since commissions can amount to considerable sums of money (especially life insurance commissions), this system has the advantage of guaranteeing a fairly high return (assuming the client has consented to the retention) without the risk of an application for a remuneration certificate being sought (subject to the court's overriding jurisdiction under section 57(5)).

Problems can arise where a solicitor receives a commission from a life office and the client fails to keep up payment of the premiums. In most cases, solicitors not authorised by the FSA will not be making arrangements for the acquisition of a policy directly from a life office. The statutory exclusion (article 29) requires the use of an authorised person; the Scope Rules generally prohibit arrangements made for packaged products. However in some circumstances following the advice of an authorised person (execution only or arrangements made as a result of management), solicitors could arrange directly with a life office and thereby receive commission. In such circumstances there may be a claw back of commission by the life office. If the solicitor has done no work other than arrange the life policy, such claw back is probably justified. If the solicitor has arranged the policy in conjunction with, for example a conveyancing transaction and the commission is retained by way of payment or part payment of his proper bill, he could be out of pocket if he has to repay the commission. Whilst in practice it may be rare for clients to default on payments of premiums where the policy is taken out in conjunction with a mortgage, solicitors who do not want to accept the risk should consider two possibilities.

An agreement could be entered into with the client reserving the right to seek further payment in the event of claw back.

Alternatively solicitors could elect to receive commissions from the life office on a 'non-indemnity' basis. In this case commission is paid by way of monthly instalment. If the client defaults on the premiums, no claw back of the commission is necessary.

This should be distinguished from the indemnity basis where the life office pays a lump sum for commission at the outset. This represents all the commission payable for the initial period (commonly 36 months) adjusted for payment in advance. If the premiums lapse the solicitor must repay some of the commission which has been received.

Finally, in relation to commissions, it should not be overlooked that Rule 10 of the Solicitors' Practice Rules 1990, and the accounting requirements in both the statutory exclusions and Law Society's Scope Rules apply to renewal commissions. Solicitors wishing to retain both the initial and renewal commissions should ensure that their client's consent is obtained for both.

CHAPTER 16

Management of investment business

INTRODUCTION

16.1   This chapter provides guidance on how firms can organise their management and administration of investment business to promote compliance with FSMA and the Law Society's Rules. Although firms not authorised by the FSA are subject to no formal management requirements, the dangers of undertaking regulated activities without authorisation (criminal and civil liability) are such that even the smallest firms should adopt appropriate systems and policies.

POLICY DECISIONS

16.2   The firm should make a number of policy decisions in respect of investment activities. These will shape the organisation of the firm for undertaking this work. It is vital for the firm to undertake this work within a framework of positive policy decisions rather than allow the organisation to develop in an unstructured way. Clear policy decisions allow all those involved in investment activities within the firm to understand their precise role. A senior partner should be responsible for ensuring that business decisions on investment activities are considered by the firm.

The policy decisions required to be taken by the firm are provided below. This may not be an exhaustive list. Further details are provided on each heading in the paragraphs which follow. The policies include:

(a)   types and extent of investment activities to be undertaken by the firm and the extent of any communications with clients and others (real time and non-real time) which might be a financial promotion;

(b)   the organisation of investment services within the firm, i.e. who should authorise departmental decisions;

(c)   arrangements for investment activities undertaken in the firm's various branches (if applicable);

(d)   appointment of a compliance officer;

(e) procedure for dealing with complaints;

(f) treatment of commission receivable.

Types and extent of investment business to be undertaken

The firm must determine its philosophy towards investment activities, in par- **16.3** ticular, it must decide which activities benefit from statutory exclusions and which activities fall within the DPB regime under FSMA, Part XX. The firm's policies on financial promotions must also be considered along with the appropriate exemptions in the FPO.

Where the FSMA, Part XX régime is used, compliance with both the Law Society's Scope Rules and Conduct of Business Rules will be necessary. Compliance with the Rules will be assisted if activities are undertaken on the basis of policies relating to the extent and type of regulated activity to be carried on. The policies can then be communicated to all fee earners so that they have a clear guide to the work in which they should and should not be involved.

Organisation of investment business

The firm must decide who is able to undertake regulated activities within **16.4** individual departments. If regulated activities are minimal, fee earners dealing with say property, trust and probate and commercial work will be able to take on such activities which arise. Where the firm regularly undertakes regulated activities, the risk of committing a criminal offence is greater and control perhaps should be in the hands of a limited number of fee earners.

Investment business undertaken at branch offices

The firm may wish to restrict the number of branches which can under- **16.5** take investment activities to ensure that competent or specialist staff deal with these matters. However, the firm may decide to allow investment activities to be undertaken at any branch without restrictions. Effective control procedures must be devised in accordance with the policies to deal with this work.

Appointment of a compliance officer

Although there is no formal requirement for a compliance officer to be **16.6** appointed, because of the risks involved in getting it wrong, it makes sense for one person to take control of the compliance requirements within the firm. In many firms the compliance officer is also the firm's money laundering reporting officer. The following is a list of duties which a compliance officer should undertake:

(a) devise or approve all the firm's procedures relating to investment activities and financial promotions including compliance systems;

(b) supervise the keeping of records under the Conduct of Business Rules;

(c) undertake internal monitoring of compliance within the firm including its branches;

(d) prepare and distribute a compliance manual or directives based on the firm's policies and procedures; and

(e) arrange training on the FSMA and the Law Society Scope and Conduct of Business Rules for appropriate personnel.

The compliance officer must have a sound knowledge of the FSMA, the Scope and Conduct of Business Rules and other Law Society Rules and have a thorough understanding of the investment activities undertaken by the firm and the fee earners involved.

Procedure for dealing with complaints

16.7 The Conduct of Business Rules contain requirements additional to the Practice Rules in respect of complaints (see above, Chapter 6). The firm must comply with Rule 15 of the Solicitors' Practice Rules 1990 and the Solicitors Costs Information and Client Care Code 1999. This requires a firm to have a written complaints procedure and ensure that complaints are handled in accordance with it; to ensure that clients are told the name of the person to contact about any problem with the service provided; and ensure that the client is given a copy of the complaints procedure on request. The Conduct of Business Rules require a statement explaining that complaints and redress mechanisms are provided through the Law Society. A recommended statement is set out in para. 6.3 above.

Commissions

16.8 The firm must put in place arrangements to comply with Practice Rule 10 and the obligations contained in the statutory exclusions and Scope Rules. In relation to Practice Rule 10 the firm should decide, for example, whether it will pass on all commissions received to clients and raise bills for fees for the services provided or seek to obtain the client's agreement to retain all or part of the commissions received. The firm should also decide, whenever possible, whether to receive commission on the indemnity or non-indemnity basis in anticipation of potential problems on claw back (see above, para. 15.5).

THE COMPLIANCE MANUAL

The FSMA, the RAO, the FPO and the Law Society's Scope and Conduct of **16.9** Business Rules require firms to comply with a fairly complex framework of rules. Full compliance with these requirements is essential.

Poor compliance in some circumstances can lead to disciplinary action being taken against the firm. This could result in the imposition of conditions on the firm's ability to conduct regulated activities or in extreme circumstances, a criminal conviction.

The firm's procedures for compliance with the rules must therefore be given attention by high level management within the firm. Once determined, the firm's policies and procedures must be communicated to all personnel who at any time may be involved in investment activities.

The most satisfactory method of recording and communicating the firm's procedures is by the use of a compliance manual. The manual should be in an easily readable form and should not attempt to reiterate all the provisions of the FSMA, the RAO, the FPO or the Law Society's Rules. Instead, it should seek to provide explanations and instructions in a practical way in respect of the investment activities as conducted by the firm. The manual should be arranged in suitable sections. It is essential that the manual is kept up to date.

The contents of the manual will vary from firm to firm. It is suggested that the following should be included in the manual:

Policy decisions

The policies which have been determined by the firm should be clearly **16.10** stated. The names of the designated personnel for complaints and approval of financial promotion material should be stated.

Brief explanation and illustration of the Act, the Regulations and the Law Society Rules as they apply to the firm

The manual should not seek to reiterate all the provisions of the Act and **16.11** other material. However, the emphasis should be on explanation and illustration of how the Act, regulations and rules apply to the firm's business.

The firm's procedures for compliance

The firm's procedures should be recorded to ensure that all personnel **16.12** understand which records need to be maintained and where they are held.

Specimen forms

16.13 All forms relating to investment activities should be included with instructions for their use. Consideration should be given to unique reference numbering and colour coding to denote departments.

Instructions to departments of the firm on procedures which relate specifically to work undertaken in those departments

16.14 Procedures to be followed when dealing with clients of the various departments should be recorded where possible using one subsection per department. The procedures should of course be consistent with the policy decisions made on the type and extent of investment activities to be undertaken, for example, procedures for use of an authorised person where the firm wishes to use the authorised person exclusion.

A list of warnings

16.15 A simple list of warnings could be included to inform staff when they are stepping outside the firm's policies or the individual's authority.

Help

16.16 No matter how well written the manual is, the Act, the Regulations and the Rules can present a considerable compliance problem. The manual should give clear instructions on how to obtain assistance and advice from within the firm. A call for help at a crucial point by a fee earner could prevent non-compliance with the Rules or a breach of the firm's internal policies.

APPENDICES

A – Statutory material

Financial Services and Markets Act 2000, sections 19–26

PART II REGULATED AND PROHIBITED ACTIVITIES

The general prohibition

19. (1) No person may carry on a regulated activity in the United Kingdom, or purport to do so, unless he is –

(a) an authorised person; or
(b) an exempt person.

(2) The prohibition is referred to in this Act as the general prohibition.

Requirement for permission

20. (1) If an authorised person carries on a regulated activity in the United Kingdom, or purports to do so, otherwise than in accordance with permission –

(a) given to him by the Authority under Part IV, or
(b) resulting from any other provision of this Act,

he is to be taken to have contravened a requirement imposed on him by the Authority under this Act.

(2) The contravention does not –

(a) make a person guilty of an offence;
(b) make any transaction void or unenforceable; or
(c) (subject to subsection (3)) give rise to any right of action for breach of statutory duty.

(3) In prescribed cases the contravention is actionable at the suit of a person who suffers loss as a result of the contravention, subject to the defences and other incidents applying to actions for breach of statutory duty.

Financial promotion

21. (1) A person ('A') must not, in the course of business, communicate an invitation or inducement to engage in investment activity.

(2) But subsection (1) does not apply if –

(a) A is an authorised person; or
(b) the content of the communication is approved for the purposes of this section by an authorised person.

(3) In the case of a communication originating outside the United Kingdom, subsection (1) applies only if the communication is capable of having an effect in the United Kingdom.

(4) The Treasury may by order specify circumstances in which a person is to be regarded for the purposes of subsection (1) as –

(a) acting in the course of business;
(b) not acting in the course of business.

(5) The Treasury may by order specify circumstances (which may include compliance with financial promotion rules) in which subsection (1) does not apply.

(6) An order under subsection (5) may, in particular, provide that subsection (1) does not apply in relation to communications –

(a) of a specified description;
(b) originating in a specified country or territory outside the United Kingdom;
(c) originating in a country or territory which falls within a specified description of country or territory outside the United Kingdom; or
(d) originating outside the United Kingdom.

(7) The Treasury may by order repeal subsection (3).

(8) 'Engaging in investment activity' means –

(a) entering or offering to enter into an agreement the making or performance of which by either party constitutes a controlled activity; or
(b) exercising any rights conferred by a controlled investment to acquire, dispose of, underwrite or convert a controlled investment.

(9) An activity is a controlled activity if –

(a) it is an activity of a specified kind or one which falls within a specified class of activity; and
(b) it relates to an investment of a specified kind, or to one which falls within a specified class of investment.

(10) An investment is a controlled investment if it is an investment of a specified kind or one which falls within a specified class of investment.

(11) Schedule 2 (except paragraph 26) applies for the purposes of subsections (9) and (10) with references to section 22 being read as references to each of those subsections.

(12) Nothing in Schedule 2, as applied by subsection (11), limits the powers conferred by subsection (9) or (10).

(13) 'Communicate' includes causing a communication to be made.

(14) 'Investment' includes any asset, right or interest.

(15) 'Specified' means specified in an order made by the Treasury.

Regulated activities

22. (1) An activity is a regulated activity for the purposes of this Act if it is an activity of a specified kind which is carried on by way of business and –

(a) relates to an investment of a specified kind; or

(b) in the case of an activity of a kind which is also specified for the purposes of this paragraph, is carried on in relation to property of any kind.

(2) Schedule 2 makes provision supplementing this section.

(3) Nothing in Schedule 2 limits the powers conferred by subsection (1).

(4) 'Investment' includes any asset, right or interest.

(5) 'Specified' means specified in an order made by the Treasury.

Offences

23. (1) A person who contravenes the general prohibition is guilty of an offence and liable –

(a) on summary conviction, to imprisonment for a term not exceeding six months or a fine not exceeding the statutory maximum, or both;

(b) on conviction on indictment, to imprisonment for a term not exceeding two years or a fine, or both.

(2) In this Act 'an authorisation offence' means an offence under this section.

(3) In proceedings for an authorisation offence it is a defence for the accused to show that he took all reasonable precautions and exercised all due diligence to avoid committing the offence.

24. (1) A person who is neither an authorised person nor, in relation to the regulated activity in question, an exempt person is guilty of an offence if he –

(a) describes himself (in whatever terms) as an authorised person;

(b) describes himself (in whatever terms) as an exempt person in relation to the regulated activity; or

(c) behaves, or otherwise holds himself out, in a manner which indicates (or which is reasonably likely to be understood as indicating) that he is –

(i) an authorised person; or

(ii) an exempt person in relation to the regulated activity.

(2) In proceedings for an offence under this section it is a defence for the accused to show that he took all reasonable precautions and exercised all due diligence to avoid committing the offence.

(3) A person guilty of an offence under this section is liable on summary conviction to imprisonment for a term not exceeding six months or a fine not exceeding level 5 on the standard scale, or both.

(4) But where the conduct constituting the offence involved or included the public display of any material, the maximum fine for the offence is level 5 on the standard scale multiplied by the number of days for which the display continued.

25. (1) A person who contravenes section 21(1) is guilty of an offence and liable –

(a) on summary conviction, to imprisonment for a term not exceeding six months or a fine not exceeding the statutory maximum, or both;

(b) on conviction on indictment, to imprisonment for a term not exceeding two years or a fine, or both.

(2) In proceedings for an offence under this section it is a defence for the accused to show –

(a) that he believed on reasonable grounds that the content of the communication was prepared, or approved for the purposes of section 21, by an authorised person; or

(b) that he took all reasonable precautions and exercised all due diligence to avoid committing the offence.

Enforceability of agreements

26. (1) An agreement made by a person in the course of carrying on a regulated activity in contravention of the general prohibition is unenforceable against the other party.

(2) The other party is entitled to recover –

(a) any money or other property paid or transferred by him under the agreement; and

(b) compensation for any loss sustained by him as a result of having parted with it.

(3) 'Agreement' means an agreement –

(a) made after this section comes into force; and

(b) the making or performance of which constitutes, or is part of, the regulated activity in question.

(4) This section does not apply if the regulated activity is accepting deposits.

Financial Services and Markets Act 2000, Part XX

PART XX PROVISION OF FINANCIAL SERVICES BY MEMBERS OF THE PROFESSIONS

325. (1) The Authority must keep itself informed about –

(a) the way in which designated professional bodies supervise and regulate the carrying on of exempt regulated activities by members of the professions in relation to which they are established;

(b) the way in which such members are carrying on exempt regulated activities.

(2) In this Part –

'exempt regulated activities' means regulated activities which may, as a result of this Part, be carried on by members of a profession which is supervised and regulated by a designated professional body without breaching the general prohibition; and

'members', in relation to a profession, means persons who are entitled to practise the profession in question and, in practising it, are subject to the rules of the body designated in relation to that profession, whether or not they are members of that body.

(3) The Authority must keep under review the desirability of exercising any of its powers under this Part.

(4) Each designated professional body must co-operate with the Authority, by the sharing of information and in other ways, in order to enable the Authority to perform its functions under this Part.

326. (1) The Treasury may by order designate bodies for the purposes of this Part.

(2) A body designated under subsection (1) is referred to in this Part as a designated professional body.

(3) The Treasury may designate a body under subsection (1) only if they are satisfied that –

(a) the basic condition, and

(b) one or more of the additional conditions,

are met in relation to it.

(4) The basic condition is that the body has rules applicable to the carrying on by members of the profession in relation to which it is established of regulated activities which, if the body were to be designated, would be exempt regulated activities.

(5) The additional conditions are that –

    (a) the body has power under any enactment to regulate the practice of the profession;

    (b) being a member of the profession is a requirement under any enactment for the exercise of particular functions or the holding of a particular office;

    (c) the body has been recognised for the purpose of any enactment other than this Act and the recognition has not been withdrawn;

    (d) the body is established in an EEA State other than the United Kingdom and in that State–

        (i) the body has power corresponding to that mentioned in paragraph (a);

        (ii) there is a requirement in relation to the body corresponding to that mentioned in paragraph (b); or

        (iii) the body is recognised in a manner corresponding to that mentioned in paragraph (c).

(6) 'Enactment' includes an Act of the Scottish Parliament, Northern Ireland legislation and subordinate legislation (whether made under an Act, an Act of the Scottish Parliament or Northern Ireland legislation).

(7) 'Recognised' means recognised by –

    (a) a Minister of the Crown;

    (b) the Scottish Ministers;

    (c) a Northern Ireland Minister;

    (d) a Northern Ireland department or its head.

327. (1) The general prohibition does not apply to the carrying on of a regulated activity by a person ('P') if –

    (a) the conditions set out in subsections (2) to (7) are satisfied; and

    (b) there is not in force –

        (i) a direction under section 328, or

        (ii) an order under section 329,

which prevents this subsection from applying to the carrying on of that activity by him.

(2) P must be –

    (a) a member of a profession; or

    (b) controlled or managed by one or more such members.

(3) P must not receive from a person other than his client any pecuniary reward or other advantage, for which he does not account to his client, arising out of his carrying on of any of the activities.

(4) The manner of the provision by P of any service in the course of carrying on the activities must be incidental to the provision by him of professional services.

(5) P must not carry on, or hold himself out as carrying on, a regulated activity other than –

    (a) one which rules made as a result of section 332(3) allow him to carry on; or

    (b) one in relation to which he is an exempt person.

(6) The activities must not be of a description, or relate to an investment of a description, specified in an order made by the Treasury for the purposes of this subsection.

(7) The activities must be the only regulated activities carried on by P (other than regulated activities in relation to which he is an exempt person).

(8) 'Professional services' means services –

(a) which do not constitute carrying on a regulated activity, and
(b) the provision of which is supervised and regulated by a designated professional body.

328. (1) The Authority may direct that section 327(1) is not to apply to the extent specified in the direction.

(2) A direction under subsection (1) –

(a) must be in writing;
(b) may be given in relation to different classes of person or different descriptions of regulated activity.

(3) A direction under subsection (1) must be published in the way appearing to the Authority to be best calculated to bring it to the attention of the public.

(4) The Authority may charge a reasonable fee for providing a person with a copy of the direction.

(5) The Authority must, without delay, give the Treasury a copy of any direction which it gives under this section.

(6) The Authority may exercise the power conferred by subsection (1) only if it is satisfied that it is desirable in order to protect the interests of clients.

(7) In considering whether it is so satisfied, the Authority must have regard amongst other things to the effectiveness of any arrangements made by any designated professional body–

(a) for securing compliance with rules made under section 332(1);
(b) for dealing with complaints against its members in relation to the carrying on by them of exempt regulated activities;
(c) in order to offer redress to clients who suffer, or claim to have suffered, loss as a result of misconduct by its members in their carrying on of exempt regulated activities;
(d) for co-operating with the Authority under section 325(4).

(8) In this Part 'clients' means –

(a) persons who use, have used or are or may be contemplating using, any of the services provided by a member of a profession in the course of carrying on exempt regulated activities;
(b) persons who have rights or interests which are derived from, or otherwise attributable to, the use of any such services by other persons; or
(c) persons who have rights or interests which may be adversely affected by the use of any such services by persons acting on their behalf or in a fiduciary capacity in relation to them.

(9) If a member of a profession is carrying on an exempt regulated activity in his capacity as a trustee, the persons who are, have been or may be beneficiaries of the trust are to be treated as persons who use, have used or are or may be contemplating using services provided by that person in his carrying on of that activity.

329. (1) Subsection (2) applies if it appears to the Authority that a person to whom, as a result of section 327(1), the general prohibition does not apply is not a fit and proper person to carry on regulated activities in accordance with that section.

(2) The Authority may make an order disapplying section 327(1) in relation to that person to the extent specified in the order.

(3) The Authority may, on the application of the person named in an order under subsection (1), vary or revoke it.

(4) 'Specified' means specified in the order.

(5) If a partnership is named in an order under this section, the order is not affected by any change in its membership.

(6) If a partnership named in an order under this section is dissolved, the order continues to have effect in relation to any partnership which succeeds to the business of the dissolved partnership.

(7) For the purposes of subsection (6), a partnership is to be regarded as succeeding to the business of another partnership only if –

(a) the members of the resulting partnership are substantially the same as those of the former partnership; and
(b) succession is to the whole or substantially the whole of the business of the former partnership.

330. (1) Before giving a direction under section 328(1), the Authority must publish a draft of the proposed direction.

(2) The draft must be accompanied by –

(a) a cost benefit analysis; and
(b) notice that representations about the proposed direction may be made to the Authority within a specified time.

(3) Before giving the proposed direction, the Authority must have regard to any representations made to it in accordance with subsection (2)(b).

(4) If the Authority gives the proposed direction it must publish an account, in general terms, of –

(a) the representations made to it in accordance with subsection (2)(b); and
(b) its response to them.

(5) If the direction differs from the draft published under subsection (1) in a way which is, in the opinion of the Authority, significant –

(a) the Authority must (in addition to complying with subsection (4)) publish details of the difference; and
(b) those details must be accompanied by a cost benefit analysis.

(6) Subsections (1) to (5) do not apply if the Authority considers that the delay involved in complying with them would prejudice the interests of consumers.

(7) Neither subsection (2)(a) nor subsection (5)(b) applies if the Authority considers –

(a) that, making the appropriate comparison, there will be no increase in costs; or
(b) that, making that comparison, there will be an increase in costs but the increase will be of minimal significance.

(8) The Authority may charge a reasonable fee for providing a person with a copy of a draft published under subsection (1).

(9) When the Authority is required to publish a document under this section it must do so in the way appearing to it to be best calculated to bring it to the attention of the public.

(10) 'Cost benefit analysis' means an estimate of the costs together with an analysis of the benefits that will arise –

    (a) if the proposed direction is given; or

    (b) if subsection (5)(b) applies, from the direction that has been given.

(11) 'The appropriate comparison' means –

    (a) in relation to subsection (2)(a), a comparison between the overall position if the direction is given and the overall position if it is not given;

    (b) in relation to subsection (5)(b), a comparison between the overall position after the giving of the direction and the overall position before it was given.

331. (1) If the Authority proposes to make an order under section 329, it must give the person concerned a warning notice.

(2) The warning notice must set out the terms of the proposed order.

(3) If the Authority decides to make an order under section 329, it must give the person concerned a decision notice.

(4) The decision notice must –

    (a) name the person to whom the order applies;

    (b) set out the terms of the order; and

    (c) be given to the person named in the order.

(5) Subsections (6) to (8) apply to an application for the variation or revocation of an order under section 329.

(6) If the Authority decides to grant the application, it must give the applicant written notice of its decision.

(7) If the Authority proposes to refuse the application, it must give the applicant a warning notice.

(8) If the Authority decides to refuse the application, it must give the applicant a decision notice.

(9) A person –

    (a) against whom the Authority have decided to make an order under section 329, or

    (b) whose application for the variation or revocation of such an order the Authority had decided to refuse,

may refer the matter to the Tribunal.

(10) The Authority may not make an order under section 329 unless –

    (a) the period within which the decision to make to the order may be referred to the Tribunal has expired and no such reference has been made; or

    (b) if such a reference has been made, the reference has been determined.

332. (1) The Authority may make rules applicable to persons to whom, as a result of section 327(1), the general prohibition does not apply.

(2) The power conferred by subsection (1) is to be exercised for the purpose of ensuring that clients are aware that such persons are not authorised persons.

(3) A designated professional body must make rules –

(a) applicable to members of the profession in relation to which it is established who are not authorised persons; and

(b) governing the carrying on by those members of regulated activities (other than regulated activities in relation to which they are exempt persons).

(4) Rules made in compliance with subsection (3) must be designed to secure that, in providing a particular professional service to a particular client, the member carries on only regulated activities which arise out of, or are complementary to, the provision by him of that service to that client.

(5) Rules made by a designated professional body under subsection (3) require the approval of the Authority.

333. (1) A person who –

(a) describes himself (in whatever terms) as a person to whom the general prohibition does not apply, in relation to a particular regulated activity, as a result of this Part, or

(b) behaves, or otherwise holds himself out, in a manner which indicates (or which is reasonably likely to be understood as indicating) that he is such a person,

is guilty of an offence if he is not such a person.

(2) In proceedings for an offence under this section it is a defence for the accused to show that he took all reasonable precautions and exercised all due diligence to avoid committing the offence.

(3) A person guilty of an offence under this section is liable on summary conviction to imprisonment for a term not exceeding six months or a fine not exceeding level 5 on the standard scale, or both.

(4) But where the conduct constituting the offence involved or included the public display of any material, the maximum fine for the offence is level 5 on the standard scale multiplied by the number of days for which the display continued.

Financial Services and Markets Act 2000 (Regulated Activities) Order 2001, SI 2001/544

(as amended by the Financial Services and Markets Act 2000 (Regulated Activities) (Amendment) Order 2001, SI 2001/3544)

PART I GENERAL

Citation

1. This Order may be cited as the Financial Services and Markets Act 2000 (Regulated Activities) Order 2001.

Commencement

2. (1) Except as provided by paragraph (2), this Order comes into force on the day on which section 19 of the Act comes into force.

(2) This Order comes into force –

(a) for the purposes of articles 59, 60 and 87 (funeral plan contracts) on 1 January 2002; and
(b) for the purposes of articles 61 to 63, 88, 90 and 91 (regulated mortgage contracts) nine months after section 19 of the Act comes into force.

Interpretation

3. (1) In this Order –

'the Act' means the Financial Services and Markets Act 2000;
'annuities on human life' does not include superannuation allowances and annuities payable out of any fund applicable solely to the relief and maintenance of persons engaged, or who have been engaged, in any particular profession, trade or employment, or of the dependants of such persons;
'buying' includes acquiring for valuable consideration;
'close relative' in relation to a person means –

(a) his spouse;
(b) his children and step children, his parents and step-parents, his brothers and sisters and his step-brothers and step-sisters; and
(c) the spouse of any person within sub-paragraph (b);

'contract of general insurance' means any contract falling within Part I of Schedule 1;
'contract of insurance' means any contract of insurance which is a contract of long-term insurance or a contract of general insurance, and includes –

(a) fidelity bonds, performance bonds, administration bonds, bail bonds, customs bonds or similar contracts of guarantee, where these are –

    (i) effected or carried out by a person not carrying on a banking business;
    (ii) not effected merely incidentally to some other business carried on by the person effecting them; and
    (iii) effected in return for the payment of one or more premiums;

(b) tontines;
(c) capital redemption contracts or pension fund management contracts, where these are effected or carried out by a person who –

    (i) does not carry on a banking business; and
    (ii) otherwise carries on a regulated activity of the kind specified by article 10(1) or (2);

(d) contracts to pay annuities on human life;
(e) contracts of a kind referred to in article 1(2)(e) of the first life insurance directive (collective insurance etc.); and
(f) contracts of a kind referred to in article 1(3) of the first life insurance directive (social insurance);

but does not include a funeral plan contract (or a contract which would be a funeral plan contract but for the exclusion in article 60);

'contract of long-term insurance' means any contract falling within Part II of Schedule 1;
'contractually based investment' means –

(a) rights under a qualifying contract of insurance;
(b) any investment of the kind specified by any of articles 83, 84, 85 and 87; or
(c) any investment of the kind specified by article 89 so far as relevant to an investment falling within (a) or (b);

'deposit' has the meaning given by article 5;
'funeral plan contract' has the meaning given by article 59;
'instrument' includes any record whether or not in the form of a document;
'joint enterprise' means an enterprise into which two or more persons ('the participators') enter for commercial purposes related to a business or businesses (other than the business of engaging in a regulated activity) carried on by them; and, where a participator is a member of a group, each other member of the group is also to be regarded as a participator in the enterprise;
'local authority' means –

(a) in England and Wales, a local authority within the meaning of the Local Government Act 1972, the Greater London Authority, the Common Council of the City of London or the Council of the Isles of Scilly;
(b) in Scotland, a local authority within the meaning of the Local Government (Scotland) Act 1973;
(c) in Northern Ireland, a district council within the meaning of the Local Government Act (Northern Ireland) 1972;

'managing agent' means a person who is permitted by the Council of Lloyd's in the conduct of his business as an underwriting agent to perform for a member of Lloyd's one or more of the following functions –

(a) underwriting contracts of insurance at Lloyd's;
(b) reinsuring such contracts in whole or in part;
(c) paying claims on such contracts;

'occupational pension scheme' means any scheme or arrangement which is comprised in one or more instruments or agreements and which has, or is capable of having, effect in relation to one or more descriptions or categories of employment so as to provide benefits, in the form of pensions or otherwise, payable on termination of service, or on death or retirement, to or in respect of earners with qualifying service in an employment of any such description or category;

'overseas person' means a person who –

(a) carries on activities of the kind specified by any of articles 14, 21, 25, 37, 40, 45, 51, 52 and 53 or, so far as relevant to any of those articles, article 64 (or activities of a kind which would be so specified but for the exclusion in article 72); but
(b) does not carry on any such activities, or offer to do so, from a permanent place of business maintained by him in the United Kingdom;

'pension fund management contract' means a contract to manage the investments of pension funds (other than funds solely for the benefit of the officers or employees of the person effecting or carrying out the contract and their dependants or, in the case of a company, partly for the benefit of officers and employees and their dependants of its subsidiary or holding company or a subsidiary of its holding company); and for the purposes of this definition, 'subsidiary' and 'holding company' are to be construed in accordance with section 736 of the Companies Act 1985 or article 4 of the Companies (Northern Ireland) Order 1986;

'property' includes currency of the United Kingdom or any other country or territory;

'qualifying contract of insurance' means a contract of long-term insurance which is not –

(a) a reinsurance contract; nor
(b) a contract in respect of which the following conditions are met –

(i) the benefits under the contract are payable only on death or in respect of incapacity due to injury, sickness or infirmity;
(ii) the contract provides that benefits are payable on death (other than death due to an accident) only where the death occurs within ten years of the date on which the life of the person in question was first insured under the contract, or where the death occurs before that person attains a specified age not exceeding seventy years;
(iii) the contract has no surrender value, or the consideration consists of a single premium and the surrender value does not exceed that premium; and
(iv) the contract makes no provision for its conversion or extension in a manner which would result in it ceasing to comply with any of the above conditions;

'regulated mortgage contract' has the meaning given by article 61(3);

'security' means (except where the context otherwise requires) any investment of the kind specified by any of articles 76 to 82 or, so far as relevant to any such investment, article 89;

'selling', in relation to any investment, includes disposing of the investment for valuable consideration, and for these purposes 'disposing' includes –

(a) in the case of an investment consisting of rights under a contract –

(i) surrendering, assigning or converting those rights; or
(ii) assuming the corresponding liabilities under the contract;

(b) in the case of an investment consisting of rights under other arrangements, assuming the corresponding liabilities under the arrangements; and

(c) in the case of any other investment, issuing or creating the investment or granting the rights or interests of which it consists;

'stakeholder pension scheme' has the meaning given by section 1 of the Welfare Reform and Pensions Act 1999;

'syndicate' means one or more persons, to whom a particular syndicate number has been assigned by or under the authority of the Council of Lloyd's, carrying out or effecting contracts of insurance written at Lloyd's;

'voting shares', in relation to a body corporate, means shares carrying voting rights attributable to share capital which are exercisable in all circumstances at any general meeting of that body corporate.

(2) For the purposes of this Order, a transaction is entered into through a person if he enters into it as agent or arranges, in a manner constituting the carrying on of an activity of the kind specified by article 25(1), for it to be entered into by another person as agent or principal.

(3) For the purposes of this Order, a contract of insurance is to be treated as falling within Part II of Schedule 1, notwithstanding the fact that it contains related and subsidiary provisions such that it might also be regarded as falling within Part I of that Schedule, if its principal object is that of a contract falling within Part II and it is effected or carried out by an authorised person who has permission to effect or carry out contracts falling within paragraph 1 of Part II of Schedule 1.

PART II   SPECIFIED ACTIVITIES

CHAPTER I   GENERAL

Specified activities: general

4.   (1) The following provisions of this Part specify kinds of activity for the purposes of section 22 of the Act (and accordingly any activity of one of those kinds, which is carried on by way of business, and relates to an investment of a kind specified by any provision of Part III and applicable to that activity, is a regulated activity for the purposes of the Act).

(2) The kinds of activity specified by articles 51 and 52 are also specified for the purposes of section 22(1)(b) of the Act (and accordingly any activity of one of those kinds, when carried on by way of business, is a regulated activity when carried on in relation to property of any kind).

(3) Subject to paragraph (4), each provision specifying a kind of activity is subject to the exclusions applicable to that provision (and accordingly any reference in this Order to an activity of the kind specified by a particular provision is to be read subject to any such exclusions).

(4) Where an investment firm –

    (a) provides core investment services to third parties on a professional basis, and
    (b) in doing so would be treated as carrying on an activity of a kind specified by a provision of this Part but for an exclusion in any of articles 15, 68, 69 and 70,

that exclusion is to be disregarded (and accordingly the investment firm is to be treated as carrying on an activity of the kind specified by the provision in question).

(5) In this article –

'core investment service' means any service listed in section A of the Annex to the investment services directive, the text of which is set out in Schedule 2; and
'investment firm' means a person whose regular occupation or business is the provision of core investment services to third parties on a professional basis, other than –

    (a) a person to whom the investment services directive does not apply by virtue of Article 2.2 of that directive (the text of which is set out in Schedule 3); or
    (b) a person to whom (if he were incorporated in or formed under the law of an EEA State or, being an individual, had his head office in an EEA State) that directive would not apply by virtue of Article 2.2 of that directive.

CHAPTER II   ACCEPTING DEPOSITS

The activity

Accepting deposits

5.   (1) Accepting deposits is a specified kind of activity if –

    (a) money received by way of deposit is lent to others; or
    (b) any other activity of the person accepting the deposit is financed wholly, or to a material extent, out of the capital of or interest on money received by way of deposit.

(2) In paragraph (1), 'deposit' means a sum of money, other than one excluded by any of articles 6 to 9, paid on terms –

    (a) under which it will be repaid, with or without interest or premium, and either on demand or at a time or in circumstances agreed by or on behalf of the person making the payment and the person receiving it; and
    (b) which are not referable to the provision of property (other than currency) or services or the giving of security.

(3) For the purposes of paragraph (2), money is paid on terms which are referable to the provision of property or services or the giving of security if, and only if –

    (a) it is paid by way of advance or part payment under a contract for the sale, hire or other provision of property or services, and is repayable only in the event that the property or services is or are not in fact sold, hired or otherwise provided;

(b) it is paid by way of security for the performance of a contract or by way of security in respect of loss which may result from the non-performance of a contract; or

(c) without prejudice to sub-paragraph (b), it is paid by way of security for the delivery up or return of any property, whether in a particular state of repair or otherwise.

Exclusions

Sums paid by certain persons

6. (1) A sum is not a deposit for the purposes of article 5 if it is –

(a) paid by any of the following persons –

(i) the Bank of England, the central bank of an EEA State other than the United Kingdom, or the European Central Bank;

(ii) an authorised person who has permission to accept deposits, or to effect or carry out contracts of insurance;

(iii) an EEA firm falling within paragraph 5(b), (c) or (d) of Schedule 3 to the Act (other than one falling within paragraph (ii) above);

(iv) the National Savings Bank;

(v) a municipal bank, that is to say a company which was, immediately before the coming into force of this article, exempt from the prohibition in section 3 of the Banking Act 1987 by virtue of section 4(1) of, and paragraph 4 of Schedule 2 to, that Act;

(vi) Keesler Federal Credit Union;

(vii) a body of persons certified as a school bank by the National Savings Bank or by an authorised person who has permission to accept deposits;

(viii) a local authority;

(ix) any body which by virtue of any enactment has power to issue a precept to a local authority in England and Wales or a requisition to a local authority in Scotland, or to the expenses of which, by virtue of any enactment, a local authority in the United Kingdom is or can be required to contribute (and in this paragraph, 'enactment' includes an enactment comprised in, or in an instrument made under, an Act of the Scottish Parliament);

(x) the European Community, the European Atomic Energy Community or the European Coal and Steel Community;

(xi) the European Investment Bank;

(xii) the International Bank for Reconstruction and Development;

(xiii) the International Finance Corporation;

(xiv) the International Monetary Fund;

(xv) the African Development Bank;

(xvi) the Asian Development Bank;

(xvii) the Caribbean Development Bank;

(xviii) the Inter-American Development Bank;

(xix) the European Bank for Reconstruction and Development;

(xx) the Council of Europe Resettlement Fund;

(b) paid by a person other than one mentioned in sub-paragraph (a) in the course of carrying on a business consisting wholly or to a significant extent of lending money;

(c) paid by one company to another at a time when both are members of the same group or when the same individual is a majority shareholder controller of both of them; or

(d) paid by a person who, at the time when it is paid, is a close relative of the person receiving it or who is, or is a close relative of, a director or manager of that person or who is, or is a close relative of, a controller of that person.

(2) For the purposes of paragraph (1)(c), an individual is a majority shareholder controller of a company if he is a controller of the company by virtue of paragraph (a), (c), (e) or (g) of section 422(2) of the Act, and if in his case the greatest percentage of those referred to in those paragraphs is 50 or more.

(3) In the application of sub-paragraph (d) of paragraph (1) to a sum paid by a partnership, that sub-paragraph is to have effect as if, for the reference to the person paying the sum, there were substituted a reference to each of the partners.

Sums received by solicitors etc.

7. (1) A sum is not a deposit for the purposes of article 5 if it is received by a practising solicitor acting in the course of his profession.

(2) In paragraph (1), 'practising solicitor' means –

(a) a solicitor who is qualified to act as such under section 1 of the Solicitors Act 1974, article 4 of the Solicitors (Northern Ireland) Order 1976 or section 4 of the Solicitors (Scotland) Act 1980;

(b) a recognised body;

(c) a registered foreign lawyer in the course of providing professional services as a member of a multi-national partnership;

(d) a registered European lawyer; or

(e) a partner of a registered European lawyer who is providing professional services in accordance with –

(i) rules made under section 31 of the Solicitors Act 1974;

(ii) regulations made under article 26 of the Solicitors (Northern Ireland) Order 1976; or

(iii) rules made under section 34 of the Solicitors (Scotland) Act 1980.

(3) In this article –

(a) 'a recognised body' means a body corporate recognised by –

(i) the Council of the Law Society under section 9 of the Administration of Justice Act 1985;

(ii) the Incorporated Law Society of Northern Ireland under article 26A of the Solicitors (Northern Ireland) Order 1976; or

(iii) the Council of the Law Society of Scotland under section 34 of the Solicitors (Scotland) Act 1980;

(b) 'registered foreign lawyer' has the meaning given by section 89 of the Courts and Legal Services Act 1990 or, in Scotland, section 65 of the Solicitors (Scotland) Act 1980;

(c) 'multi-national partnership' has the meaning given by section 89 of the Courts and Legal Services Act 1990 but, in Scotland, is a reference to a 'multi-national practice' within the meaning of section 60A of the Solicitors (Scotland) Act 1980, 'registered European lawyer' has the meaning given by regulation 2(1) of the European Communities (Lawyer's Practice) Regulations 2000 or regulation 2(1) of the European Communities (Lawyer's Practice) (Scotland) Regulation 2000.

Sums received by persons authorised to deal etc.

8. A sum is not a deposit for the purposes of article 5 if it is received by a person who is –

(a) an authorised person with permission to carry on an activity of the kind specified by any of articles 14, 21, 25, 37, 51 and 52, or

(b) an exempt person in relation to any such activity,

in the course of, or for the purpose of, carrying on any such activity (or any activity which would be such an activity but for any exclusion made by this Part) with or on behalf of the person by or on behalf of whom the sum is paid.

Sums received in consideration for the issue of debt securities

9. (1) Subject to paragraph (2), a sum is not a deposit for the purposes of article 5 if it is received by a person as consideration for the issue by him of any investment of the kind specified by article 77 or 78.

(2) The exclusion in paragraph (1) does not apply to the receipt by a person of a sum as consideration for the issue by him of commercial paper unless –

(a) the commercial paper is issued to persons –

    (i) whose ordinary activities involve them in acquiring, holding, managing or disposing of investments (as principal or agent) for the purposes of their businesses; or

    (ii) who it is reasonable to expect will acquire, hold, manage or dispose of investments (as principal or agent) for the purposes of their businesses; and

(b) the redemption value of the commercial paper is not less than £100,000 (or an amount of equivalent value denominated wholly or partly in a currency other than sterling), and no part of the commercial paper may be transferred unless the redemption value of that part is not less than £100,000 (or such an equivalent amount).

(3) In paragraph (2), 'commercial paper' means an investment of the kind specified by article 77 or 78 which must be redeemed before the first anniversary of the date of issue.

CHAPTER III   INSURANCE

The activities

Effecting and carrying out contracts of insurance

10. (1) Effecting a contract of insurance as principal is a specified kind of activity.

(2) Carrying out a contract of insurance as principal is a specified kind of activity.

Exclusions

Community co-insurers

11. (1) There is excluded from article 10(1) or (2) the effecting or carrying out of a contract of insurance by an EEA firm falling within paragraph 5(d) of Schedule 3 to the Act –

(a) other than through a branch in the United Kingdom; and
(b) pursuant to a Community co-insurance operation in which the firm is participating otherwise than as the leading insurer.

(2) In paragraph (1), 'Community co-insurance operation' and 'leading insurer' have the same meaning as in the Council Directive of 30 May 1978 on the co-ordination of laws, regulations and administrative provisions relating to Community co-insurance (No. 78/473/EEC).

Breakdown insurance

12. (1) There is excluded from article 10(1) or (2) the effecting or carrying out, by a person who does not otherwise carry on an activity of the kind specified by that article, of a contract of insurance which –

(a) is a contract under which the benefits provided by that person ('the provider') are exclusively or primarily benefits in kind in the event of accident to or breakdown of a vehicle; and
(b) contains the terms mentioned in paragraph (2).

(2) Those terms are that –

(a) the assistance takes either or both of the forms mentioned in paragraph (3)(a) and (b);
(b) the assistance is not available outside the United Kingdom and the Republic of Ireland except where it is provided without the payment of additional premium by a person in the country concerned with whom the provider has entered into a reciprocal agreement; and
(c) assistance provided in the case of an accident or breakdown occurring in the United Kingdom or the Republic of Ireland is, in most circumstances, provided by the provider's servants.

(3) The forms of assistance are –

(a) repairs to the relevant vehicle at the place where the accident or breakdown has occurred; this assistance may also include the delivery of parts, fuel, oil, water or keys to the relevant vehicle;
(b) removal of the relevant vehicle to the nearest or most appropriate place at which repairs may be carried out, or to –

(i) the home, point of departure or original destination within the United Kingdom of the driver and passengers, provided the accident or breakdown occurred within the United Kingdom;
(ii) the home, point of departure or original destination within the Republic of Ireland of the driver and passengers, provided the accident or break-down occurred within the Republic of Ireland or within Northern Ireland;

(iii) the home, point of departure or original destination within Northern Ireland of the driver and passengers, provided the accident or breakdown occurred within the Republic of Ireland;

and this form of assistance may include the conveyance of the driver or passengers of the relevant vehicle, with the vehicle, or (where the vehicle is to be conveyed only to the nearest or most appropriate place at which repairs may be carried out) separately, to the nearest location from which they may continue their journey by other means.

(4) A contract does not fail to meet the condition in paragraph (1)(a) solely because the provider may reimburse the person entitled to the assistance for all or part of any sums paid by him in respect of assistance either because he failed to identify himself as a person entitled to the assistance or because he was unable to get in touch with the provider in order to claim the assistance.

(5) In this article –

'the assistance' means the benefits to be provided under a contract of the kind mentioned in paragraph (1);
'breakdown' means an event –

(a) which causes the driver of the relevant vehicle to be unable to start a journey in the vehicle or involuntarily to bring the vehicle to a halt on a journey because of some malfunction of the vehicle or failure of it to function, and
(b) after which the journey cannot reasonably be commenced or continued in the relevant vehicle;

'the relevant vehicle' means the vehicle (including a trailer or caravan) in respect of which the assistance is required.

Supplemental

Application of sections 327 and 332 of the Act to insurance market activities

13. (1) In sections 327(5) and (7) and 332(3)(b) of the Act (exemption from the general prohibition for members of the professions, and rules in relation to such persons), the references to 'a regulated activity' and 'regulated activities' do not include –

(a) any activity of the kind specified by article 10(1) or (2), where –

    (i) P is a member of the Society; and
    (ii) by virtue of section 316 of the Act (application of the Act to Lloyd's underwriting), the general prohibition does not apply to the carrying on by P of that activity; or

(b) any activity of the kind specified by article 10(2), where –

    (i) P is a former underwriting member; and
    (ii) the contract of insurance in question is one underwritten by P at Lloyd's.

(2) In paragraph (1) –

'member of the Society' has the same meaning as in Lloyd's Act 1982; and
'former underwriting member' has the meaning given by section 324(1) of the Act.

CHAPTER IV   DEALING IN INVESTMENTS AS PRINCIPAL

The activity

Dealing in investments as principal

14.   Buying, selling, subscribing for or underwriting securities or contractually based investments (other than investments of the kind specified by article 87, or article 89 so far as relevant to that article) as principal is a specified kind of activity.

Exclusions

Absence of holding out etc.

15.   (1) Subject to paragraph (3), a person ('A') does not carry on an activity of the kind specified by article 14 by entering into a transaction which relates to a security or is the assignment (or, in Scotland, the assignation) of a qualifying contract of insurance (or an investment of the kind specified by article 89, so far as relevant to such a contract), unless –

- (a) A holds himself out as willing, as principal, to buy, sell or subscribe for investments of the kind to which the transaction relates at prices determined by him generally and continuously rather than in respect of each particular transaction;
- (b) A holds himself out as engaging in the business of buying investments of the kind to which the transaction relates, with a view to selling them;
- (c) A holds himself out as engaging in the business of underwriting investments of the kind to which the transaction relates; or
- (d) A regularly solicits members of the public with the purpose of inducing them, as principals or agents, to enter into transactions constituting activities of the kind specified by article 14, and the transaction is entered into as a result of his having solicited members of the public in that manner.

(2) In paragraph (1)(d), 'members of the public' means any persons other than –

- (a) authorised persons or persons who are exempt persons in relation to activities of the kind specified by article 14;
- (b) members of the same group as A;
- (c) persons who are or who propose to become participators with A in a joint enterprise;
- (d) any person who is solicited by A with a view to the acquisition by A of 20 per cent or more of the voting shares in a body corporate;
- (e) if A (either alone or with members of the same group as himself) holds more than 20 per cent of the voting shares in a body corporate, any person who is solicited by A with a view to –
  - (i) the acquisition by A of further shares in the body corporate; or
  - (ii) the disposal by A of shares in the body corporate to the person solicited or to a member of the same group as the person solicited;
- (f) any person who –
  - (i) is solicited by A with a view to the disposal by A of shares in a body corporate to the person solicited or to a member of the same group as that person; and

(ii) either alone or with members of the same group holds 20 per cent or more of the voting shares in the body corporate;

(g) any person whose head office is outside the United Kingdom, who is solicited by an approach made or directed to him at a place outside the United Kingdom and whose ordinary business involves him in carrying on activities of the kind specified by any of articles 14, 21, 25, 37, 40, 45, 51, 52 and 53 or (so far as relevant to any of those articles) article 64, or would do so apart from any exclusion from any of those articles made by this Order.

(3) This article does not apply where A enters into the transaction as bare trustee or, in Scotland, as nominee for another person and is acting on that other person's instructions (but the exclusion in article 66(1) applies if the conditions set out there are met).

Dealing in contractually based investments

16. A person who is not an authorised person does not carry on an activity of the kind specified by article 14 by entering into a transaction relating to a contractually based investment –

(a) with or through an authorised person, or an exempt person acting in the course of a business comprising a regulated activity in relation to which he is exempt; or

(b) through an office outside the United Kingdom maintained by a party to the transaction, and with or through a person whose head office is situated outside the United Kingdom and whose ordinary business involves him in carrying on activities of the kind specified by any of articles 14, 21, 25, 37, 40, 45, 51, 52 and 53 or, so far as relevant to any of those articles, article 64 (or would do so apart from any exclusion from any of those articles made by this Order).

Acceptance of instruments creating or acknowledging indebtedness

17. (1) A person does not carry on an activity of the kind specified by article 14 by accepting an instrument creating or acknowledging indebtedness in respect of any loan, credit, guarantee or other similar financial accommodation or assurance which he has made, granted or provided.

(2) The reference in paragraph (1) to a person accepting an instrument includes a reference to a person becoming a party to an instrument otherwise than as a debtor or a surety.

Issue by a company of its own shares etc.

18. (1) There is excluded from article 14 the issue by a company of its own shares or share warrants, and the issue by any person of his own debentures or debenture warrants.

(2) In this article –

(a) 'company' means any body corporate other than an open-ended investment company;

(b) 'shares' and 'debentures' include any investment of the kind specified by article 76 or 77;

(c) 'share warrants' and 'debenture warrants' mean any investment of the kind specified by article 79 which relates to shares in the company concerned or, as the case may be, debentures issued by the person concerned.

Risk management

19. (1) A person ('B') does not carry on an activity of the kind specified by article 14 by entering as principal into a transaction with another person ('C') if –

(a) the transaction relates to investments of the kind specified by any of articles 83 to 85 (or article 89 so far as relevant to any of those articles);

(b) neither B nor C is an individual;

(c) the sole or main purpose for which B enters into the transaction (either by itself or in combination with other such transactions) is that of limiting the extent to which a relevant business will be affected by any identifiable risk arising otherwise than as a result of the carrying on of a regulated activity; and

(d) the relevant business consists mainly of activities other than –

(i) regulated activities; or

(ii) activities which would be regulated activities but for any exclusion made by this Part.

(2) In paragraph (1), 'relevant business' means a business carried on by –

(a) B;

(b) a member of the same group as B; or

(c) where B and another person are, or propose to become, participators in a joint enterprise, that other person.

Other exclusions

20. Article 14 is also subject to the exclusions in articles 66 (trustees etc.), 68 (sale of goods and supply of services), 69 (groups and joint enterprises), 70 (sale of body corporate), 71 (employee share schemes) and 72 (overseas persons).

CHAPTER V DEALING IN INVESTMENTS AS AGENT

The activity

Dealing in investments as agent

21. Buying, selling, subscribing for or underwriting securities or contractually based investments (other than investments of the kind specified by article 87, or article 89 so far as relevant to that article) as agent is a specified kind of activity.

Exclusions

Deals with or through authorised persons

22. (1) A person who is not an authorised person does not carry on an activity of the kind specified by article 21 by entering into a transaction as agent for another person ('the client') with or through an authorised person if –

(a) the transaction is entered into on advice given to the client by an authorised person; or

(b) it is clear, in all the circumstances, that the client, in his capacity as an investor, is not seeking and has not sought advice from the agent as to the merits of the client's entering into the transaction (or, if the client has sought such advice, the agent has declined to give it but has recommended that the client seek such advice from an authorised person).

(2) But the exclusion in paragraph (1) does not apply if the agent receives from any person other than the client any pecuniary reward or other advantage, for which he does not account to the client, arising out of his entering into the transaction.

Risk management

23. (1) A person ('B') does not carry on an activity of the kind specified by article 21 by entering as agent for a relevant person into a transaction with another person ('C') if –

(a) the transaction relates to investments of the kind specified by any of articles 83 to 85 (or article 89 so far as relevant to any of those articles);

(b) neither B nor C is an individual;

(c) the sole or main purpose for which B enters into the transaction (either by itself or in combination with other such transactions) is that of limiting the extent to which a relevant business will be affected by any identifiable risk arising otherwise than as a result of the carrying on of a regulated activity; and

(d) the relevant business consists mainly of activities other than –

    (i) regulated activities; or

    (ii) activities which would be regulated activities but for any exclusion made by this Part.

(2) In paragraph (1), 'relevant person' means –

(a) a member of the same group as B; or

(b) where B and another person are, or propose to become, participators in a joint enterprise, that other person;

and 'relevant business' means a business carried on by a relevant person.

Other exclusions

24. Article 21 is also subject to the exclusions in articles 67 (profession or non-investment business), 68 (sale of goods and supply of services), 69 (groups and joint enterprises), 70 (sale of body corporate), 71 (employee share schemes) and 72 (overseas persons).

CHAPTER VI   ARRANGING DEALS IN INVESTMENTS

The activities

Arranging deals in investments

25. (1) Making arrangements for another person (whether as principal or agent) to buy, sell, subscribe for or underwrite a particular investment which is –

(a) a security,

(b) a contractually based investment, or

(c) an investment of the kind specified by article 86, or article 89 so far as relevant to that article,

is a specified kind of activity.

(2) Making arrangements with a view to a person who participates in the arrangements buying, selling, subscribing for or underwriting investments falling within paragraph (1)(a), (b) or (c) (whether as principal or agent) is also a specified kind of activity.

Exclusions

Arrangements not causing a deal

26. There are excluded from article 25(1) arrangements which do not or would not bring about the transaction to which the arrangements relate.

Enabling parties to communicate

27. A person does not carry on an activity of the kind specified by article 25(2) merely by providing means by which one party to a transaction (or potential transaction) is able to communicate with other such parties.

Arranging transactions to which the arranger is a party

28. (1) There are excluded from article 25(1) any arrangements for a transaction into which the person making the arrangements enters or is to enter as principal or as agent for some other person.

(2) There are excluded from article 25(2) any arrangements which a person makes with a view to transactions into which he enters or is to enter as principal or as agent for some other person.

Arranging deals with or through authorised persons

29. (1) There are excluded from article 25(1) and (2) arrangements made by a person ('A') who is not an authorised person for or with a view to a transaction which is or is to be entered into by a person ('the client') with or though an authorised person if –

(a) the transaction is or is to be entered into on advice to the client by an authorised person; or

(b) it is clear, in all the circumstances, that the client, in his capacity as an investor, is not seeking and has not sought advice from A as to the merits of the client's entering into the transaction (or, if the client has sought such advice, A has declined to give it but has recommended that the client seek such advice from an authorised person).

(2) But the exclusion in paragraph (1) does not apply if A receives from any person other than the client any pecuniary reward or other advantage, for which he does not account to the client, arising out of his making the arrangements.

Arranging transactions in connection with lending on the security of insurance policies

30. (1) There are excluded from article 25(1) and (2) arrangements made by a money-lender under which either –

(a) a relevant authorised person or a person acting on his behalf will introduce to the money-lender persons with whom the relevant authorised person has entered, or proposes to enter, into a relevant transaction, or he will advise such persons to approach the money-lender, with a view to the money-lender lending money on the security of any contract effected pursuant to a relevant transaction; or

(b) a relevant authorised person gives an assurance to the money-lender as to the amount which, on the security of any contract effected pursuant to a relevant transaction, will or may be received by the money-lender should the money-lender lend money to a person introduced to him pursuant to the arrangements.

(2) In paragraph (1) –

'money-lender' means a person who is –

(a) a money-lending company within the meaning of section 338 of the Companies Act 1985;

(b) a body corporate incorporated under the law of, or of any part of, the United Kingdom relating to building societies; or

(c) a person whose ordinary business includes the making of loans or the giving of guarantees in connection with loans;

'relevant authorised person' means an authorised person who has permission to effect qualifying contracts of insurance or to sell investments of the kind specified by article 89, so far as relevant to such contracts;

'relevant transaction' means the effecting of a qualifying contract of insurance or the sale of an investment of the kind specified by article 89, so far as relevant to such contracts.

Arranging the acceptance of debentures in connection with loans

31. (1) There are excluded from article 25(1) and (2) arrangements under which a person accepts or is to accept, whether as principal or agent, an instrument creating or acknowledging indebtedness in respect of any loan, credit, guarantee or other similar financial accommodation or assurance which is, or is to be, made, granted or provided by that person or his principal.

(2) The reference in paragraph (1) to a person accepting an instrument includes a reference to a person becoming a party to an instrument otherwise than as a debtor or a surety.

Provision of finance

32. There are excluded from article 25(2) arrangements having as their sole purpose the provision of finance to enable a person to buy, sell, subscribe for or underwrite investments.

Introducing

33. There are excluded from article 25(2) arrangements where –

(a) they are arrangements under which persons ('clients') will be introduced to another person;

(b) the person to whom introductions are to be made is –

(i) an authorised person;

(ii) an exempt person acting in the course of a business comprising a regulated activity in relation to which he is exempt; or

(iii) a person who is not unlawfully carrying on regulated activities in the United Kingdom and whose ordinary business involves him in engaging in an activity of the kind specified by any of articles 14, 21, 25, 37, 40, 45, 51, 52 and 53 (or, so far as relevant to any of those articles, article 64), or would do so apart from any exclusion from any of those articles made by this Order; and

(c) the introduction is made with a view to the provision of independent advice or the independent exercise of discretion in relation to investments generally or in relation to any class of investments to which the arrangements relate.

Arrangements for the issue of shares etc.

34. (1) There are excluded from article 25(1) and (2) –

(a) arrangements made by a company for the purposes of issuing its own shares or share warrants; and

(b) arrangements made by any person for the purposes of issuing his own debentures or debenture warrants;

and for the purposes of article 25(1) and (2), a company is not, by reason of issuing its own shares or share warrants, and a person is not, by reason of issuing his own debentures or debenture warrants, to be treated as selling them.

(2) In paragraph (1), 'company', 'shares', 'debentures', 'share warrants' and 'debenture warrants' have the meanings given by article 18(2).

International securities self-regulating organisations

35. (1) There are excluded from article 25(1) and (2) any arrangements made for the purposes of carrying out the functions of a body or association which is approved under this article as an international securities self-regulating organisation, whether the arrangements are made by the organisation itself or by a person acting on its behalf.

(2) The Treasury may approve as an international securities self-regulating organisation any body corporate or unincorporated association with respect to which the conditions mentioned in paragraph (3) appear to them to be met if, having regard to such matters affecting international trade, overseas earnings and the balance of payments or otherwise as they consider relevant, it appears to them that to do so would be desirable and not result in any undue risk to investors.

(3) The conditions are that –

(a) the body or association does not have its head office in the United Kingdom;

(b) the body or association is not eligible for recognition under section 287 or 288 of the Act (applications by investment exchanges and clearing houses) on the ground that (whether or not it has applied, and whether or not it would be eligible on other grounds) it is unable to satisfy the requirements of one or both of paragraphs (a) and (b) of section 292(3) of the Act (requirements for overseas investment exchanges and overseas clearing houses);

(c) the body or association is able and willing to co-operate with the Authority by the sharing of information and in other ways;

(d) adequate arrangements exist for co-operation between the Authority and those responsible for the supervision of the body or association in the country or territory in which its head office is situated;

(e) the body or association has a membership composed of persons falling within any of the following categories, that is to say, authorised persons, exempt persons, and persons whose head offices are outside the United Kingdom and whose ordinary business involves them in engaging in activities which are activities of a kind specified by this Order (or would be apart from any exclusion made by this Part); and

(f) the body or association facilitates and regulates the activity of its members in the conduct of international securities business.

(4) In paragraph (3)(f), 'international securities business' means the business of buying, selling, subscribing for or underwriting investments (or agreeing to do so), either as principal or agent, where –

(a) the investments are securities or contractually based investments and are of a kind which, by their nature, and the manner in which the business is conducted, may be expected normally to be bought or dealt in by persons sufficiently expert to understand the risks involved; and

(b) either the transaction is international or each of the parties may be expected to be indifferent to the location of the other;

and, for the purposes of this definition, it is irrelevant that the investments may ultimately be bought otherwise than in the course of such business by persons not so expert.

(5) Any approval under this article is to be given by notice in writing; and the Treasury may by a further notice in writing withdraw any such approval if for any reason it appears to them that it is not appropriate to it to continue in force.

Other exclusions

36. Article 25 is also subject to the exclusions in articles 66 (trustees etc.), 67 (profession or non-investment business), 68 (sale of goods and supply of services), 69 (groups and joint enterprises), 70 (sale of body corporate), 71 (employee share schemes) and 72 (overseas persons).

CHAPTER VII MANAGING INVESTMENTS

The activity

Managing investments

37. Managing assets belonging to another person, in circumstances involving the exercise of discretion, is a specified kind of activity if —

(a) the assets consist of or include any investment which is a security or a contractually based investment; or

(b) the arrangements for their management are such that the assets may consist of or include such investments, and either the assets have at any time since 29 April 1988 done so, or the arrangements have at any time (whether before or after that date) been held out as arrangements under which the assets would do so.

Exclusions

Attorneys

38. A person does not carry on an activity of the kind specified by article 37 if –

(a) he is a person appointed to manage the assets in question under a power of attorney; and

(b) all routine or day-to-day decisions, so far as relating to investments of a kind mentioned in article 37(a), are taken on behalf of that person by –

    (i) an authorised person with permission to carry on activities of the kind specified by article 37;

    (ii) a person who is an exempt person in relation to activities of that kind;

    (iii) an overseas person.

Other exclusions

39. Article 37 is also subject to the exclusions in articles 66 (trustees etc.), 68 (sale of goods and supply of services) and 69 (groups and joint enterprises).

CHAPTER VIII   SAFEGUARDING AND ADMINISTERING INVESTMENTS

The activity

Safeguarding and administering investments

40. (1) The activity consisting of both –

(a) the safeguarding of assets belonging to another, and

(b) the administration of those assets,

or arranging for one or more other persons to carry on that activity, is a specified kind of activity if the condition in sub-paragraph (a) or (b) of paragraph (2) is met.

(2) The condition is that –

(a) the assets consist of or include any investment which is a security or a contractually based investment; or

(b) the arrangements for their safeguarding and administration are such that the assets may consist of or include such investments, and either the assets have at any time since 1 June 1997 done so, or the arrangements have at any time (whether before or after that date) been held out as ones under which such investments would be safeguarded and administered.

(3) For the purposes of this article –

(a) it is immaterial that title to the assets safeguarded and administered is held in uncertificated form;

(b) it is immaterial that the assets safeguarded and administered may be transferred to another person, subject to a commitment by the person safeguarding and administering them, or arranging for their safeguarding and administration, that they will be replaced by equivalent assets at some future date or when so requested by the person to whom they belong.

Exclusions

Acceptance of responsibility by third party

41. (1) There are excluded from article 40 any activities which a person carries on pursuant to arrangements which –

   (a) are ones under which a qualifying custodian undertakes to the person to whom the assets belong a responsibility in respect of the assets which is no less onerous than the qualifying custodian would have if the qualifying custodian were safeguarding and administering the assets; and
   (b) are operated by the qualifying custodian in the course of carrying on in the United Kingdom an activity of the kind specified by article 40.

(2) In paragraph (1), 'qualifying custodian' means a person who is –

   (a) an authorised person who has permission to carry on an activity of the kind specified by article 40, or
   (b) an exempt person acting in the course of a business comprising a regulated activity in relation to which he is exempt.

Introduction to qualifying custodians

42. (1) There are excluded from article 40 any arrangements pursuant to which introductions are made by a person ('P') to a qualifying custodian with a view to the qualifying custodian providing in the United Kingdom a service comprising an activity of the kind specified by article 40, where the qualifying person (or other person who is to safeguard and administer the assets in question) is not connected with P.

(2) For the purposes of paragraph (1) –

   (a) 'qualifying custodian' has the meaning given by article 41(2); and
   (b) a person is connected with P if either he is a member of the same group as P, or P is remunerated by him.

Activities not constituting administration

43. The following activities do not constitute the administration of assets for the purposes of article 40 –

   (a) providing information as to the number of units or the value of any assets safeguarded;
   (b) converting currency;
   (c) receiving documents relating to an investment solely for the purpose of onward transmission to, from or at the direction of the person to whom the investment belongs.

Other exclusions

44. Article 40 is also subject to the exclusions in articles 66 (trustees etc.), 67 (profession or non-investment business), 68 (sale of goods and supply of services), 69 (groups and joint enterprises) and 71 (employee share schemes).

CHAPTER IX   SENDING DEMATERIALISED INSTRUCTIONS

The activities

Sending dematerialised instructions

45. (1) Sending, on behalf of another person, dematerialised instructions relating to a security is a specified kind of activity, where those instructions are sent by means of a relevant system in respect of which an Operator is approved under the 1995 Regulations.

(2) Causing dematerialised instructions relating to a security to be sent on behalf of another person by means of such a system is also a specified kind of activity where the person causing them to be sent is a system-participant.

(3) In this Chapter –

(a) 'the 1995 Regulations' means the Uncertified Securities Regulations 1995; and
(b) 'dematerialised instruction', 'Operator', 'settlement bank' and 'system-participant' have the meaning given by regulation 3 of the 1995 Regulations.

Exclusions

Instructions on behalf of participating issuers

46. There is excluded from article 45 the act of sending, or causing to be sent, a dematerialised instruction where the person on whose behalf the instruction is sent or caused to be sent is a participating issuer within the meaning of the 1995 Regulations.

Instructions on behalf of settlement banks

47. There is excluded from article 45 the act of sending, or causing to be sent, a dematerialised instruction where the person on whose behalf the instruction is sent or caused to be sent is a settlement bank in its capacity as such.

Instructions in connection with takeover offers

48. (1) There is excluded from article 45 the act of sending, or causing to be sent, a dematerialised instruction where the person on whose behalf the instruction is sent or caused to be sent is an offeror making a takeover offer.

(2) In this article –

(a) 'offeror' means, in the case of a takeover offer made by two or more persons jointly, the joint offers or any of them;
(b) 'takeover offer' means –

(i) an offer to acquire shares (which in this sub-paragraph has the same meaning as in section 428(1) of the Companies Act 1985) in a body corporate incorporated in the United Kingdom which is a takeover offer within the meaning of Part XIIIA of that Act (or would be such an offer if that Part of that Act applied in relation to any body corporate);
(ii) an offer to acquire all or substantially all the shares, or all the shares of a particular class, in a body corporate incorporated outside the United Kingdom; or

(iii) an offer made to all the holders of shares, or shares of a particular class, in a body corporate to acquire a specified proportion of those shares;

but in determining whether an offer falls within paragraph (ii) there are to be disregarded any shares which the offeror or any associate of his (within the meaning of section 430E of the Companies Act 1985) holds or has contracted to acquire; and in determining whether an offer falls within paragraph (iii) the offeror, any such associate and any person whose shares the offeror or any such associate has contracted to acquire is not to be regarded as a holder of shares.

Instructions in the course of providing a network

49. There is excluded from article 45 the act of sending, or causing to be sent, a dematerialised instruction as a necessary part of providing a network, the purpose of which is to carry dematerialised instructions which are at all times properly authenticated (within the meaning of the 1995 Regulations).

Other exclusions

50. Article 45 is also subject to the exclusions in articles 66 (trustees etc.) and 69 (groups and joint enterprises).

CHAPTER X   COLLECTIVE INVESTMENT SCHEMES

The activities

Establishing etc. a collective investment scheme

51.   (1) The following are specified kinds of activity –

(a) establishing, operating or winding up a collective investment scheme;
(b) acting as trustee of an authorised unit trust scheme;
(c) acting as the depositary or sole director of an open-ended investment company.

(2) In this article, 'trustee', 'authorised unit trust scheme' and 'depositary' have the meaning given by section 237 of the Act.

CHAPTER XI   STAKEHOLDER PENSION SCHEMES

The activities

Establishing etc. a stakeholder pension scheme

52.   Establishing, operating or winding up a stakeholder pension scheme is a specified kind of activity.

CHAPTER XII   ADVISING ON INVESTMENTS

The activity

Advising on investments

53.   Advising a person is a specified kind of activity if the advice is –

(a) given to the person in his capacity as an investor or potential investor, or in his capacity as agent for an investor or a potential investor; and

(b) advice on the merits of his doing any of the following (whether as principal or agent) –

(i) buying, selling, subscribing for or underwriting a particular investment which is a security or a contractually based investment, or

(ii) exercising any right conferred by such an investment to buy, sell, subscribe for or underwrite such an investment.

Exclusions

Advice given in newspapers etc.

54. (1) There is excluded from article 53 the giving of advice in writing or other legible form if the advice is contained in a newspaper, journal, magazine, or other periodical publication, or is given by way of a service comprising regularly updated news or information, if the principal purpose of the publication or service, taken as a whole and including any advertisements or other promotional material contained in it, is neither –

(a) that of giving advice of a kind mentioned in article 53; nor

(b) that of leading or enabling persons to buy, sell, subscribe for or underwrite securities or contractually based investments.

(2) There is also excluded from article 53 the giving of advice in any service consisting of the broadcast or transmission of television or radio programmes, if the principal purpose of the service, taken as a whole and including any advertisements or other promotional material contained in it, is neither of those mentioned in paragraph (1)(a) and (b).

(3) The Authority may, on the application of the proprietor of any such publication or service as is mentioned in paragraph (1) or (2), certify that it is of the nature described in that paragraph, and may revoke any such certificate if it considers that it is no longer justified.

(4) A certificate given under paragraph (3) and not revoked is conclusive evidence of the matters certified.

Other exclusions

55. Article 53 is also subject to the exclusions in articles 66 (trustees etc.), 67 (profession or non-investment business), 68 (sale of goods and supply of services), 69 (groups and joint enterprises), 70 (sale of body corporate) and 72 (overseas persons).

CHAPTER XIII   LLOYD'S

The activities

Advice on syndicate participation at Lloyd's

56. Advising a person to become, or continue or cease to be, a member of a particular Lloyd's syndicate is a specified kind of activity.

Managing the underwriting capacity of a Lloyd's syndicate

57. Managing the underwriting capacity of a Lloyd's syndicate as a managing agent at Lloyd's is a specified kind of activity.

Arranging deals in contracts of insurance written at Lloyd's

58. The arranging, by the society incorporated by Lloyd's Act 1871 by the name of Lloyd's, of deals in contracts of insurance written at Lloyd's, is a specified kind of activity.

CHAPTER XIV   FUNERAL PLAN CONTRACTS

The activity

Funeral plan contracts

59. (1) Entering as provider into a funeral plan contract is a specified kind of activity.
  (2) A 'funeral plan contract' is a contract (other than one excluded by article 60) under which –

(a) a person ('the customer') makes one or more payments to another person ('the provider'); and
(b) the provider undertakes to provide, or secure that another person provides, a funeral in the United Kingdom for the customer (or some other person who is living at the date when the contract is entered into) on his death;

unless, at the time of entering into the contract, the customer and the provider intend or expect the funeral to occur within one month.

Exclusion

Plans covered by insurance or trust arrangements

60. (1) There is excluded from article 59 any contract under which –

(a) the provider undertakes to secure that sums paid by the customer under the contract will be applied towards a contract of whole life insurance on the life of the customer (or other person for whom the funeral is to be provided), effected and carried out by an authorised person who has permission to effect and carry out such contracts of insurance, for the purpose of providing the funeral; or
(b) the provider undertakes to secure that sums paid by the customer under the contract will be held on trust for the purpose of providing the funeral, and that the following requirements are or will be met with respect to the trust –

(i)   the trust must be established by a written instrument;
(ii)   more than half of the trustees must be unconnected with the provider;
(iii) the trustees must appoint, or have appointed, an independent fund manager who is an authorised person who has permission to carry on an activity of the kind specified by article 37, and who is a person who is unconnected with the provider, to manage the assets of the trust;
(iv) annual accounts must be prepared, and audited by a person who is eligible for appointment as a company auditor under section 25 of the

Companies Act 1989, with respect to the assets and liabilities of the trust; and

(v) the assets and liabilities of the trust must, at least once every three years, be determined, calculated and verified by an actuary who is a Fellow of the Institute of Actuaries or of the Faculty of Actuaries.

(2) For the purposes of paragraph (1)(b)(ii) and (iii), a person is unconnected with the provider if he is a person other than –

(a) the provider;

(b) a member of the same group as the provider;

(c) a director, other officer or employee of the provider, or of any member of the same group as the provider;

(d) a partner of the provider;

(e) a close relative of a person falling within sub-paragraph (a), (c) or (d); or

(f) an agent of any person falling within sub-paragraphs (a) to (e).

CHAPTER XV   REGULATED MORTGAGE CONTRACTS

The activities

Regulated mortgage contracts

61.   (1) Entering into a regulated mortgage contract as lender is a specified kind of activity.

(2) Administering a regulated mortgage contract is also a specified kind of activity, where the contract was entered into by way of business after the coming into force of this article.

(3) In this Chapter –

(a) a contract is a 'regulated mortgage contract' if, at the time it is entered into, the following conditions are met –

(i) the contract is one under which a person ('the lender') provides credit to an individual or to trustees ('the borrower');

(ii) the contract provides for the obligation of the borrower to repay to be secured by a first legal mortgage on land (other than timeshare accommodation) in the United Kingdom;

(iii) at least 40 per cent of that land is used, or is intended to be used, as or in connection with a dwelling by the borrower or (in the case of credit provided to trustees) by an individual who is a beneficiary of the trust, or by a related person;

(b) 'administering' a regulated mortgage contract means either or both of –

(i) notifying the borrower of changes in interest rates or payments due under the contract, or of other matters of which the contract requires him to be notified; and

(ii) taking any necessary steps for the purposes of collecting or recovering payments due under the contract from the borrower;

but a person is not to be treated as administering a regulated mortgage contract merely because he has, or exercises, a right to take action for the purposes of enforcing the contract (or to require that such action is or is not taken);

(c) 'credit' includes a cash loan, and any other form of financial accommodation.

(4) For the purposes of paragraph (3)(a) –

(a) a 'first legal mortgage' means a legal mortgage ranking in priority ahead of all other mortgages (if any) affecting the land in question, where 'mortgage' includes charge and (in Scotland) a heritable security;

(b) the area of any land which comprises a building or other structure containing two or more storeys is to be taken to be the aggregate of the floor areas of each of those storeys;

(c) 'related person', in relation to the borrower or (in the case of credit provided to trustees) a beneficiary of the trust, means –

    (i) that person's spouse;

    (ii) a person (whether or not of the opposite sex) whose relationship with that person has the characteristics of the relationship between husband and wife; or

    (iii) that person's parent, brother, sister, child, grandparent or grandchild; and

(d) 'timeshare accommodation' has the meaning given by section 1 of the Timeshare Act 1992.

Exclusions

Arranging administration by authorised person

62. A person who is not an authorised person does not carry on an activity of the kind specified by article 61(2) in relation to a regulated mortgage contract where he –

(a) arranges for another person, being an authorised person with permission to carry on an activity of that kind, to administer the contract; or

(b) administers the contract himself during a period of not more than one month beginning with the day on which any such arrangement comes to an end.

Administration pursuant to agreement with authorised person

63. A person who is not an authorised person does not carry on an activity of the kind specified by article 61(2) in relation to a regulated mortgage contract where he administers the contract pursuant to an agreement with an authorised person who has permission to carry on an activity of that kind.

CHAPTER XVI   AGREEING TO CARRY ON ACTIVITIES

The activity

Agreeing to carry on specified kinds of activity

64. Agreeing to carry on an activity of the kind specified by any other provision of this Part (other than article 5, 10, 51 or 52) is a specified kind of activity.

Exclusion

Overseas persons

65. Article 64 is subject to the exclusion in article 72 (overseas persons).

CHAPTER XVII EXCLUSIONS APPLYING TO SEVERAL SPECIFIED KINDS OF ACTIVITY

Trustees, nominees and personal representatives

66. (1) A person ('X') does not carry on an activity of the kind specified by article 14 where he enters into a transaction as bare trustee or, in Scotland, as nominee for another person ('Y') and –

    (a) X is acting on Y's instructions; and

    (b) X does not hold himself out as providing a service of buying and selling securities or contractually based investments.

(2) Subject to paragraph (7), there are excluded from article 25(1) and (2) arrangements made by a person acting as trustee or personal representative for or with a view to a transaction which is or is to be entered into –

    (a) by that person and a fellow trustee or personal representative (acting in their capacity as such); or

    (b) by a beneficiary under the trust, will or intestacy.

(3) Subject to paragraph (7), there is excluded from article 37 any activity carried on by a person acting as trustee or personal representative, unless –

    (a) he holds himself out as providing a service comprising an activity of the kind specified by article 37; or

    (b) the assets in question are held for the purposes of an occupational pension scheme, and, by virtue of article 4 of the Financial Services and Markets Act 2000 (Carrying on Regulated Activities by Way of Business) Order 2001, he is to be treated as carrying on that activity by way of business.

(4) Subject to paragraph (7), there is excluded from article 40 any activity carried on by a person acting as trustee or personal representative, unless he holds himself out as providing a service comprising an activity of the kind specified by article 40.

(5) A person does not, by sending or causing to be sent a dematerialised instruction (within the meaning of article 45), carry on an activity of the kind specified by that article if the instruction relates to an investment which that person holds as trustee or personal representative.

(6) Subject to paragraph (7), there is excluded from article 53 the giving of advice by a person acting as trustee or personal representative where he gives the advice to –

    (a) a fellow trustee or personal representative for the purposes of the trust or the estate; or

    (b) a beneficiary under the trust, will or intestacy concerning his interest in the trust fund or estate.

(7) Paragraphs (2), (3), (4) and (6) do not apply if the person carrying on the activity is remunerated for what he does in addition to any remuneration he receives as trustee or personal representative, and for these purposes a person is not to be

regarded as receiving additional remuneration merely because his remuneration is calculated by reference to time spent.

Activities carried on in the course of a profession or non-investment business

67.　(1) There is excluded from articles 21, 25(1) and (2), 40 and 53 any activity which –

(a) is carried on in the course of carrying on any profession or business which does not otherwise consist of the carrying on of regulated activities in the United Kingdom; and

(b) may reasonably be regarded as a necessary part of other services provided in the course of that profession or business.

(2) But the exclusion in paragraph (1) does not apply if the activity in question is remunerated separately from the other services.

Activities carried on in connection with the sale of goods or supply of services

68.　(1) Subject to paragraphs (9), (10) and (11), this article concerns certain activities carried on for the purposes of or in connection with the sale of goods or supply of services by a supplier to a customer, where –

'supplier' means a person whose main business is to sell goods or supply services and not to carry on any activities of the kind specified by any of articles 14, 21, 25, 37, 40, 45, 51, 52 and 53 and, where the supplier is a member of a group, also means any other member of that group; and

'customer' means a person, other than an individual, to whom a supplier sells goods or supplies services, or agrees to do so, and, where the customer is a member of a group, also means any other member of that group;

and in this article 'related sale or supply' means a sale of goods or supply of services to the customer otherwise than by the supplier, but for or in connection with the same purpose as the sale or supply mentioned above.

(2) There is excluded from article 14 any transaction entered into by a supplier with a customer, if the transaction is entered into for the purposes of or in connection with the sale of goods or supply of services, or a related sale or supply.

(3) There is excluded from article 21 any transaction entered into by a supplier as agent for a customer, if the transaction is entered into for the purposes of or in connection with the sale of goods or supply of services, or a related sale or supply, and provided that –

(a) where the investment to which the transaction relates is a security, the supplier does not hold himself out (other than to the customer) as engaging in the business of buying securities of the kind to which the transaction relates with a view to selling them, and does not regularly solicit members of the public for the purpose of inducing them (as principals or agents) to buy, sell, subscribe for or underwrite securities;

(b) where the investment to which the transaction relates is a contractually based investment, the supplier enters into the transaction –

(i) with or through an authorised person, or an exempt person acting in the course of a business comprising a regulated activity in relation to which he is exempt; or

    (ii) through an office outside the United Kingdom maintained by a party to the transaction, and with or through a person whose head office is situated outside the United Kingdom and whose ordinary business involves him in carrying on activities of the kind specified by any of articles 14, 21, 25, 37, 40, 45, 51, 52 and 53 or, so far as relevant to any of those articles, article 64, or would do so apart from any exclusion from any of those articles made by this Order.

(4) In paragraph (3)(a), 'members of the public' has the meaning given by article 15(2), references to 'A' being read as references to the supplier.

(5) There are excluded from article 25(1) and (2) arrangements made by a supplier for, or with a view to, a transaction which is or is to be entered into by a customer for the purposes of or in connection with the sale of goods or supply of services, or a related sale or supply.

(6) There is excluded from article 37 any activity carried on by a supplier where the assets in question –

    (a) are those of a customer; and
    (b) are managed for the purposes of or in connection with the sale of goods or supply of services, or a related sale or supply.

(7) There is excluded from article 40 any activity carried on by a supplier where the assets in question are or are to be safeguarded and administered for the purposes of or in connection with the sale of goods or supply of services, or a related sale or supply.

(8) There is excluded from article 53 the giving of advice by a supplier to a customer for the purposes of or in connection with the sale of goods or supply of services, or a related sale or supply, or to a person with whom the customer proposes to enter into a transaction for the purposes of or in connection with such a sale or supply or related sale or supply.

(9) Paragraphs (2), (3) and (5) do not apply in the case of a transaction for the sale or purchase of a qualifying contract of insurance, an investment of the kind specified by article 81, or an investment of the kind specified by article 89 so far as relevant to such a contract or such an investment.

(10) Paragraph (6) does not apply where the assets managed consist of qualifying contracts of insurance, investments of the kind specified by article 81, or investments of the kind specified by article 89 so far as relevant to such contracts or such investments.

(11) Paragraph (8) does not apply in the case of advice in relation to an investment which is a qualifying contract of insurance, is of the kind specified by article 81, or is of the kind specified by article 89 so far as relevant to such a contract or such an investment.

Groups and joint enterprises

69. (1) There is excluded from article 14 any transaction into which a person enters as principal with another person if that other person is also acting as principal and –

    (a) they are members of the same group; or
    (b) they are, or propose to become, participators in a joint enterprise and the transaction is entered into for the purposes of or in connection with that enterprise.

(2) There is excluded from article 21 any transaction into which a person enters as agent for another person if that other person is acting as principal, and the condition in paragraph (1)(a) or (b) is met, provided that –

(a) where the investment to which the transaction relates is a security, the agent does not hold himself out (other than to members of the same group or persons who are or propose to become participators with him in a joint enterprise) as engaging in the business of buying securities of the kind to which the transaction relates with a view to selling them, and does not regularly solicit members of the public for the purpose of inducing them (as principals or agents) to buy, sell, subscribe for or underwrite securities;

(b) where the investment to which the transaction relates is a contractually based investment, the agent enters into the transaction –

(i) with or through an authorised person, or an exempt person acting in the course of a business comprising a regulated activity in relation to which he is exempt; or

(ii) through an office outside the United Kingdom maintained by a party to the transaction, and with or through a person whose head office is situated outside the United Kingdom and whose ordinary business involves him in carrying on activities of the kind specified by any of articles 14, 21, 25, 37, 40, 45, 51, 52 and 53 or, so far as relevant to any of those articles, article 64, or would do so apart from any exclusion from any of those articles made by this Order.

(3) In paragraph (2)(a), 'members of the public' has the meaning given by article 15(2), references to 'A' being read as references to the agent.

(4) There are excluded from article 25(1) and (2) arrangements made by a person if –

(a) he is a member of a group and the arrangements in question are for, or with a view to, a transaction which is or is to be entered into, as principal, by another member of the same group; or

(b) he is or proposes to become a participator in a joint enterprise, and the arrangements in question are for, or with a view to, a transaction which is or is to be entered into, as principal, by another person who is or proposes to become a participator in that enterprise, for the purposes of or in connection with that enterprise.

(5) There is excluded from article 37 any activity carried on by a person if –

(a) he is a member of a group and the assets in question belong to another member of the same group; or

(b) he is or proposes to become a participator in a joint enterprise with the person to whom the assets belong, and the assets are managed for the purposes of or in connection with that enterprise.

(6) There is excluded from article 40 any activity carried on by a person if –

(a) he is a member of a group and the assets in question belong to another member of the same group; or

(b) he is or proposes to become a participator in a joint enterprise, and the assets in question –

(i) belong to another person who is or proposes to become a participator in that joint enterprise; and

(ii) are or are to be safeguarded and administered for the purposes of or in connection with that enterprise.

(7) A person who is a member of a group does not carry on an activity of the kind specified by article 45 where he sends a dematerialised instruction, or causes one to be sent, on behalf of another member of the same group, if the investment to which the instruction relates is one in respect of which a member of the same group is registered as holder in the appropriate register of securities, or will be so registered as a result of the instruction.

(8) In paragraph (7), 'dematerialised instruction' and 'register of securities' have the meaning given by regulation 3 of the Uncertificated Securities Regulations 1995.

(9) There is excluded from article 53 the giving of advice by a person if –

(a) he is a member of a group and gives the advice in question to another member of the same group; or

(b) he is, or proposes to become, a participator in a joint enterprise and the advice in question is given to another person who is, or proposes to become, a participator in that enterprise for the purposes of or in connection with that enterprise.

Activities carried on in connection with the sale of a body corporate

70. (1) A person does not carry on an activity of the kind specified by article 14 by entering as principal into a transaction if –

(a) the transaction is one to acquire or dispose of shares in a body corporate other than an open-ended investment company, or is entered into for the purposes of such an acquisition or disposal; and

(b) either –

(i) the conditions set out in paragraph (2) are met; or

(ii) those conditions are not met, but the object of the transaction may nevertheless reasonably be regarded as being the acquisition of day to day control of the affairs of the body corporate.

(2) The conditions mentioned in paragraph (1)(b) are that –

(a) the shares consist of or include 50 per cent or more of the voting shares in the body corporate; or

(b) the shares, together with any already held by the person acquiring them, consist of or include at least that percentage of such shares; and

(c) in either case, the acquisition or disposal is between parties each of whom is a body corporate, a partnership, a single individual or a group of connected individuals.

(3) In paragraph (2)(c), 'a group of connected individuals' means –

(a) in relation to a party disposing of shares in a body corporate, a single group of persons each of whom is –

(i) a director or manager of the body corporate;

(ii) a close relative of any such director or manager;

(iii) a person acting as trustee for any person falling within paragraph (i) or (ii); and

(b) in relation to a party acquiring shares in a body corporate, a single group of persons each of whom is –

(i)   a person who is or is to be a director or manager of the body corporate;

(ii)   a close relative of any such person; or

(iii) a person acting as trustee for any person falling within paragraph (i) or (ii).

(4) A person does not carry on an activity of the kind specified by article 21 by entering as agent into a transaction of the kind described in paragraph (1).

(5) There are excluded from article 25(1) and (2) arrangements made for, or with a view to, a transaction of the kind described in paragraph (1).

(6) There is excluded from article 53 the giving of advice in connection with a transaction (or proposed transaction) of the kind described in paragraph (1).

Activities carried on in connection with employee share schemes

71. (1) A person ('C'), a member of the same group as C or a relevant trustee does not carry on an activity of the kind specified by article 14 by entering as principal into a transaction the purpose of which is to enable or facilitate –

(a)   transactions in shares in, or debentures issued by, C between, or for the benefit of, any of the persons mentioned in paragraph (2); or

(b)   the holding of such shares or debentures by, or for the benefit of, such persons.

(2) The persons referred to in paragraph (1) are –

(a)   the *bona fide* employees or former employees of C or of another member of the same group as C;

(b)   the wives, husbands, widows, widowers, or children or step-children under the age of eighteen of such employees or former employees.

(3) C, a member of the same group as C or a relevant trustee does not carry on an activity of the kind specified by article 21 by entering as agent into a transaction of the kind described in paragraph (1).

(4) There are excluded from article 25(1) or (2) arrangements made by C, a member of the same group as C or a relevant trustee if the arrangements in question are for, or with a view to, a transaction of the kind described in paragraph (1).

(5) There is excluded from article 40 any activity if the assets in question are, or are to be, safeguarded and administered by C, a member of the same group as C or a relevant trustee for the purpose of enabling or facilitating transactions of the kind described in paragraph (1).

(6) In this article –

(a)   'shares' and 'debentures' include –

(i)   any investment of the kind specified by article 76 or 77;

(ii)   any investment of the kind specified by article 79 or 80 so far as relevant to articles 76 and 77; and

(iii) any investment of the kind specified by article 89 so far as relevant to investments of the kind mentioned in paragraph (i) or (ii);

(b)   'relevant trustee' means a person who, in pursuance of the arrangements made for the purpose mentioned in paragraph (1), holds, as trustee, shares in or debentures issued by C.

Overseas persons

72. (1) An overseas person does not carry on an activity of the kind specified by article 14 by –

    (a) entering into a transaction as principal with or through an authorised person, or an exempt person acting in the course of a business comprising a regulated activity in relation to which he is exempt; or

    (b) entering into a transaction as principal with a person in the United Kingdom, if the transaction is the result of a legitimate approach.

(2) An overseas person does not carry on an activity of the kind specified by article 21 by –

    (a) entering into a transaction as agent for any person with or through an authorised person or an exempt person acting in the course of a business comprising a regulated activity in relation to which he is exempt; or

    (b) entering into a transaction with another party ('X') as agent for any person ('Y'), other than with or through an authorised person or such an exempt person, unless –

        (i) either X or Y is in the United Kingdom; and

        (ii) the transaction is the result of an approach (other than a legitimate approach) made by or on behalf of, or to, whichever of X or Y is in the United Kingdom.

(3) There are excluded from article 25(1) arrangements made by an overseas person with an authorised person, or an exempt person acting in the course of a business comprising a regulated activity in relation to which he is exempt.

(4) There are excluded from article 25(2) arrangements made by an overseas person with a view to transactions which are, as respects transactions in the United Kingdom, confined to –

    (a) transactions entered into by authorised persons as principal or agent; and

    (b) transactions entered into by exempt persons, as principal or agent, in the course of business comprising regulated activities in relation to which they are exempt.

(5) There is excluded from article 53 the giving of advice by an overseas person as a result of a legitimate approach.

(6) There is excluded from article 64 any agreement made by an overseas person to carry on an activity of the kind specified by article 25(1) or (2), 37, 40 or 45 if the agreement is the result of a legitimate approach.

(7) In this article, 'legitimate approach' means –

    (a) an approach made to the overseas person which has not been solicited by him in any way, or has been solicited by him in a way which does not contravene section 21 of the Act; or

    (b) an approach made by or on behalf of the overseas person in a way which does not contravene that section.

PART III   SPECIFIED INVESTMENTS

Investments: general

73.   The following kinds of investment are specified for the purposes of section 22 of the Act.

Deposits

74.   A deposit.

Contracts of insurance

75.   Rights under a contract of insurance.

Shares etc.

76.   (1) Shares or stock in the share capital of –

(a) any body corporate (wherever incorporated), and
(b) any unincorporated body constituted under the law of a country or territory outside the United Kingdom.

(2) Paragraph (1) includes –

(a) any shares of a class defined as deferred shares for the purposes of section 119 of the Building Societies Act 1986; and
(b) any transferable shares in a body incorporated under the law of, or any part of, the United Kingdom relating to industrial and provident societies or credit unions, or in a body constituted under the law of another EEA State for purposes equivalent to those of such a body.

(3) But subject to paragraph (2) there are excluded from paragraph (1) shares or stock in the share capital of –

(a) an open-ended investment company;
(b) a building society incorporated under the law of, or any part of, the United Kingdom;
(c) a body incorporated under the law of, or any part of, the United Kingdom relating to industrial and provident societies or credit unions;
(d) any body constituted under the law of an EEA State for purposes equivalent to those of a body falling within sub-paragraph (b) or (c).

Instruments creating or acknowledging indebtedness

77.   (1) Subject to paragraph (2), such of the following as do not fall within article 78 –

(a) debentures;
(b) debenture stock;
(c) loan stock;
(d) bonds;
(e) certificates of deposit;
(f) any other instrument creating or acknowledging indebtedness.

(2) If and to the extent that they would otherwise fall within paragraph (1), there are excluded from that paragraph –

    (a) an instrument acknowledging or creating indebtedness for, or for money borrowed to defray, the consideration payable under a contract for the supply of goods or services;

    (b) a cheque or other bill of exchange, a banker's draft or a letter of credit (but not a bill of exchange accepted by a banker);

    (c) a banknote, a statement showing a balance on a current, deposit or savings account, a lease or other disposition of property, or a heritable security; and

    (d) a contract of insurance.

(3) An instrument excluded from paragraph (1) of article 78 by paragraph (2)(b) of that article is not thereby to be taken to fall within paragraph (1) of this article.

Government and public securities

78. (1) Subject to paragraph (2), loan stock, bonds and other instruments creating or acknowledging indebtedness, issued by or on behalf of any of the following –

    (a) the government of the United Kingdom;

    (b) the Scottish Administration;

    (c) the Executive Committee of the Northern Ireland Assembly;

    (d) the National Assembly for Wales;

    (e) the government of any country or territory outside the United Kingdom;

    (f) a local authority in the United Kingdom or elsewhere; or

    (g) a body the members of which comprise –

        (i) states including the United Kingdom or another EEA State; or

        (ii) bodies whose members comprise states including the United Kingdom or another EEA State.

(2) There are excluded from paragraph (1) –

    (a) so far as applicable, the instruments mentioned in article 77(2)(a) to (d);

    (b) any instrument creating or acknowledging indebtedness in respect of –

        (i) money received by the Director of Savings as deposits or otherwise in connection with the business of the National Savings Bank;

        (ii) money raised under the National Loans Act 1968 under the auspices of the Director of Savings or treated as so raised by virtue of section 11(3) of the National Debt Act 1972.

Instruments giving entitlements to investments

79. (1) Warrants and other instruments entitling the holder to subscribe for any investment of the kind specified by article 76, 77 or 78.

(2) It is immaterial whether the investment to which the entitlement relates is in existence or identifiable.

(3) An investment of the kind specified by this article is not to be regarded as falling within article 83, 84 or 85.

Certificates representing certain securities

80. (1) Subject to paragraph (2), certificates or other instruments which confer contractual or property rights (other than rights consisting of an investment of the kind specified by article 83) –

(a) in respect of any investment of the kind specified by any of articles 76 to 79, being an investment held by a person other than the person on whom the rights are conferred by the certificate or instrument; and

(b) the transfer of which may be effected without the consent of that person.

(2) There is excluded from paragraph (1) any certificate or other instrument which confers rights in respect of two or more investments issued by different persons, or in respect of two or more different investments of the kind specified by article 78 and issued by the same person.

Units in a collective investment scheme

81.   Units in a collective investment scheme (within the meaning of Part XVII of the Act).

Rights under a stakeholder pension scheme

82.   Rights under a stakeholder pension scheme.

Options

83.   Options to acquire or dispose of –

(a) a security or contractually based investment (other than one of a kind specified by this article);

(b) currency of the United Kingdom or any other country or territory;

(c) palladium, platinum, gold or silver; or

(d) an option to acquire or dispose of an investment of the kind specified by this article by virtue of paragraph (a), (b) or (c).

Futures

84.   (1) Subject to paragraph (2), rights under a contract for the sale of a commodity or property of any other description under which delivery is to be made at a future date and at a price agreed on when the contract is made.

(2) There are excluded from paragraph (1) rights under any contract which is made for commercial and not investment purposes.

(3) A contract is to be regarded as made for investment purposes if it is made or traded on a recognised investment exchange, or is made otherwise than on a recognised investment exchange but is expressed to be as traded on such an exchange or on the same terms as those on which an equivalent contract would be made on such an exchange.

(4) A contract not falling within paragraph (3) is to be regarded as made for commercial purposes if under the terms of the contract delivery is to be made within seven days, unless it can be shown that there existed an understanding that (notwithstanding the express terms of the contract) delivery would not be made within seven days.

(5) The following are indications that a contract not falling within paragraph (3) or (4) is made for commercial purposes and the absence of them is an indication that it is made for investment purposes –

(a) one or more of the parties is a producer of the commodity or other property, or uses it in his business;

(b) the seller delivers or intends to deliver the property or the purchaser takes or intends to take delivery of it.

(6) It is an indication that a contract is made for commercial purposes that the prices, the lot, the delivery date or other terms are determined by the parties for the purposes of the particular contract and not by reference (or not solely by reference) to regularly published prices, to standard lots or delivery dates or to standard terms.

(7) The following are indications that a contract is made for investment purposes –

(a) it is expressed to be as traded on an investment exchange;
(b) performance of the contract is ensured by an investment exchange or a clearing house;
(c) there are arrangements for the payment or provision of margin.

(8) For the purposes of paragraph (1), a price is to be taken to be agreed on when a contract is made –

(a) notwithstanding that it is left to be determined by reference to the price at which a contract is to be entered into on a market or exchange or could be entered into at a time and place specified in the contract; or
(b) in a case where the contract is expressed to be by reference to a standard lot and quality, notwithstanding that provision is made for a variation in the price to take account of any variation in quantity or quality on delivery.

Contracts for differences etc.

85. (1) Subject to paragraph (2), rights under –

(a) a contract for differences; or
(b) any other contract the purpose or pretended purpose of which is to secure a profit or avoid a loss by reference to fluctuations in –

(i) the value or price of property of any description; or
(ii) an index or other factor designated for that purpose in the contract.

(2) There are excluded from paragraph (1) –

(a) rights under a contract if the parties intend that the profit is to be secured or the loss is to be avoided by one or more of the parties taking delivery of any property to which the contract relates;
(b) rights under a contract under which money is received by way of deposit on terms that any interest or other return to be paid on the sum deposited will be calculated by reference to fluctuations in an index or other factor;
(c) rights under any contract under which –

(i) money is received by the Director of Savings as deposits or otherwise in connection with the business of the National Savings Bank; or
(ii) money is raised under the National Loans Act 1968 under the auspices of the Director of Savings or treated as so raised by virtue of section 11(3) of the National Debt Act 1972;

(d) rights under a qualifying contract of insurance.

Lloyd's syndicate capacity and syndicate membership

86. (1) The underwriting capacity of a Lloyd's syndicate.

(2) A person's membership (or prospective membership) of a Lloyd's syndicate.

Funeral plan contracts

87. Rights under a funeral plan contract.

Regulated mortgage contracts

88. Rights under a regulated mortgage contract.

Rights to or interests in investments

89. (1) Subject to paragraphs (2) to (4), any right to or interest in anything which is specified by any other provision of this Part (other than article 88).

(2) Paragraph (1) does not include interests under the trusts of an occupational pension scheme.

(3) Paragraph (1) does not include –

(a) rights to or interests in a contract of insurance of the kind referred to in paragraph (1)(a) of article 60; or
(b) interests under a trust of the kind referred to in paragraph (1)(b) of that article.

(4) Paragraph (1) does not include anything which is specified by any other provision of this Part.

PART IV   CONSEQUENTIAL PROVISIONS

Regulated mortgage contracts: consequential provisions

Consequential amendments of the Consumer Credit Act 1974

90. (1) The Consumer Credit Act 1974 is amended as follows.

(2) In section 16 (exempt agreements), after subsection (6B) insert –

'(6C) This Act does not regulate a consumer credit agreement if –

(a) it is secured by a land mortgage; and
(b) entering into that agreement as lender is a regulated activity for the purposes of the Financial Services and Markets Act 2000.

(6D) But section 126, and any other provision so far as it relates to section 126, applies to an agreement which would (but for subsection (6C)) be a regulated agreement.
(6E) Subsection (6C) must be read with –

(a) section 22 of the Financial Services and Markets Act 2000 (regulated activities: power to specify classes of activity and categories of investment);
(b) any order for the time being in force under that section; and
(c) Schedule 2 to that Act.'

(3) In section 43 (advertisements), after subsection (3) insert –

'(3A) An advertisement does not fall within subsection (1)(a) in so far as it is a communication of an invitation or inducement to engage in investment activity within the meaning of section 21 of the Financial Services and Markets Act 2000, other than an exempt generic communication.

(3B) An "exempt generic communication" is a communication to which subsection (1) of section 21 of the Financial Services and Markets Act 2000 does not apply, as a result of an order under subsection (5) of that section, because it does not identify a person as providing an investment or as carrying on an activity to which the communication relates.'

(4) In section 52 (quotations), after subsection (2) insert –

'(3) In this section, "quotation" does not include –

(a) any document which is a communication of an invitation or inducement to engage in investment activity within the meaning of section 21 of the Financial Services and Markets Act 2000; or

(b) any document (other than one falling within paragraph (a)) provided by an authorised person (within the meaning of that Act) in connection with an agreement which would or might be an exempt agreement as a result of section 16(6C).'

(5) In section 53 (duty to display information), after 'land' insert '(other than credit provided under an agreement which is an exempt agreement as a result of section 16(6C))'.

(6) In section 137 (extortionate credit bargains), in subsection (2)(a), after 'any agreement' insert '(other than an agreement which is an exempt agreement as a result of section 16(6C))'.

(7) In section 151 (advertisements for the purposes of ancillary credit business), after subsection (2) insert –

'(2A) An advertisement does not fall within subsection (1) or (2) in so far as it is a communication of an invitation or inducement to engage in investment activity within the meaning of section 21 of the Financial Services and Markets Act 2000, other than an exempt generic communication (as defined in section 43(3B)).'

Consequential amendments of subordinate legislation under the Consumer Credit Act 1974

91. (1) In the Consumer Credit (Advertisements) Regulations 1989, after paragraph (2) of regulation 9 (application of Regulations) insert –

'(3) These Regulations do not apply to any advertisement in so far as it is a communication of an invitation or inducement to engage in investment activity within the meaning of section 21 of the Financial Services and Markets Act 2000, other than an exempt generic communication.

(4) An "exempt generic communication" is a communication to which subsection (1) of section 21 of the Financial Services and Markets Act 2000 does not apply, as a result of an order under subsection (5) of that section, because it does not identify a person as providing an investment or as carrying on an activity to which the communication relates.'

(2) In the Consumer Credit (Content of Quotations) and Consumer Credit (Advertisements) (Amendment) Regulations 1999, in the definition of 'quotation' in paragraph (1) of regulation 2 (interpretation of Part II) –

(a) omit 'or' at the end of sub-paragraph (c); and

(b) after sub-paragraph (d) insert –

'(e) any document which is a communication of an invitation or inducement to engage in investment activity within the meaning of section 21 of the Financial Services and Markets Act 2000; or

(f) any document (other than one falling within sub-paragraph (e)), provided by an authorised person (within the meaning of that Act) in connection with an agreement which would or might be an exempt agreement as a result of section 16(6C) of the Act.'

SCHEDULE 1

Article 3(1)

CONTRACTS OF INSURANCE

PART I   CONTRACTS OF GENERAL INSURANCE

Accident

1.   Contracts of insurance providing fixed pecuniary benefits or benefits in the nature of indemnity (or a combination of both) against risks of the person insured or, in the case of a contract made by virtue of section 140, 140A or 140B of the Local Government Act 1972 (or, in Scotland, section 86(1) of the Local Government (Scotland) Act 1973), a person for whose benefit the contract is made –

   (a) sustaining injury as the result of an accident or of an accident of a specified class; or
   (b) dying as a result of an accident or of an accident of a specified class; or
   (c) becoming incapacitated in consequence of disease or of disease of a specified class,

including contracts relating to industrial injury and occupational disease but excluding contracts falling within paragraph 2 of Part I of, or paragraph IV of Part II of, this Schedule.

Sickness

2.   Contracts of insurance providing fixed pecuniary benefits or benefits in the nature of indemnity (or a combination of both) against risks of loss to the persons insured attributable to sickness or infirmity but excluding contracts falling within paragraph IV of Part II of this Schedule.

Land vehicles

3.   Contracts of insurance against loss of or damage to vehicles used on land, including motor vehicles but excluding railway rolling stock.

Railway rolling stock

4.   Contract of insurance against loss of or damage to railway rolling stock.

Aircraft

5. Contracts of insurance upon aircraft or upon the machinery, tackle, furniture or equipment of aircraft.

Ships

6. Contracts of insurance upon vessels used on the sea or on inland water, or upon the machinery, tackle, furniture or equipment of such vessels.

Goods in transit

7. Contracts of insurance against loss of or damage to merchandise, baggage and all other goods in transit, irrespective of the form of transport.

Fire and natural forces

8. Contracts of insurance against loss of or damage to property (other than property to which paragraphs 3 to 7 relate) due to fire, explosion, storm, natural forces other than storm, nuclear energy or land subsidence.

Damage to property

9. Contracts of insurance against loss of or damage to property (other than property to which paragraphs 3 to 7 relate) due to hail or frost or any other event (such as theft) other than those mentioned in paragraph 8.

Motor vehicle liability

10. Contracts of insurance against damage arising out of or in connection with the use of motor vehicles on land, including third-party risks and carrier's liability.

Aircraft liability

11. Contracts of insurance against damage arising out of or in connection with the use of aircraft, including third-party risks and carrier's liability.

Liability of ships

12. Contracts of insurance against damage arising out of or in connection with the use of vessels on the sea or on inland water, including third-party risks and carrier's liability.

General liability

13. Contracts of insurance against risks of the persons insured incurring liabilities to third parties, the risks in question not being risks to which paragraph 10, 11 or 12 relates.

Credit

14. Contracts of insurance against risks of loss to the persons insured arising from the insolvency of debtors of theirs or from the failure (otherwise than through insolvency) of debtors of theirs to pay their debts when due.

Suretyship

15. (1) Contracts of insurance against the risks of loss to the persons insured arising from their having to perform contracts of guarantee entered into by them.

(2) Fidelity bonds, performance bonds, administration bonds, bail bonds or customs bonds or similar contracts of guarantee, where these are –

(a) effected or carried out by a person not carrying on a banking business;
(b) not effected merely incidentally to some other business carried on by the person effecting them; and
(c) effected in return for the payment of one or more premiums.

Miscellaneous financial loss

16. Contracts of insurance against any of the following risks, namely –

(a) risks of loss to the persons insured attributable to interruptions of the carrying on of business carried on by them or to reduction of the scope of business so carried on;
(b) risks of loss to the persons insured attributable to their incurring unforeseen expense (other than loss such as is covered by contracts falling within paragraph 18);
(c) risks which do not fall within sub-paragraph (a) or (b) and which are not of a kind such that contracts of insurance against them fall within any other provision of this Schedule.

Legal expenses

17. Contracts of insurance against risks of loss to the persons insured attributable to their incurring legal expenses (including costs of litigation).

Assistance

18. Contracts of insurance providing either or both of the following benefits, namely –

(a) assistance (whether in cash or in kind) for persons who get into difficulties while travelling, while away from home or while away from their permanent residence; or
(b) assistance (whether in cash or in kind) for persons who get into difficulties otherwise than as mentioned in sub-paragraph (a).

PART II   CONTRACTS OF LONG-TERM INSURANCE

Life and annuity

I. Contracts of insurance on human life or contracts to pay annuities on human life, but excluding (in each case) contracts within paragraph III.

Marriage and birth

II. Contract of insurance to provide a sum on marriage or on the birth of a child, being contracts expressed to be in effect for a period of more than one year.

Linked long term

III. Contracts of insurance on human life or contracts to pay annuities on human life where the benefits are wholly or partly to be determined by references to the value of, or the income from, property of any description (whether or not specified in the contracts) or by reference to fluctuations in, or in an index of, the value of property of any description (whether or not so specified).

Permanent health

IV. Contracts of insurance providing specified benefits against risks of persons becoming incapacitated in consequence of sustaining injury as a result of an accident or of an accident of a specified class or of sickness or infirmity, being contracts that –

(a) are expressed to be in effect for a period of not less than five years, or until the normal retirement age for the persons concerned, or without limit of time; and

(b) either are not expressed to be terminable by the insurer, or are expressed to be so terminable only in special circumstances mentioned in the contract.

Tontines

V. Tontines.

Capital redemption contracts

VI. Capital redemption contracts, where effected or carried out by a person who does not carry on a banking business, and otherwise carries on a regulated activity of the kind specified by article 10(1) or (2).

Pension fund management

VII.

(a) Pension fund management contracts, and

(b) pension fund management contracts which are combined with contracts of insurance covering either conservation of capital or payment of a minimum interest,

where effected or carried out by a person who does not carry on a banking business, and otherwise carries on a regulated activity of the kind specified by article 10(1) or (2).

Collective insurance etc.

VIII. Contracts of a kind referred to in article 1(2)(e) of the first life insurance directive.

Social insurance

IX. Contracts of a kind referred to in article 1(3) of the first life insurance directive.

SCHEDULE 2

Article 4

ANNEX TO THE INVESTMENT SERVICES DIRECTIVE

'ANNEX

Section A Services

1.

    (a) Reception and transmission, on behalf of investors, of orders in relation to one or more instruments listed in Section B.

    (b) Execution of such orders other than for own account.

2.   Dealing in any of the instruments listed in Section B for own account.

3.   Managing portfolios of investments in accordance with mandates given by investors on a discretionary, client-by-client basis where such portfolios include one or more of the instruments listed in Section B.

4.   Underwriting in respect of issues of any of the instruments listed in Section B and/or the placing of such issues.

Section B Investments

1.

    (a) Transferable securities.

    (b) Units in collective investment undertakings.

2.   Money-market instruments.

3.   Financial-futures contracts, including equivalent cash-settled instruments.

4.   Forward interest-rate agreements (FRAs).

5.   Interest-rate, currency and equity swaps.

6.   Options to acquire or dispose of any instruments falling within this section of the Annex, including equivalent cash-settled instruments. This category includes in particular options on currency and on interest rates.

Section C Non-core services

1.   Safekeeping and administration in relation to one or more of the instruments listed in Section B.

2.   Safe custody services.

3.   Granting credits or loans to an investor to allow him to carry out a transaction in one or more of the instruments listed in Section B, where the firm granting the credit or loan is involved in the transaction.

4.   Advice to undertakings on capital structure, industrial strategy and related matters and advice and service relating to mergers and the purchase of undertakings.

5.   Services related to underwriting.

6. Investment advice concerning one or more of the instruments listed in Section B.

7. Foreign-exchange services where these are connected with the provision of investment services.'

SCHEDULE 3

Article 4

ARTICLE 2.2 OF THE INVESTMENT SERVICES DIRECTIVE

'This Directive shall not apply to:

    (a) insurance undertakings as defined in Article 1 of Directive 73/239/EEC or Article 1 of Directive 79/267/EEC or undertakings carrying on the reinsurance and retrocession activities referred to in Directive 64/225/EEC;

    (b) firms which provide investment services exclusively for their parent undertakings, for their subsidiaries or for other subsidiaries of their parent undertakings;

    (c) persons providing an investment service where that service is provided in an incidental manner in the course of a professional activity and that activity is regulated by legal or regulatory provisions or a code of ethics governing the profession which do not exclude the provision of that service;

    (d) firms that provide investment services consisting exclusively in the administration of employee participation schemes;

    (e) firms that provide investment services that consist in providing both the services referred to in (b) and those referred to in (d);

    (f) the central banks of Member States and other national bodies performing similar functions and other public bodies charged with or intervening in the management of the public debt;

    (g) firms

      – which may not hold clients' funds or securities and which for that reason may not at any time place themselves in debit with their clients, and

      – which may not provide any investment service except the reception and transmission of orders in transferable securities and units in collective investment undertakings, and

      – which in the course of providing that service may transmit orders only to

        (i) investment firms authorised in accordance with this Directive;

        (ii) credit institutions authorised in accordance with Directives 77/80/EEC and 89/646/EEC;

        (iii) branches of investment firms or of credit institutions which are authorised in a third country and which are subject to and comply with prudential rules considered by the competent authorities as at least as stringent as those laid down in this Directive, in Directive 89/646/EEC or in Directive 93/6/EEC;

        (iv) collective investment undertakings authorised under the law of a Member State to market units to the public and to the managers of such undertakings;

(v)   investment companies with fixed capital, as defined in Article 15(4) of Directive 79/91/EEC, the securities of which are listed or dealt in on a regulated market in a Member State;

– the activities of which are governed at national level by rules or by a code of ethics;

(h) collective investment undertakings whether coordinated at Community level or not and the depositaries and managers of such undertakings;

(i) persons whose main business is trading in commodities amongst themselves or with producers or professional users of such products and who provide investment services only for such producers and professional users to the extent necessary for their main business;

(j) firms that provide investment services consisting exclusively in dealing for their own account on financial-futures or options markets or which deal for the accounts of other members of those markets or make prices for them and which are guaranteed by clearing members of the same markets. Responsibility for ensuring the performance of contracts entered into by such firms must be assumed by clearing members of the same markets;

(k) associations set up by Danish pension funds with the sole aim of managing the assets of pension funds that are members of those associations;

(l) "*agenti di cambio*" whose activities and functions are governed by Italian Royal Decree No. 222 of 7 March 1925 and subsequent provisions amending it, and who are authorised to carry on their activities under Article 19 of Italian Law No 1 of 2 January 1991.'

Financial Services and Markets Act 2000 (Financial Promotion) Order 2001, SI 2001/1335

(as amended by the Financial Services and Markets Act 2000 (Financial Promotion) (Amendment) Order 2001, SI 2001/2633 – extracts)

PART III EXEMPTIONS: INTERPRETATION AND APPLICATION

Interpretation: real time communications

7. (1) In this Order, references to a real time communication are references to any communication made in the course of a personal visit, telephone conversation or other interactive dialogue.

(2) A non-real time communication is a communication not falling within paragraph (1).

(3) For the purposes of this Order, non-real time communications include communications made by letter or e-mail or contained in a publication.

(4) For the purposes of this Order, the factors in paragraph (5) are to be treated as indications that a communication is a non-real time communication.

(5) The factors are that –

    (a) the communication is made to or directed at more than one recipient in identical terms (save for details of the recipient's identity);

    (b) the communication is made or directed by way of a system which in the normal course constitutes or creates a record of the communication which is available to the recipient to refer to at a later time;

    (c) the communication is made or directed by way of a system which in the normal course does not enable or require the recipient to respond immediately to it.

Interpretation: solicited and unsolicited real time communications

8. (1) A real time communication is solicited where it is made in the course of a personal visit, telephone call or other interactive dialogue if that call, visit or dialogue –

    (a) was initiated by the recipient of the communication; or

    (b) takes place in response to an express request from the recipient of the communication.

(2) A real time communication is unsolicited where it is made otherwise than as described in paragraph (1).

(3) For the purposes of paragraph (1) –

(a) a person is not to be treated as expressly requesting a call, visit or dialogue –

    (i) because he omits to indicate that he does not wish to receive any or any further visits or calls or to engage in any or any further dialogue;

    (ii) because he agrees to standard terms that state that such visits, calls or dialogue will take place, unless he has signified clearly that, in addition to agreeing to the terms, he is willing for them to take place;

(b) a communication is solicited only if it is clear from all the circumstance when the call, visit or dialogue is initiated or requested that during the course of the visit, call or dialogue communications will be made concerning the kind of controlled activities or investments to which the communications in fact made relate;

(c) it is immaterial whether the express request was made before or after this article comes into force.

(4) Where a real time communication is solicited by a recipient ('R'), it is treated as having also been solicited by any other person to whom it is made at the same time as it is made to R if that other recipient is –

(a) a close relative of R; or

(b) expected to engage in any investment activity jointly with R.

PART IV   EXEMPT COMMUNICATIONS: ALL CONTROLLED ACTIVITIES

Follow up non-real time communications and solicited real time communications

14. (1) Where a person makes or directs a communication ('the first communication') which is exempt from the financial promotion restriction because, in compliance with the requirements of another provision of this Order, it is accompanied by certain indications or contains certain information, then the financial promotion restriction does not apply to any subsequent communication which complies with the requirements of paragraph (2).

(2) The requirements of this paragraph are that the subsequent communication –

(a) is a non-real time communication or a solicited real time communication;

(b) is made by the same person who made the first communication;

(c) is made to a recipient of the first communication;

(d) relates to the same controlled activity and the same controlled investment as the first communication; and

(e) is made within 12 months of the recipient receiving the first communication.

(3) A communication made or directed before this article comes into force is to be treated as a first communication falling within paragraph (1) if it would have fallen within that paragraph had it been made or directed after this article comes into force.

Introductions

15. (1) If the requirements of paragraph (2) are met, the financial promotion restriction does not apply to any real time communication which is made with a view to or for the purposes of introducing the recipient to –

(a) an authorised person who carries on the controlled activity to which the communication relates; or

(b) an exempt person where the communication relates to a controlled activity which is also a regulated activity in relation to which he is an exempt person.

(2) The requirements of this paragraph are that –

(a) the maker of the communication ('A') is not a close relative of, nor a member of the same group as, the person to whom the introduction is, or is to be, made;

(b) A does not receive from any person other than the recipient any pecuniary reward or other advantage arising out of his making the introduction; and

(c) it is clear in all the circumstances that the recipient, in his capacity as an investor, is not seeking and has not sought advice from A as to the merits of the recipient engaging in investment activity (or, if the client has sought such advice, A has declined to give it, but has recommended that the recipient seek such advice from an authorised person).

PART VI   EXEMPT COMMUNICATIONS: CERTAIN CONTROLLED ACTIVITIES

One off non-real time communications and solicited real time communications

28. (1) The financial promotion restriction does not apply to a one off communication which is either a non-real time communication or a solicited real time communication.

(2) If all the conditions set out in paragraph (3) are met in relation to a communication it is to be regarded as a one off communication. In any other case in which one or more of those conditions are met, that fact is to be taken into account in determining whether the communication is a one off communication (but a communication may still be regarded as a one off communication even if none of the conditions in paragraph (3) is met).

(3) The conditions are that –

(a) the communication is made only to one recipient or only to one group of recipients in the expectation that they would engage in any investment activity jointly;

(b) the identity of the product or service to which the communication relates has been determined having regard to the particular circumstances of the recipient;

(c) the communication is not part of an organised marketing campaign.

(4) Notwithstanding article 11, the financial promotion restriction does not apply to a one off solicited real time communication relating to the controlled activity falling within paragraph 10 of Schedule 1 (or within paragraph 11 in so far as it relates to that activity) even if the communication also relates to the controlled activity falling within paragraph 1 of that Schedule.

One off unsolicited real time communications

28A. (1) The financial promotion restriction does not apply to an unsolicited real time communication if the conditions in paragraph (2) are met.

(2) The conditions in this paragraph are that –

   (a) the communication is a one off communication;

   (b) the communicator believes on reasonable grounds that the recipient understands the risks associated with engaging in the investment activity to which the communication relates;

   (c) at the time that the communication is made, the communicator believes on reasonable grounds that the recipient would expect to be contacted by him in relation to the investment activity to which the communication relates.

(3) Paragraphs (2) and (3) of article 28 apply in determining whether a communication is a one off communication for the purposes of this article as they apply for the purposes of article 28.

Certified high net worth individuals

48. (1) If the requirements of paragraph (4) are met, the financial promotion restriction does not apply to any communication which –

   (a) is a non-real time communication or a solicited real time communication;

   (b) is made to a certified high net worth individual;

   (c) does not invite or induce the recipient to engage in investment activity with the person who has signed the certificate of high net worth referred to in paragraph (2)(a);
   and

   (d) relates only to one or more investments falling within paragraph (5).

(2) 'Certified high net worth individual' means any individual –

   (a) who has a current certificate of high net worth; and

   (b) who has signed, within the period of twelve months ending with the day on which the communication is made, a statement in the following terms:

> 'I make this statement so that I am able to receive promotions which are exempt from the restriction on financial promotion in section 21 of the Financial Services and Markets Act 2000. The exemption relates to certified high net worth individuals and I declare that I qualify as such. I accept that the content of promotions and other material that I receive may not have been approved by a person who has been authorised under that Act and that their content may not therefore be subject to controls which would apply if the promotion were made or approved by an authorised person. I am aware that it is open to me to seek advice from someone who is authorised under the Act and who specialises in advising on this kind of investment.'

(3) For the purposes of paragraph (2)(a) a certificate of high net worth –

   (a) must be in writing or other legible form;

   (b) is current if it is signed and dated within the period of twelve months ending with the day on which the communication is made;

   (c) must state that in the opinion of the person signing the certificate, the person to whom the certificate relates either –

     (i) had, during the financial year immediately preceding the date on which the certificate is signed, an annual income of not less than £100,000; or

     (ii) held, throughout the financial year immediately preceding the date on which the certificate is signed, net assets to the value of not less than £250,000;

(d) must be signed by the recipient's accountant or by the recipient's employer.

(4) The requirements of this paragraph are that the communication is accompanied by an indication –

(a) that it is exempt from the general restriction (in section 21 of the Financial Services and Markets Act 2000) on the communication of invitations or inducements to engage in investment activity on the grounds that it is made to a certified high net worth individual;

(b) of the requirements that must be met for a person to qualify as a certified high net worth individual;

(c) that the content of the communication has not been approved by an authorised person and that such approval is, unless this exemption or any other exemption applies, required by section 21 of the Act;

(d) that reliance on the communication for the purpose of engaging in any investment activity may expose the individual to a significant risk of losing all of the property invested;

(e) that any person who is in any doubt about the investment to which the communication relates should consult an authorised person specialising in advising on investments of the kind in question.

(5) An investment falls within this paragraph if –

(a) it is an investment falling within paragraph 14 of Schedule 1 being stock or shares in an unlisted company;

(b) it is an investment falling within paragraph 15 of Schedule 1 being an instrument acknowledging the indebtedness of an unlisted company;

(c) it is an investment falling within paragraph 17 or 18 of Schedule 1 conferring entitlement or rights with respect to investments falling within sub-paragraph (a) or (b);

(d) it comprises units in a collective investment scheme being a scheme which invests wholly or predominantly in investments falling within sub-paragraph (a) or (b);

(e) it is an investment falling within paragraph 21 of Schedule 1 to acquire or dispose of an investment falling within sub-paragraph (a), (b) or (c);

(f) it is an investment falling within paragraph 22 of Schedule 1 being rights under a contract for the sale of an investment falling within sub-paragraph (a), (b) or (c);

(g) it is an investment falling within paragraph 23 of Schedule 1 being a contract relating to, or to fluctuations in the value or price of, an investment falling within sub-paragraph (a), (b) or (c),

provided in each case that it is an investment under the terms of which the investor cannot incur a liability or obligation to pay or contribute more than he commits by way of investment.

(6) In determining an individual's 'net assets' no account shall be taken of –

(a) the property which is his primary residence or any loan secured on that residence;

(b) any rights of his under a qualifying contract of insurance; or

(c) any benefits (in the form of pensions or otherwise) which are payable on the termination of his service or on his death or retirement and to which he is (or his dependants are), or may be, entitled.

High net worth companies, unincorporated associations etc.

49. (1) The financial promotion restriction does not apply to any communication which –

- (a) is made only to recipients whom the person making the communication believes on reasonable grounds to be persons to whom paragraph (2) applies; or
- (b) may reasonably be regarded as directed only at persons to whom paragraph (2) applies.

(2) This paragraph applies to –

- (a) any body corporate which has a called-up share capital or net asset of –
  - (i) in the case of a body corporate which has more than 20 members or which is a subsidiary undertaking of a parent undertaking which has more than 20 members, not less than £500,000;
  - (ii) in the case of any other body corporate, not less than £5 million;
- (b) any unincorporated association or partnership which has net assets of not less than £5 million;
- (c) the trustee of a high value trust;
- (d) any person ('A') whilst acting in the capacity of director, officer or employee of a person ('B') falling within any of sub-paragraphs (a) to (c) where A's responsibilities when acting in that capacity, involve him in B's engaging in investment activity;
- (e) any person to whom the communication may otherwise lawfully be made.

(3) For the purposes of paragraph (1)(b) –

- (a) if all the conditions set out in paragraph (4)(a) to (c) are met, the communication is to be regarded as directed at persons to whom paragraph (2) applies;
- (b) in any other case in which one or more of those conditions are met, that fact is to be taken into account in determining whether the communication is directed at persons to whom paragraph (2) applies (but a communication may still be regarded as so directed even if none of the conditions in paragraph (4) is met).

(4) The conditions are that –

- (a) the communication includes an indication of the description of persons to whom it is directed and an indication of the fact that the controlled investment or controlled activity to which it relates is available only to such persons;
- (b) the communication includes an indication that persons of any other description should not act upon it;
- (c) there are in place proper systems and procedures to prevent recipients other than persons to whom paragraph (2) applies engaging in the investment activity to which the communication relates with the person directing the communication, a close relative of his or a member of the same group.

(5) 'Called-up share capital' has the meaning given in the 1985 Act or in the 1986 Order.

(6) 'High value trust' means a trust where the aggregate value of the cash and investments which form part of the trust's assets (before deducting the amount of its liabilities) –

(a) is £10 million or more; or

(b) has been £10 million or more at any time during the year immediately preceding the date on which the communication in question was first made or directed.

(7) 'Net assets' has the meaning given by section 264 of the 1985 Act or the equivalent provision of the 1986 Order.

Settlors, trustees and personal representatives

53. The financial promotion restriction does not apply to any communication which is made between –

(a) a person when acting as a settlor or grantor of a trust, a trustee or a personal representative; and

(b) a trustee of the trust, a fellow trustee or a fellow personal representative (as the case may be),

if the communication is made for the purposes of the trust or estate.

Beneficiaries of trust, will or intestacy

54. The financial promotion restriction does not apply to any communication which is made –

(a) between a person when acting as a settlor or grantor of a trust, trustee or personal representative and a beneficiary under the trust, will or intestacy; or

(b) between a beneficiary under a trust, will or intestacy and another beneficiary under the same trust, will or intestacy,

if the communication relates to the management or distribution of that trust fund or estate.

Communications by members of professions

55. (1) The financial promotion restriction does not apply to a real time communication (whether solicited or unsolicited) which –

(a) is made by a person ('P') who carries on a regulated activity to which the general prohibition does not apply by virtue of section 327 of the Act; and

(b) is made to a recipient who has, prior to the communication being made, engaged P to provide professional services,

where the controlled activity to which the communication relates is an excluded activity which would be undertaken by P for the purposes of, and incidental to, the provision by him of professional services to or at the request of the recipient.

(2) 'Professional services' has the meaning given in section 327 of the Act.

(3) An 'excluded activity' is an activity to which the general prohibition would apply but for the application of –

(a) section 327 of the Act; or

(b) article 67 of the Regulated Activities Order.

Non-real time communication by members of professions

55A. (1) The financial promotion restriction does not apply to a non-real time communication which is –

(a) made by a person ('P') who carries on Part XX activities; and

(b) limited to what is required or permitted by paragraphs (2) and (3).

(2) The communication must be in the following terms –

'This [firm/company] is not authorised under the Financial Services and Markets Act 2000 but we are able in certain circumstances to offer a limited range of investment services to clients because we are members of [relevant designated professional body]. We can provide these investment services if they are an incidental part of the professional services we have been engaged to provide.'

(3) The communication may in addition set out the Part XX activities which P is able to offer to his clients, provided it is clear that these are the investment services to which the statement in paragraph (2) relates.

(4) 'Part XX activities' means the regulated activities to which the general prohibition does not apply when they are carried on by P by virtue of section 327 of the Act.

B – Rules of practice

Solicitors' Financial Services (Scope) Rules 2001

These rules, dated [the date of the Master of the Rolls' concurrence], are made by the Council of the Law Society with the concurrence of the Master of the Rolls under section 31 of the Solicitors Act 1974, section 9 of the Administration of Justice Act 1985 and for the purposes of section 332 of the Financial Services and Markets Act 2000, regulating the practices of:

solicitors and recognised bodies in any part of the world,
registered European lawyers in any part of the United Kingdom, and
registered foreign lawyers in England and Wales,

in carrying out 'regulated activities' in, into or from the United Kingdom.

1. Purpose

1. The Law Society is a designated professional body under Part XX of *the Act*, and *firms* may therefore carry on certain *regulated activities* without being regulated by the *FSA*, if they can meet the conditions specified in section 327 of *the Act*. As a designated professional body the Law Society is required to make rules governing the carrying on by *firms* of *regulated* activities. The purpose of these rules is to set out the scope of the *regulated activities* which may be undertaken by *firms* which are not regulated by the *FSA*.
2. These rules:

   - prohibit *firms* which are not regulated by the *FSA* from carrying on certain *regulated activities*;
   - set out the basic conditions which those *firms* must satisfy when carrying on any *regulated activities*;
   - set out other restrictions on *regulated activities* carried on by those *firms*.

2. Application

These rules apply only to *firms* which are not regulated by the *FSA*.

3. Prohibited activities

A *firm* must not carry on, or agree to carry on, any of the following activities:

   (a) *market making* in *investments*;
   (b) *buying*, selling, subscribing for or underwriting *investments* as principal where the *firm*:

      i   holds itself out as engaging in the business of *buying* such *investments* with a view to selling them;

      ii   holds itself out as engaging in the business of underwriting *investments* of the kind to which the *transaction* relates; or

      iii   regularly solicits members of the public with the purpose of inducing them, as principals or agents, to enter into *transactions* and the *transaction* is entered into as a result of the *firm* having solicited members of the public in that manner.

(c) *buying* or selling *investments* with a view to stabilising or maintaining the market price of the *investments*;

(d) acting as a *stakeholder pension scheme* manager;

(e) entering into a *broker funds arrangement*;

(f) effecting and carrying out *contracts of insurance* as principal;

(g) establishing, operating or winding up a *collective investment scheme*;

(h) establishing, operating or winding up a *stakeholder pension scheme*;

(i) managing the underwriting capacity of a Lloyd's syndicate as a managing agent at Lloyd's;

(j) advising a person to become a member of a particular Lloyd's syndicate;

(k) entering as provider into a *funeral plan contract*; or

(l) entering into a *regulated mortgage contract* as lender or administering a *regulated mortgage contract*.

4. Basic conditions

A *firm* which carries on any *regulated activities* must ensure that:

(a) the activities arise out of, or are complementary to, the provision of a particular *professional service* to a particular *client*;

(b) the manner of the provision by the *firm* of any service in the course of carrying on the activities is incidental to the provision by the *firm* of *professional services*;

(c) the *firm* accounts to the *client* for any pecuniary reward or other advantage which the *firm* receives from a third party;

(d) the activities are not of a description, nor do they relate to an investment of a description, specified in any order made by the Treasury under section 327(6) of *the Act*;

(e) the *firm* does not carry on, or hold itself out as carrying on, a *regulated activity* other than one which is allowed by these rules or one in relation to which the *firm* is an *exempt person*;

(f) there is not in force any order or direction of the *FSA* under sections 328 or 329 of *the Act* which prevents the *firm* from carrying on the activities; and

(g) the activities are not otherwise prohibited by these rules.

5. Other restrictions

(1) Packaged products (except personal pension schemes)

A *firm* must not recommend, or make arrangements for, a *client* to *buy* a *packaged product* **except where**:

(a) recommending, or arranging for, a *client* to *buy* a *packaged product* by means of an assignment;

(b) the arrangements are made as a result of a *firm* managing assets within the exception to rule 5(4) below; or

(c) arranging a *transaction* for a *client* where the *firm* assumes on reasonable grounds that the *client* is not relying on the *firm* as to the merits or suitability of that *transaction*.

(2) Personal pension schemes

(a) A firm must not recommend a *client* to *buy* or dispose of any rights or interests in a *personal pension scheme*.

(b) A *firm* must not make arrangements for a *client* to *buy* any rights or interests in a *personal pension scheme* **except where** the *firm* assumes on reasonable grounds that the *client* is not relying on the *firm* as to the merits or suitability of that *transaction* but this exception does not apply where the *transaction* involves:

  i   a *pension transfer*; or
  ii   an *opt-out*.

(3) Securities and contractually based investments (except packaged products)

(a) A firm must not recommend a *client* to *buy* or subscribe for a *security* or a *contractually based investment* where the *transaction* would be made:

  i   with a person acting in the course of carrying on the business of *buying*, selling, subscribing for or underwriting the *investment*, whether as principal or agent;
  ii   on an investment exchange or any other market to which that *investment* is admitted for dealing; or
  iii in response to an invitation to subscribe for an *investment* which is, or is to be, admitted for dealing on an investment exchange or any other market.

(b) This rule does not apply where the *client* is:

  i   not an individual;
  ii   an individual who acts in connection with the carrying on of a business of any kind by himself or by an undertaking of which the *client* is, or would become as a result of the *transaction* to which the recommendation relates, a *controller*; or
  iii acting in his capacity as a trustee of an occupational pension scheme.

(4) Discretionary management

A *firm* must not manage *assets* belonging to another person in circumstances which involve the exercise of discretion **except where** the *firm* or a *partner*, *officer* or *employee* of the *firm* is a trustee, personal representative, donee of a power of attorney or receiver appointed by the Court of Protection, and either:

(a) all routine or day to day decisions, so far as relating to that activity, are taken by an *authorised person* with permission to carry on that activity or an *exempt person*; or

(b) any decision to enter into a transaction, which involves *buying* or subscribing for an *investment*, is undertaken in accordance with the advice of an *authorised person* with permission to give advice in relation to such an activity or an *exempt person*.

(5) Corporate finance

A *firm* must not act as any of the following:

(a) sponsor to an issue in respect of securities to be admitted for dealing on the London Stock Exchange; or
(b) nominated adviser to an issue in respect of securities to be admitted for dealing on the Alternative Investment Market of the London Stock Exchange.

6. Effect of a breach of these rules

(1) The Law Society may exercise its statutory powers in respect of any *firm* which breaches these rules.
(2) In determining whether or not there has been a breach of these rules the Law Society will take account of whether the *firm* has given due regard to the guidance issued by the Law Society on how to determine whether *regulated activities* are carried on in accordance with these rules.
(3) A *firm* which breaches these rules may:

    (a) be committing a criminal offence under section 23 of *the Act*;
    (b) be made subject to an order by the *FSA* under section 329 of *the Act* which could prevent the *firm* from carrying on any *regulated activities*.

7. Repeal and commencement

(1) These rules repeal the Solicitors' Investment Business Rules 1995.
(2) These rules come into force on [the date of the coming into force of section 19 of *the Act*].

8. Interpretation

(1) In these rules unless the context otherwise requires:

the Act means the Financial Services and Markets Act 2000;
AIM means The Alternative Investment Market of the London Stock Exchange;
asset means an *investment*;
authorised person has the meaning given in section 31 of *the Act*;
broker funds arrangement means an arrangement between a *firm* and a *life office* (or operator of a *regulated collective investment scheme*) under which the *life office* (or operator of the *regulated collective investment scheme*) agrees to establish a separate fund whose composition may be determined by instructions from the *firm* and in which it is possible for more than one *client* to invest;
buy or *buying* includes acquiring for valuable consideration;
client, in relation to any *regulated activities* carried on by a *firm* for a trust or the estate of a deceased person (including a controlled trust), means the trustees or personal representatives in their capacity as such and not any person who is a beneficiary under the trust or interested in the estate;
collective investment scheme means (in accordance with section 235 of *the Act* (Collective investment schemes)) any arrangements with respect to property

of any description, including money, the purpose or effect of which is to enable persons taking part in the arrangements (whether by becoming owners of the property or any part of it or otherwise) to participate in or receive profits or income arising from the acquisition, holding, management or disposal of the property or sums paid out of such profits or income, which are not excluded by the Financial Services and Markets Act (Collective Investment Schemes) Order 2001 (SI 2001/1062);

contract of insurance has the meaning given by article 3(1) of the *Regulated Activities Order*;

contractually based investment has the meaning given by article 3(1) of the *Regulated Activities Order* but does not include an investment which falls within the definition of a *packaged product*;

controller has the meaning given in section 422 of *the Act*;

employee means an individual who is employed in connection with the *firm's regulated activities* under a contract of service or under a contract for services such that he or she is held out as an employee or consultant of the *firm*;

exempt person means a person who is exempt from the *general prohibition* as a result of an exemption order made under section 38(1) or as a result of section 39(1) or 285(2) or (3) of *the Act* and who, in engaging in the activity in question, is acting in the course of business in respect of which that person is exempt;

firm means:

(a) a sole solicitor or *registered European lawyer*;

(b) a lawyers' *partnership* which includes at least one solicitor, *registered European lawyer* or *recognised body*, and which is permitted by rule 7(6)(a)–(c) of the Solicitors' Practice Rules 1990; or

(c) a *recognised body*,

FSA means the Financial Services Authority;

funeral plan contract has the meaning given in article 59 of the *Regulated Activities Order*;

general prohibition has the meaning given in section 19(2) of *the Act*;

individual pension contract means a *pension policy* or *pension contract* under which contributions are paid to:

(a) a personal pension scheme approved under section 630 of the Income and Corporation Taxes Act 1988, whose sole purpose is the provision of annuities or lump sums under arrangements made by individuals in accordance with the scheme;

(b) a retirement benefits scheme approved under section 591(2)(g) of the Income and Corporation Taxes Act 1988, for the provision of relevant benefits by means of an annuity contract made with an insurance company of the employee's choice;

Individual Savings Account means an account which is a scheme of investment satisfying the conditions prescribed in the *Individual Savings Account* Regulations 1998 (S.I. 1998/1870);

investment means any of the investments specified in Part III of the *Regulated Activities Order*;

investment trust means a closed-ended company which is listed in the United Kingdom or another member state and:

(a) is approved by the Inland Revenue under section 842 of the Income and Corporation Taxes Act 1988 (or, in the case of a newly formed company, has declared its intention to conduct its affairs so as to obtain approval); or

(b) is resident in another member state and would qualify for approval if resident and listed in the United Kingdom;

investment trust savings scheme means a dedicated service for investment in the securities of one or more *investment trusts* within a particular marketing group (and references to an *investment trust savings scheme* include references to securities to be acquired through that scheme);

ISA means an *Individual Savings Account*;

life office means a person with permission to effect or carry out *long term insurance contracts*;

life policy means a *long term insurance contract* other than a *pure protection contract* or a reinsurance contract, but including a *pension policy*;

long term insurance contract has the meaning given in Part II of Schedule 1 to the *Regulated Activities Order*;

market making means where a *firm* holds itself out as willing, as principal, to buy, sell or subscribe for *investments* of the kind to which the *transaction* relates at prices determined by the *firm* generally and continuously rather than in respect of each particular *transaction*;

occupational pension scheme means any scheme or arrangement which is comprised in one or more documents or agreements and which has, or is capable of having, effect in relation to one or more descriptions or categories of employment so as to provide benefits, in the form of pensions or otherwise, payable on termination of service, or on death or retirement, to or in respect of earners with qualifying service in an employment of any such description or category;

officer means a director or secretary of a *recognised body* which is a company, or a member of a *recognised body* which is a limited liability partnership;

opt-out means a *transaction* resulting from a decision by an individual to opt out of or decline to join a final salary or money-purchase *occupational pension scheme* of which he or she is a current member, or which he or she is, or at the end of a waiting period will become, eligible to join, in favour of an *individual pension contract* or contracts;

packaged product means a *life policy*, a unit or share in a *regulated collective investment scheme,* or an *investment trust savings scheme* whether or not held within an *ISA* or *PEP*, or a *stakeholder pension scheme*;

partner and *partnership* refer only to an unincorporated *firm* and not to a *firm* which is incorporated as a limited liability partnership;

pension contract means a right to benefits obtained by the making of contributions to an *occupational pension scheme* or to *a personal pension scheme,* where the contributions are paid to a *regulated collective investment scheme*;

pension policy means a right to benefits obtained by the making of contributions to an *occupational pension scheme* or to *a personal pension scheme,* where the contributions are paid to a *life office*;

pension transfer means a *transaction* resulting from a decision by an individual to transfer deferred benefits from a final salary *occupational pension scheme,* or from a money-purchase *occupational pension scheme,* in favour of an *individual pension contract* or contracts;

PEP means a personal equity plan within the Personal Equity Plan Regulations 1989;

personal pension scheme means a scheme of investment in accordance with section 630 of the Income and Corporation Taxes Act 1988;

245

professional services means services provided by a *firm* in the course of its practice and which do not constitute carrying on a *regulated activity*;

pure protection contract means a *long term insurance contract*:

(a) under which the benefits are payable only in respect of death or of incapacity due to injury, sickness or infirmity:

(b) which provides that benefits are payable on death (other than a death due to accident) only where the death occurs within ten years of the date on which the life of the *person* in question was first insured under the contract, or where the death occurs before that person attains a specified age not exceeding 70 years;

(c) which has no surrender value or the consideration consists of a single premium and the surrender value does not exceed that premium; and

(d) which makes no provision for its conversion or extension in a manner which would result in its ceasing to comply with (a), (b) and (c);

recognised body means a body corporate recognised by the Council under the Solicitors' Incorporated Practice Rules 2001;

registered European lawyer means a person whose name is on the register of European lawyers maintained by the Law Society under regulation 15 of the European Communities (Lawyer's Practice) Regulations 2000;

Regulated Activities Order means the Financial Services and Markets Act 2000 (Regulated Activities) Order 2001;

regulated activity means an activity which is specified in the *Regulated Activities Order*;

regulated collective investment scheme means:

(a) an investment company with variable capital;

(b) an authorised unit trust scheme as defined in section 237(3) of *the Act*; or

(c) a scheme recognised under sections 264, 270 or 272 of *the Act*;

regulated mortgage contract has the meaning given by article 61(3) of the *Regulated Activities Order*;

security has the meaning given by article 3(1) of the *Regulated Activities Order* but does not include an *investment* which falls within the definition of a *packaged product*;

stakeholder pension scheme means a scheme established in accordance with Part I of the Welfare and Pensions Reform Act 1999 and the Stakeholder Pension Scheme Regulations 2000; and

transaction means the purchase, sale, subscription or underwriting of a particular *investment*.

(2) In these rules references to statutes, rules, codes or regulations, statements or principles etc. other than these rules include any modification or replacement thereof.

(3) As the context requires, other words and expressions shall have the meanings assigned to them by the Interpretation Act 1978, *the Act* and the Solicitors Act 1974.

(4) References in these rules to activities carried on by a *firm* include activities carried on by an individual as a principal, *officer* or *employee* of the *firm*.

Solicitors' Financial Services (Conduct of Business) Rules 2001

These rules, dated [the date of the Master of the Rolls' concurrence], are made by the Council of the Law Society with the concurrence of the Master of the Rolls under section 31 of the Solicitors Act 1974 and section 9 of the Administration of Justice Act 1985, regulating the practices of:

- *solicitors and recognised bodies in any part of the world,*
- *registered European lawyers in any part of the United Kingdom, and*
- *registered foreign lawyers in England and Wales,*

in carrying out 'regulated activities' in, into or from the United Kingdom.

1. Purpose

(1) The Law Society is a designated professional body under Part XX *of the Act*, and *firms* may therefore carry on certain regulated activities without being regulated by the FSA.

(2) The Solicitors' Financial Services (Scope) Rules [2001] set out the scope of the *regulated activities* which may be undertaken by *firms* which are not regulated by the FSA. These rules regulate the way in which *firms* carry on such exempt *regulated activities*.

2. Application

Apart from rule 3 (status disclosure), these rules apply to:

(a) *firms* which are not regulated by the FSA; and
(b) *firms* which are regulated by the FSA

but these rules only apply to such firms in respect of their *non-mainstream regulated activities*.

3. Status disclosure

(1) This rule applies only to *firms* which are not regulated by the FSA.

(2) A *firm* shall give the *client* the following information in writing before the *firm* provides a service which includes the carrying on of a *regulated activity*:

(a) a statement that the firm is not authorised by the FSA;
(b) the nature of the regulated activities carried on by the firm, and the fact that they are limited in scope;
(c) a statement that the firm is regulated by the Law Society; and

(d) a statement explaining that complaints and redress mechanisms are provided through Law Society regulation.

Guidance note

1. There is no prescribed form in which this information must be given to the client. It may be included in the firm's client care letter or in a separate letter.
2. A statement on the firm's stationery to the effect that the firm is regulated by the Law Society would assist in meeting the requirements of this rule.

4. Execution of transactions

A *firm* shall ensure that where it has agreed or decided in its discretion to effect a *transaction*, it shall do so as soon as possible, unless it reasonably believes that it is in the *client's* best interests not to do so.

Guidance note

1. Rule 1 of the Solicitors' Practice Rules 1990 emphasises a solicitor's duty to act in the best interests of the client. Accordingly, in cases where there is any doubt on the point, firms should ensure that transactions are effected on the best terms reasonably available.
2. Rule 15 of the Solicitors' Practice Rules 1990 provides that clients should be kept fully informed of transactions effected on their behalf, unless clients have indicated to the contrary.

5. Records of transactions

(1) Where a *firm* receives instructions from a *client* to effect a *transaction*, or makes a decision to effect a *transaction* in its discretion, it shall keep a record of:

(a) the name of the *client*;
(b) the terms of the instructions or decision; and
(c) in the case of instructions, the date when they were received.

(2) Where a *firm* gives instructions to another person to effect a *transaction*, it shall keep a record of:

(a) the name of the *client;*
(b) the terms of the instructions;
(c) the date when the instructions were given; and
(d) the name of the other person instructed.

Guidance note

It is not necessary for the firm to make a separate record. Normal file notes or letters on the file will meet the requirements of this rule provided that they include the appropriate information. If instructions are given or received over the telephone, an appropriate attendance note would satisfy this rule.

6. Record of commissions

Where a *firm* receives commission which is attributable to *regulated activities* carried on by the *firm*, it shall keep a record of:

(a) the amount of the commission; and

(b) how the firm has accounted to the client.

Guidance note

1. Any commission received by the firm has to be dealt with in accordance with Rule 10 of the Solicitors' Practice Rules 1990. However, firms should bear in mind that in the case of commissions attributable to regulated activities, the exception for commissions received of £20 or less, does not apply because it is overridden by the condition in section 327(3) of the Act.
2. The record could be a letter or bill of costs provided the information is clear.

7. Safekeeping of clients' investments

(1) Where a *firm* undertakes the *regulated* activity of safeguarding and administering investments, the *firm* must operate appropriate systems, including the keeping of appropriate records, which provide for the safekeeping of *assets* entrusted to the *firm* by *clients* and others.

(2) Where such assets are passed to a third party:

(a) an acknowledgement of receipt of the property should be obtained; and

(b) if they have been passed to a third party on the *client's* instructions, such instructions should be obtained in writing.

8. Packaged products – execution only business

If a *firm* arranges for a client on an *execution only* basis any *transaction* involving a *packaged product*, the *firm* shall send the *client* written confirmation to the effect that:

(a) the *client* had not sought and was not given any advice from the *firm* in connection with the transaction; or

(b) the *client* was given advice from the *firm* in connection with that *transaction* but nevertheless persisted in wishing the *transaction* to be effected;

and in either case the *transaction* is effected on the *client's* explicit instructions.

9. Retention of records

Each record made under these rules shall be kept for at least six years.

Guidance note

The six years shall run from the date on which the relevant record has been made.

10. Waivers

(1) In any particular case or cases the Council shall have power to waive in writing any of the provisions of these rules, but shall not do so unless it appears that:

(a) compliance with them would be unduly burdensome having regard to the benefit which compliance would confer on investors; and

(b) the exercise of the power would not result in any undue risk to investors.

(2) The Council shall have power to revoke any waiver.

11. Commencement

These rules come into force on [the date of the coming into force of section 19 of the Act].

12. Interpretation

(1) The interpretation of these rules is governed by rule 7(1)–(4) of the Solicitors' Financial Services (Scope) Rules 2001.

(2) In these rules:

execution only (transaction) means a *transaction* which is effected by a *firm* for a *client* where the *firm* assumes on reasonable grounds that the *client* is not relying on the *firm* as to the merits or suitability of that *transaction*;

Guidance note

1. Whether a transaction is 'execution only' will depend on the existing relationship between the client and the firm and the circumstances surrounding that transaction. Generally, a transaction will be 'execution only' if the client instructs the firm to effect it without having received advice from the firm. Even though this is the case, however, the transaction may still not qualify as 'execution only' because, in view of the relationship, the client may reasonably expect the firm to indicate if the transaction is inappropriate. In any event, a firm may be negligent (and possibly in breach of Rule 1 of the Solicitors' Practice Rules 1990) if it fails to advise on the appropriateness or otherwise.
2. A transaction will also be 'execution only' if the firm has advised the client that the transaction is unsuitable, but the client persists in wishing the transaction to be carried out. In those circumstances it is good practice (and in some cases a requirement) for the firm to confirm in writing that its advice has not been accepted, and that the transaction is being effected on an 'execution only' basis.
3. Where the transaction involves a packaged product, there is a specific requirement to confirm in writing the 'execution only' nature of a transaction (see Rule 8 above).

non-mainstream regulated activity means a regulated activity of a *firm* regulated by the FSA in relation to which the conditions in the Professional Firms Sourcebook (5.2.1R) are satisfied.

(3) These rules are to be interpreted in the light of the guidance notes.

C – Guidance

APPENDIX C1

Professional firms – the need for authorisation under the Financial Services and Markets Act 2000

FSA Guidance – August 2001 (extracts)

1.1 Introduction

1.1.1 The Financial Services Authority ('the *FSA*') issues this guidance under the powers granted to it in section 157 of the Financial Services and Markets Act 2000 ('the *Act*'). The content of the guidance has no special authority under the *Act*. The interpretation of the Act is ultimately a matter for the courts to determine and the views expressed by the *FSA* in this guidance will not bind a court of law. Nevertheless, any *person* acting in line with the guidance may have recourse to the defence provided in sections 23(3) (Contravention of the general prohibition) and 25(2) (Contravention of section 21) of the *Act* that he took all reasonable precautions and exercised all due diligence to avoid committing an offence. Furthermore, acting in line with the guidance is likely to be a factor (see sections 28(3) (Agreements made unenforceable by section 26 or 27) and 30(4) (Enforceability of agreements resulting from unlawful communications) of the *Act*) which the courts would wish to take into account in considering whether it would be just and equitable to allow agreements, which were it not for the court's discretion would otherwise be unenforceable, to be enforced.

1.2 Purpose

1.2.1 The purpose of the guidance is to help *professional firms* to determine whether they will require *authorisation* under the *Act* at the date of entry into force of the main provisions of the *Act* – in essence the *general prohibition* in section 19 (The general prohibition). This date has been set at 1 December 2001.

1.3 Summary

1.3.1 The guidance:

(1) outlines the scope of the *Act* and changes made from the scope of the Financial Services Act 1986 ('the FS Act') which are likely to be of particular relevance to professional firms (see 1.6 and 1.12);

(2) describes the operation and scope of the exemption régime under Part XX of the *Act* ('the Part XX exemption') (see 1.8); and

(3) outlines the restrictions on the making of *financial promotions* (see 1.26).

1.4   Background

1.4.1 Approximately 15,000 *professional firms* currently have authorisation from their professional body under the FS Act. A considerable number of these firms are authorised primarily as a precaution against the possibility that they may conduct activities which constitute investment business. The *FSA* understands that, of these firms, some 13,000 conduct only investment business which arises out of their professional business.

1.4.2 The existing recognised professional body régime is not to be continued under the *Act*. However, the Government has determined that only those *professional firms* whose activities are not incidental to their professional business or who are providing services which call for *FSA* regulation for reasons of investor protection or market integrity (for example, pension transfer business) should have to seek *authorisation* from the *FSA*.

1.4.3 To achieve this the Government has:

(1)   clarified the definitions of certain activities carried over from the FS Act;
(2)   extended the scope of certain exclusions currently available under the FS Act and provided new exclusions; and
(3)   created a special exemption régime for incidental business.

1.5   Application of the Act to professional firms

1.5.1 Under section 19 of the *Act* (The general prohibition) no *person* may carry on or purport to carry on a *regulated activity* in the *UK* unless he is authorised or exempt. The meaning of *regulated activity* is in the Financial Services and Markets Act 2000 (Regulated Activities) Order 2001 ('the *Regulated Activities Order*').

1.5.2 Before deciding whether they need authorisation *professional firms* should take account of all aspects of their business and the regulatory implications for them of becoming authorised or of their being unauthorised and, if necessary, relying on the Part XX exemption. More particularly, to determine whether *authorisation* is needed a *professional firm* (whether a company, partnership or sole trader) will need to consider the following questions:

(1)   will the firm be able to conduct all of its financial services activities, which would otherwise be *regulated activities*, within the terms of the exclusions in Part II of the *Regulated Activities Order*?
(2)   if not, are the firm's activities subject to any of the exclusions contained in Part II of the *Regulated Activities Order*?
(3)   if not, will the firm satisfy the terms of the Part XX exemption in relation to all of its activities which are *regulated activities*?

If the answer to (3) is no then the firm will need *authorisation* (or another form of exemption).

1.5.3 *Professional firms* will also wish to take account of the implications for their activities, if they intend to operate without *authorisation*, of the restrictions placed on the making of *financial promotions* in section 21 of the *Act* (Restrictions on financial promotion) (see 1.26).

1.6 Regulated activities

1.6.1 *Regulated activities* under Part II of the *Regulated Activities Order* are generally expressed as relating to particular investments or groups of investments. The exceptions to this concern *collective investment schemes* and stakeholder pension schemes where *regulated activities* connected with such schemes are expressed as relating to property of any kind. The activities that are regulated are listed below under the investments (or property) to which they relate. The *Regulated Activities Order* should be consulted to determine the precise meaning of the provisions mentioned.

(1) Deposits:

    (a) accepting deposits (article 5 of the *Regulated Activities Order*).

(2) Contracts of insurance:

    (a) effecting contracts of insurance as principal (article 10);
    (b) carrying out contracts of insurance as principal (article 10);
    (c) arranging deals in contracts of insurance written at Lloyd's (applies only to the Society of Lloyd's itself) (article 58).

(3) *Securities* (for example, shares, debentures, government and public securities, warrants, certificates representing certain securities, units in collective investment schemes and rights to or interests in any of these) and *contractually based investments* (for example, futures, options, contracts for differences, most long-term insurance contracts other than pure risk only contracts and rights to or interests in any of these as well as (with effect from 1 January 2002) funeral plan contracts and rights to or interests in such contracts):

    (a) dealing as principal (article 14) (does not apply to funeral plan contracts);
    (b) dealing as agents (article 21) (does not apply to funeral plan contracts);
    (c) arranging deals in investments (article 25);
    (d) managing investments (article 37);
    (e) safeguarding and administering investments (article 40);
    (f) advising on investments (article 53).

(4) *Securities* only:

    (a) sending (or causing the sending of) dematerialised instructions (article 45).

(5) Any property:

    (a) establishing, operating or winding up a collective investment scheme (article 51);
    (b) acting as trustee of an authorised unit trust scheme (article 51);
    (c) acting as depository or sole director of an *open-ended investment company* (article 51);
    (d) establishing, operating or winding up a stakeholder pension scheme (article 52).

(6) Lloyd's syndicate capacity and syndicate membership:

    (a) arranging deals in syndicate capacity or syndicate membership (article 25);
    (b) advising an underwriting member of Lloyd's to become, or to continue or cease to be, a member of a particular syndicate (article 56);
    (c) managing the underwriting capacity of a Lloyd's syndicate as a managing agent at Lloyd's (article 57).

(7) (With effect from 1 January 2002) rights under a funeral plan contract:

    (a) entering as provider into a funeral plan contract (article 59);

    (b) the regulated activities referred to in 1.6.1 G(3)(c) to (f).

(8) (With effect from 1 September 2002) rights under a regulated mortgage contract:

    (a) entering into a regulated mortgage contract as lender (article 61);

    (b) administering a regulated mortgage contract (article 61).

1.6.2 In addition to actually carrying out these activities, entering into agreements to do most of them is itself a *regulated activity* (article 64 of the *Regulated Activities Order*), even if the contracted activities are delegated to a third party.

1.6.3 The *regulated activities* represent, for the most part, the activities currently regulated under the FS Act, the Banking Act 1987 ('the BA') and the Insurance Companies Act 1982 ('the ICA') as well as certain activities which have not been subject to statutory regulation before (see 1.21.1 G). Certain types of investment business under the FS Act have been amended to clarify their scope. These changes are referred to in 1.13.

1.7   Exclusions

1.7.1 In general terms, the exclusions in Part II of the *Regulated Activities Order* carry forward the existing exclusions under Parts III and IV of Schedule 1 to the FS Act together with similar provisions under the BA and the ICA. Certain of these exclusions have been amended so as to extend their scope and some new ones have been added. Those of particular relevance to *professional firms* are referred to in greater detail in 1.14 to 1.20.

1.8   The Part XX exemption régime

1.8.1 The Government introduced the exemption régime within Part XX of the Act in response to concerns about 'precautionary authorisation' of *professional firms* and about dual regulation of those firms who provide financial services only as part of their professional services. It is designed to exclude *professional firms* that are not carrying on mainstream financial services activities from the requirement to be authorised by the *FSA*.

1.8.2 Under section 326 of the Act (Designation of professional bodies) the Treasury may designate a *professional body* which meets certain conditions. These include that it must have rules governing the carrying on by its members of *regulated activities* which are subject to the exemption. The following *professional bodies* have been designated:

(1) the Law Society of England and Wales;
(2) the Law Society of Scotland;
(3) the Law Society of Northern Ireland;
(4) the Institute of Chartered Accountants in England and Wales;
(5) the Institute of Chartered Accountants of Scotland;
(6) the Institute of Chartered Accountants in Ireland;
(7) the Association of Chartered Certified Accountants; and
(8) the Institute of Actuaries.

1.8.3 Section 327 of the *Act* (Exemption from the general prohibition) exempts from the need for *authorisation* a *person* who is a member of a profession or controlled or managed by one or more members subject to the following conditions:

(1) there must not be a direction or order made by the *FSA* under sections 328 or 329 of the *Act* which has the effect of disapplying section 327 of the *Act* in relation to that person;

(2) the *person* must not receive any pecuniary reward or other advantage in connection with the carrying on of *regulated activities* other than from his client or for which he accounts to his client (see 1.9 for guidance on the meaning of 'accounts to his client');

(3) any *regulated activities* carried on by him must be incidental to the provision by him of professional services (see 1.10 for guidance on the meaning of 'incidental');

(4) the *person* must not carry on, or hold himself out as carrying on, a *regulated activity* other than:

(a) one which the rules of his *designated professional body* allow him to carry on; or

(b) for which he is otherwise an *exempt person* (for example, an *appointed representative* or an insolvency practitioner – see 1.24);

(5) the activities must not be of a description, or relate to an investment of a description, specified in an order made by the Treasury under section 327(6) of the *Act* (i.e. the Financial Services and Markets Act 2000 (Professions) (Non-Exempt Activities) Order 2001 – 'the *Non-Exempt Activities Order*' – see 1.11);

(6) the *regulated activities* (other than any in respect of which he is otherwise exempt) must be the only ones he carries on (for example, he cannot use the Part XX exemption if he is an *authorised person* or if he is otherwise carrying on *regulated activities* for which he should be authorised).

1.9 Meaning of 'accounts to his client' in section 327(3) of the Act

1.9.1 The *FSA* considers that, in order for a *professional firm* to be accounting to his client for the purposes of section 327(3) of the *Act*, the firm must treat any commission or other pecuniary benefit received from third parties and which results from *regulated activities* carried on by the firm, as held to the order of the client. A *professional firm* will not be accounting to his client simply by telling the client that the firm will receive commission. Unless the client agrees to the firm keeping the commission it belongs to the client and must be paid to the client. There is no de minimis below which the *professional firm* may retain the sum. In the *FSA*'s opinion, the condition would be satisfied by the *professional firm* paying over to the client any third party payment it receives. Otherwise, it would be satisfied by the *professional firm* informing the client of the sum and that he has the right to require the firm to pay the sum concerned to the client, thus allowing the sum to be used to offset fees due from the client in respect of professional services provided to him or in recognition of other services provided by the firm. However, it does not permit a *professional firm* to retain third party payments by seeking its client's agreement through standard terms and conditions. Similarly, a mere notification to the client that a particular sum has been received coupled with the *professional firm*'s request to retain it does not satisfy the condition.

1.10   Meaning of 'incidental' in section 327(4) of the Act

1.10.1 The *FSA* considers that to satisfy the condition in section 327(4) of the *Act regulated activities* cannot be a major part of the practice of the firm. The *FSA* also considers the following further factors to be among those that are relevant:

    (1) the scale of *regulated activity* in proportion to other professional services provided;

    (2) whether and to what extent services that are *regulated activities* are held out as separate services; and

    (3) the impression given of how the firm provides *regulated activities*, for example, through its advertising or other promotions of its services.

1.10.2 In the *FSA*'s opinion, one consequence of this is that the *professional firm* cannot provide services which are *regulated activities* if they amount to a separate business conducted in isolation from the provision of professional services. This does not, however, preclude the firm operating its professional business in a way which involves separate teams or departments one of which handles the *regulated activities*.

1.10.3 For the purpose of section 327(4), professional services are services which do not constitute carrying on a *regulated activity*, and the provision of which is supervised and regulated by a *designated professional body*.

1.11   Designated professional body rules: the Non-Exempt Activities Order

1.11.1 To determine whether he is able to carry on a particular *regulated activity* under the Part XX exemption, a *person* must pay due regard to both the rules of his *designated professional body* and the *Non-Exempt Activities Order* and the interaction between them.

1.11.2 The rules of a *person's designated professional body* must be designed to ensure that, in providing a professional service to a client, the member carries on only *regulated activities* which arise out of, or are complementary to, his providing that service to that client.

1.11.3 Each *designated professional body* has its own rules for this purpose and it would not be appropriate for the *FSA* to attempt to summarise the effect of each *designated professional body*'s rules in this guidance. It is a matter for each *designated professional body* to issue guidance on its rules and the *FSA* understands that they have done or propose to do so.

1.11.4 The *Non-Exempt Activities Order* precludes the Part XX exemption from applying to certain *regulated activities*. Some of these activities are precluded entirely, others in part.

1.11.5 The activities precluded entirely are:

    (1) accepting deposits (article 5 of the *Regulated Activities Order*);

    (2) effecting and carrying out contracts of insurance (article 10 of the *Regulated Activities Order*);

    (3) dealing in investments as principal (article 14 of the *Regulated Activities Order*);

    (4) establishing, operating and winding up a *collective investment scheme* including acting as trustee of an authorised unit trust scheme or sole director of an *open-ended investment company* (article 51 of the *Regulated Activities Order*);

(5) establishing, operating and winding up a *stakeholder pension scheme* (article 52 of the *Regulated Activities Order*);

(6) managing the underwriting capacity of a Lloyd's syndicate (article 57 of the *Regulated Activities Order*);

(7) (with effect from 1 January 2002) entering as provider into funeral plan contracts (article 59 of the *Regulated Activities Order*); and

(8) (with effect from 1 September 2002) entering into as lender and administering regulated mortgage contracts (article 61 of the *Regulated Activities Order*).

1.11.6 The activities precluded in part are those referred to in 1.11.7 G to 1.11.14 G.

1.11.7 Managing investments (article 37 of the *Regulated Activities Order*) is a precluded activity insofar as it involves the exercise of discretion in connection with buying or subscribing for a *security* or a *contractually based investment* unless either:

(1) all routine or day to day decisions are taken by an *authorised person* who has *permission* to manage investments or an *exempt person* who is exempt for that activity; or

(2) where such decisions are taken by the *exempt professional firm*, they are taken in line with advice given by an *authorised person* who has *permission* to give such advice or an *exempt person* whose exemption covers giving such advice.

1.11.8 *Exempt professional firms* are thus free (subject to their complying with the terms of the Part XX exemption and their *designated professional body*'s rules) to make decisions at their own discretion in the course of managing investments where the decisions are of the following kind:

(1) decisions to sell or not to sell existing investments;

(2) strategic decisions such as decisions on the mix of different types of investments;

(3) decisions on the appointment or removal of external fund managers or the apportionment of funds for investment between fund managers; and

(4) any other decision which does not concern the acquisition of a particular investment.

Decisions of the kind referred to in (3) would not include decisions which concern the acquisition of a pooled investment product, such as units in a *collective investment scheme*, where the operator is an external fund manager. Such decisions would concern the acquisition of particular investments. But decisions to place funds with an external fund manager who maintains segregated funds for individual investors will fall under (3) even if the fund manager (or a group company of his) also operates pooled investment vehicles and has discretion to invest funds in those vehicles.

1.11.9 *Exempt professional firms* are also able to make decisions on the acquisition of particular investments where the decision is not routine or day to day in nature. This is discussed further in 1.18.2 G below which deals with the exclusion in article 38 of the *Regulated Activities Order* for attorneys managing investments.

1.11.10 Any other decisions (that is, decisions concerning the acquisition of a particular investment which are not routine or day to day decisions) will be subject to the requirement that they be delegated to or made in line with advice received from a suitably authorised or *exempt person*. It follows that *exempt professional firms* are not required to follow the advice of an *authorised person* other than where it concerns the acquisition of a particular investment.

1.11.11 Advising on investments (article 53 of the *Regulated Activities Order*) in the manner set out in 1.11.11 G(1) and (2) is a precluded activity other than when the advice is given in certain circumstances. These circumstances are where the advice endorses a corresponding recommendation given by an *authorised person* who has *permission* to give advice on the proposed transaction or an *exempt person* whose exemption *covers* giving such advice. Subject to this exception, advising on investments is precluded:

(1) where the advice:

    (a) is given to an individual (or his agent) other than:

        (i) in connection with the individual carrying on a business of which he is or is to be a *controller* ('*controller*' being defined in section 422 of the *Act* (Controller) as, in broad terms, a *person* who has a 10 per cent or greater shareholding in the business undertaking or is able to exercise a significant influence over its management); or

        (ii) where the individual is acting as trustee of an *occupational pension scheme*;

    (b) is a recommendation to buy or subscribe for a particular *security* or *contractually based investment*; and

    (c) relates to a transaction which would be made:

        (i) with a *person* in the course of his carrying on a business of dealing in investments of the kind to which the transaction relates (for instance, advice to buy XYZ plc shares from a stockbroker or to buy an investment product from the provider of that product);

        (ii) on an investment exchange or market (for example, buying listed securities on the LSE); A 'market' for these purposes would include non-centralised arrangements such as the traded endowment market but not private arrangements such as a private auction of shares in a family business; or

        (iii) in response to an invitation to subscribe for investments which are, or are to be, admitted for dealing on an investment exchange or market (for example, a public offer or flotation of *securities* in respect of which an application for listing has been made); or

(2) where the advice is a recommendation to a member of a *personal pension scheme* (or his agent) to dispose of any rights or interests which he has under the scheme.

1.11.12 An *exempt professional firm* is thus able (subject to its complying with the terms of the Part XX exemption and its *designated professional body*'s rules) to advise on investments where the advice is a recommendation not to buy or subscribe for investments or where the advice relates to the disposal of investments other than rights under a *personal pension scheme*. An *exempt professional firm* is also able, in most circumstances, to give advice which relates to the acquisition of investments issued by an unquoted company or where all of the parties to the transaction are private individuals. Furthermore, an *exempt professional firm* may provide advice to its client on the merits of advice given by an appropriately *authorised* or *exempt person* or advise its client to seek further information or clarification from the *authorised* or *exempt person* provided it does not recommend that its client purchase a particular investment other than that recommended by the *authorised* or *exempt person*. For the avoidance of doubt, it is not necessary for a *professional firm* to endorse a recommendation for the same reasons as given by the *authorised person*.

1.11.13 Advising a *person* to become a member of a particular Lloyd's syndicate (article 56 of the *Regulated Activities Order*) is precluded except where the advice endorses that of an appropriately *authorised* or *exempt person*. An *exempt professional firm* may thus advise a client (subject again to the terms of the Part XX exemption and its *designated professional body*'s rules) not to become or to cease or continue to be a member of a particular syndicate.

1.11.14 Agreeing to carry on any of the *regulated activities* which are precluded under the *Non-Exempt Activities Order*, where such agreeing is itself a *regulated activity*, is also a precluded activity.

1.11.15 In summary, in addition to the activities capable of being undertaken in limited circumstances as explained in 1.11.7 G to 1.11.14 G, a *professional firm* will not be precluded under the *Non-Exempt Activities Order* from undertaking the following *regulated activities*:

(1) dealing in investments as agent (article 21 of the *Regulated Activities Order*);
(2) arranging deals in investments (article 25 of the *Regulated Activities Order*);
(3) safeguarding and administering investments (article 40 of the *Regulated Activities Order*);
(4) sending dematerialised instructions (article 45 of the *Regulated Activities Order*).

1.12 The Part XX Exemption – general issues

1.12.1 A *professional firm* which wishes to carry on *regulated activities* which are precluded under the *Non-Exempt Activities Order* will need to be authorised (or otherwise exempt). Any *professional firm* carrying on *regulated activities* which are not precluded under the *Non-Exempt Activities Order* and in an incidental manner to his professional services will need to consider whether those activities are permitted under its *designated professional body*'s rules as referred to in 1.8.2 G and 1.8.3 G.

1.12.2 An issue arises, as regards the Part XX exemption, where a *professional firm* is an individual who is also a member or former underwriting member of the Society of Lloyd's. Such an individual will or may be carrying on the *regulated activities* of effecting or carrying out contracts of insurance as principal or both. Such *regulated activities* would ordinarily be precluded under the *Non-Exempt Activities Order* but, under article 13 of the *Regulated Activities Order*, they may be disregarded for the purposes of determining whether the Part XX exemption applies.

1.12.3 Annex 1G to this guidance contains a table indicating the correlation between the *regulated activities* in the *Regulated Activities Order* and those precluded under the *Non-Exempt Activities Order*.

1.13 Regulated activities – amendments to definitions in the FS Act

1.13.1 As mentioned in 1.6.3 G, the definitions of certain *regulated activities* which are carried forward from the FS Act have been amended so as to clarify their scope. The *Regulated Activities Order* should be consulted to determine the precise meaning of provisions to which reference is made.

1.13.2 Under article 53 of the *Regulated Activities Order*, the *regulated activity* of advising on investments requires that advice given must relate to the merits of buying or selling a 'particular' investment. This clarifies that giving generic or other advice relating to investments generally or to a class of investments will not require *authorisation*.

1.13.3 Under article 37 of the *Regulated Activities Order*, the *regulated activity* of managing investments requires the exercise of discretion. Hence, any form of non-discretionary management will only require *authorisation* if it involves another *regulated activity* such as dealing or arranging deals in investments, safeguarding and administering investments or advising on investments.

1.14 Exclusions

1.14.1 In general terms, the existing exclusions under Parts III and IV of Schedule 1 to the FS Act have been carried forward into the *Regulated Activities Order*. Several of these have been modified and other exclusions added. Those likely to be of particular relevance to *professional firms* are referred to in general terms in 1.15 to 1.19. The *Regulated Activities Order* should be consulted to determine the precise meaning and effect of the provisions to which reference is made. The *FSA* anticipates that these exclusions and the modifications referred to in 1.13.2 G and 1.13.3 G may enable a number of *professional firms* to avoid conducting *regulated activities* at all.

1.15 Accepting deposits (article 5 of the Regulated Activities Order)

1.15.1 Article 7 of the *Regulated Activities Order* excludes from the definition of a deposit a sum of money received by a practising solicitor (as defined) in the course of his profession. This continues the exemption currently contained in article 8 of the Banking Act 1987 (Exempt Transactions) Regulations 1997.

1.16 Dealing as agent (article 21 of the Regulated Activities Order)

1.16.1 Article 22 of the *Regulated Activities Order* excludes an *unauthorised person* who enters into a transaction as agent for another *person* ('the client') with or through an *authorised person* if:

(1) the transaction is entered into on advice given to the client by an *authorised person* (whether or not the authorised person with or through whom the transaction is entered into); or

(2) it is clear that the client, in his capacity as investor, has not sought advice from the agent as to the merits of entering into the transaction or, if he has, the agent has declined to give it and has suggested that the client seek advice from an *authorised person*;

and provided, in either case, that the agent does not receive any pecuniary reward other than from the client or for which he accounts to the client (see 1.9 for guidance on the meaning of 'accounts to his client' in this context).

1.16.2 It is, therefore, permissible for a *professional firm* to have given legal, accountancy, or other professional advice to the client, not being advice on the merits of the client entering into the transaction as an investor, and still be able to use this exclusion.

1.16.3 For the purposes of the article 22 exclusion, and in the *FSA's* view, an agent will be entering into a transaction 'through' an *authorised person* in the following circumstances:

(1) where the *authorised person* also enters into the transaction as agent (whether for the agent's client or the counterparty to the trade) or arranges for the transaction to be effected;

(2) where the transaction is arranged by an *appointed representative* of an *authorised person* acting in accordance with section 39 of the *Act* and the Appointed Representatives Regulations (see 1.24).

1.16.4 Many *professional firms* are understood at present to conduct investment business in this manner and as referred to in 1.17.1 G (the so-called 'authorised third party' route).

1.17   Arranging deals in investments (article 25 of the Regulated Activities Order)

1.17.1 Article 29 of the *Regulated Activities Order* excludes an *unauthorised person* who arranges deals on behalf of a client with or through an *authorised person* subject to conditions identical to those referred to in 1.16.1 G.

1.17.2 Article 33 of the *Regulated Activities Order* reproduces in substantially the same form the introducers' exclusion presently contained in Note (6) to paragraph 13 of Schedule 1 to the FS Act. This allows arrangements to be made provided they are restricted to introducing persons to an *authorised, exempt* or overseas *person* for the purpose of the provision of independent advice or independent exercise of discretion relating to investments generally or to a class of investments. The exemption relates only to the activity of making arrangements with a view to a *person* who participates in them buying or selling an investment (article 25(2) of the *Regulated Activities Order*). It does not apply to the activity of arranging for a *person* to buy or sell a particular investment (article 25(1)) but, in the *FSA's* view, that activity does not apply to introducing because arrangements under article 25(1) must bring about the particular transaction (article 26 of the *Regulated Activities Order*). Mere introductions will not, in the *FSA's* view, bring about transactions. *Professional firms* making use of this exclusion to make arrangements with a view to introducing clients to an *authorised* or *exempt person* will continue to be able to receive payments under those arrangements if the other terms of the exclusion are met. However, firms which do retain commission for introductions made under article 33 of the *Regulated Activities Order* must bear in mind that this may prevent them from making use of the exemption for *real time financial promotions* concerning introductions in article 15 of the *Financial Promotion Order*. This is explained in greater detail in 1.26.23 G.

1.17.3 In the *FSA*'s opinion, the exclusion in article 33 is only effective where arrangements do not go beyond introductions. The *FSA* takes this to mean that the *person* making the arrangements will do no more than bring together the investor and the firm to whom the introduction is made for the purpose referred to in article 33. The *FSA* would regard arrangements as going beyond introductions if the introducer retained some ongoing role as a form of conduit. For example, where a *professional firm* agrees to procure advice on behalf of a client from an *authorised person*, with a view to presenting the advice to its client and offering comment which does not amount to advice on the merits of the client following the *authorised person*'s recommendation (for example, a mere explanation of the meaning of certain terms in a proposed contract). This would be the type of arrangement for which article 29 of the *Regulated Activities Order* is designed. Article 29, as explained in 1.9.1 G, requires firms to account to their clients as respects payments received from third parties.

1.18   Managing investments (article 37 of the Regulated Activities Order)

1.18.1 Article 38 of the *Regulated Activities Order* excludes a *person* who manages investments if he is appointed to do so under a power of attorney and all routine day to day decisions concerning *securities* or *contractually based investments* are taken by either:

(1) an *authorised person* with *appropriate permission* to manage investments; or

(2) an *exempt person* whose exemption covers such managing activities.

1.18.2 The *FSA* takes the following views in relation to the meaning of 'all routine or day to day decisions';

(1) a 'routine' decision is any decision other than one which may properly be regarded as exceptional. In determining whether or not decisions are routine, due account would need to be taken of the usual types of decision which the attorney takes or expects to be taking. Examples of possible non-routine decisions which an attorney might take include where the appointed fund manager has a conflict of interest or decisions relating to certain specified situations (for example, where the appointed fund manager proposes to invest in a particular type of investment such as a company associated with the tobacco or arms supply industries);

(2) a 'day to day' decision is a decision which relates to the everyday management of the assets in question. It will not include strategic decisions such as decisions on the proportion of the assets which should be invested in equities as compared to fixed interest securities, or decisions on which investment manager(s) to appoint or to whom to apportion cash for investment purposes from time to time;

(3) the exclusion requires that the attorney takes only decisions which are neither 'routine' nor 'day to day' in nature.

1.18.3 It is usually the case that where a *professional firm* provides attorney services it will be an individual partner or employee of the firm who becomes the attorney. The question then arises as to whether it is the firm or the actual attorney who is potentially covered by the exclusion. It is the *FSA*'s view that, provided it is the case that the firm has offered to provide the services of a partner or employee to act as attorney and that the client accounts to the firm for fees payable for the services of the attorney, it will be the firm which has and needs the benefit of the exclusion. This is because the attorney will be carrying on the firm's business and not his own business. It follows that if the attorney, in implementing a decision which is not a routine or day to day decision, uses other employees, officers or partners of the firm to execute or arrange the transaction, the firm would be entitled to make use of any exclusion which may be available to a *person* acting as attorney.

1.19   Safeguarding and administration of investments (article 40 of the Regulated Activities Order)

1.19.1 It is understood that some *professional firms* may operate separate nominee companies for holding investments belonging to their clients. Article 41 of the *Regulated Activities Order* continues the exclusion in Note (1) to paragraph 13A of Schedule 1 to the FS Act for sub-custodians where a primary custodian (being an *authorised person* or an *exempt person* acting in the course of his exempt activities) takes responsibility for the sub-custodian's safeguarding and administration activities.

1.19.2 *Professional firms* using the Part XX exemption will not be able to use this exclusion as they will not be authorised. Nor will they be *exempt persons* for this purpose. However, *professional firms'* nominee companies would only require *authorisation* if:

(1) they are undertaking or arranging both the safeguarding and administration of investments; and

(2) in so doing, they are carrying on the activities as a business.

1.19.3 Where a nominee company exists purely to hold title to investments and other assets and has no staff or resources it is likely that it will only be safeguarding the assets and that it is the *person* who controls the nominee company who has undertaken to provide the service of safeguarding and administration and who undertakes the actual administration. Furthermore, it is unlikely that such a nominee company would be regarded as carrying on business of any kind.

1.20   Exclusions of general application

1.20.1 Article 66 of the *Regulated Activities Order* reproduces the existing exclusions for trustees and personal representatives in paragraph 22 of Schedule 1 to the FS Act. These relate to the *regulated activities* of dealing in investments as principal, arranging deals in investments, managing investments, safeguarding and administration of investments, sending dematerialised instructions and advising on investments and are subject to various conditions.

1.20.2 For the activities of arranging deals in investments, managing investments, safeguarding and administration of investments and advising on investments, the trustee or personal representative must not receive remuneration for providing *regulated activities* in addition to any remuneration he may receive for providing the services of a trustee or personal representative. Article 66 also makes it clear that a trustee or personal representative is not to be regarded as receiving additional remuneration merely because his remuneration as trustee or personal representative is calculated by reference to time spent. Hence, the mere fact that a trustee may spend, for example, an hour of his time taking part in a meeting at which decisions are made does not, of itself, mean that the trustee is additionally remunerated for undertaking investment management duties by virtue of his being paid by the hour for providing trustee services.

1.20.3 In addition, for the activities of dealing in investments, managing investments and safeguarding and administration of investments, it is necessary that the trustee or personal representative does not hold himself out as providing such a service. In the *FSA*'s opinion, trustees (or personal representatives) will be holding themselves out as providing services of this kind only where they offer to provide services over and above those which trustees normally provide; and professional trustees will so hold themselves out where they offer to provide services over and above those provided by trustees generally, rather than those provided by professional trustees.

1.20.4 It is the *FSA*'s view that where a firm provides the services of a trustee or personal representative it is, for similar reasons to those given in 1.18.3 G, the firm itself which benefits from the trustees' exclusion (on the basis, amongst other things, that the individual partner or employee is not himself carrying on a business of any kind).

1.20.5 Article 67 of the *Regulated Activities Order* continues the 'necessary' exclusions currently in paragraph 24 of Schedule 1 to the FS Act. In general terms, these exclusions relate to the *regulated activities* of arranging deals in investments, safeguarding and administration of investments and advising on investments where such services are a necessary part of professional (non-investment) services and are not remunerated separately. However, the requirement that the arranging, safeguarding and administration or advice be a 'necessary' part of the services provided in the course of the profession or other business (not being a *regulated activity*) is now qualified by a 'reasonableness' test. Hence, if it should turn out that something done by a *professional firm* was not, in fact, necessary, the firm will not have conducted a *regulated activity* provided it was reasonable for it to have regarded the action to be necessary at the time it was taken.

1.20.6 Examples of situations where the 'necessary' exclusion may apply for *professional firms* include an accountant advising a client on the tax implications of entering into an investment agreement or a lawyer advising a client on the legal implications of doing so. Much of the work undertaken by lawyers in negotiating and putting into effect matrimonial or structured settlements may reasonably be regarded to be a necessary part of their professional services. For example, following the provision of necessary advice in a matrimonial dispute it may reasonably be regarded to be necessary for the solicitor to instigate the sale of an insurance policy by instructing an authorised intermediary to find a buyer at the best price and then to arrange the deal. It would be unlikely, however, that it would reasonably be regarded as necessary for the solicitor to undertake the role of that authorised intermediary.

1.20.7 Article 68 of the *Regulated Activities Order* continues the exclusions in paragraph 19 of Schedule 1 to the FS Act for the *regulated activities* of dealing in investments as principal or agent, arranging deals in investments, managing investments, safeguarding and administration of investments and advising on investments, where the activities are undertaken for the purpose of or in connection with the sale of goods or supply of services. This exclusion may be of potential use to *professional firms* who undertake *regulated activities* in the course of providing professional services to a client provided:

    (1)   the client is not an individual; and

    (2)   the *regulated activities* concerned do not involve contracts of insurance which are *contractually based investments* or *units* in a *collective investment scheme*.

1.20.8   An example where this exclusion may be available to *professional firms* would be where the firm is paid for providing professional services to a corporate client by means of it being issued with *securities* rather than being paid in cash.

1.20.9   Article 70 of the *Regulated Activities Order* continues the 'sale of a business' exclusion contained in paragraph 21 of Schedule 1 to the FS Act. However, a number of changes have been made with a view to broadening the scope of the exclusion. There are not two separate circumstances in which the exclusion applies.

1.20.10   The exclusion applies to the *regulated activities* of dealing in investments as principal or agent, arranging deals in investments or advising on investments where the dealing, arranging or advice relate to a transaction which, in general terms, is one to acquire or dispose of shares in a body corporate, and either:

    (1)   it is the case that:

        (a)   the shares, in addition, where appropriate, to any shares already held by the buyer, amount to 50 per cent or more of the voting shares in the body corporate; and

        (b)   the party who is the seller is a body corporate, a partnership, a single individual or a group of connected individuals and the buyer is also one or other of these (but not necessarily the same type as the seller); or

    (2)   where the conditions in (1.20.10 G(1)) are not met, but the object of the transaction may reasonably be regarded as being the acquisition of day to day control of the affairs of the body corporate.

1.20.11   A group of connected individuals is defined in article 70(3) of the *Regulated Activities Order* as being a group of *persons* each of whom is (as respects sellers) or is to be (as respects buyers):

    (1)   a director or manager of the body corporate;

    (2)   a close relative of such a *person*; or

    (3)   a *person* acting as trustee for a *person* as referred to in 1.20.11 G(1) or (2).

1.20.12   In the *FSA*'s view, the aim of the exclusion is to remove from the scope of regulation *persons* involved with the sale of a corporate business by a *person* who, either alone or with others, controls the business to another *person* who, either alone or with others, proposes to control the business.

1.20.13   In any case where the conditions referred to in 1.20.10 G(1) are not met, it will be necessary to consider the circumstances in which the transaction takes place in order to determine whether its objective is the acquisition of day to day control. In situations where the 50 per cent holding of voting shares test is not met it remains possible that the objective of a transaction could still be the acquisition of day to day control – for instance, because the remaining shareholders represent a large number of small shareholders who it is reasonable to suppose will not regularly act in concert.

1.20.14 Where the nature of the parties test is not met (typically because there are two or more parties involved as buyer or seller and they do not collectively represent a group of connected individuals as defined) it may still be the case that the objective of the transaction is the acquisition of day to day control when due account is taken of the purpose for which the *person* concerned holds or proposes to hold the voting shares. This may typically occur, for example, where shares are or are to be held by:

(1) a *person* (of either sex) with whom a manager or director cohabits;

(2) a venture capital company which has invested, or proposes to invest, in the company and which provides or is to provide a representative to act as a manager or director of the company; or

(3) a private company used as a vehicle to hold shares by a person who is or is to be a manager or director of the company (or his close relative).

1.21   New regulated activities: regulated mortgage contracts

1.21.1 Certain activities are subject to statutory regulation for the first time under the Act. These are:

(1) arranging deals in syndicate capacity or membership (article 25 of the *Regulated Activities Order*);

(2) advice on syndicate participation at Lloyd's (article 56 of the *Regulated Activities Order*);

(3) managing the underwriting capacity of a Lloyd's syndicate (article 57 of the *Regulated Activities Order*);

(4) entering as provider into funeral plan contracts (article 59 of the *Regulated Activities Order*); and

(5) entering into as lender or administering a regulated mortgage contract (article 61 of the *Regulated Activities Order*).

1.21.2 The activity of entering as provider into funeral plan contracts does not become a *regulated activity* until 1 January 2002. It is subject to an exclusion in article 60 of the *Regulated Activities Order* for insurance-based or trust-based arrangements which meet certain conditions.

1.21.3 Of these new *regulated activities* those which may be of most relevance to *professional firms* are entering into as lender or administering regulated mortgage contracts in article 61 of the *Regulated Activities Order*. This may be of particular concern to firms of solicitors who may provide mortgages or secured bridging loans whether as a trustee or otherwise. Article 61 does not come into effect until 1 September 2002. These activities are explained in greater detail in 1.21.4 G to 1.21.7 G.

1.21.4 The activity of entering into a regulated mortgage contract as lender is a *regulated activity*. A regulated mortgage contract is one where, in general terms:

(1) the obligation of the borrower to repay is secured by a first legal mortgage on land;

(2) the land is in the *United Kingdom*; and

(3) at least 40 per cent of the land is or is to be used as a dwelling by the borrower or, where the borrower is a trustee, by a beneficiary of the trust.

1.21.5 The activity of entering into a regulated mortgage contract will count as a *regulated activity* only in relation to regulated mortgage contracts that are entered into after article 61 comes into force (that is, after 1 September 2002). In addition to excluding most regulated mortgage contracts that are entered into before that date, this will, in most circumstances, also exclude any contract entered into after that date which is not, at the point it is entered into, a regulated mortgage contract but which subsequently becomes one. This might happen, for example, where the proportion of land subject to the mortgage which is used as a dwelling is increased to 40 per cent or more or where the redemption of an earlier mortgage means that the mortgage in question becomes the first mortgage. However, there may be instances where a contract is replaced rather than varied as a result of a change (whether the change is initiated by the customer or by the lender). This could affect contracts initially entered into before article 61 enters into force as well as those entered into after that date.

1.21.6 The activity of administering any regulated mortgage contract that is entered into after article 61 has entered into force (that is, 1 September 2002) is also a *regulated activity*. A *person* administers a contract for these purposes if he notifies the borrower of matters required to be notified under the contract (such as changes in interest rate or payments due). A *person* will also be considered to administer a regulated mortgage contract if he takes any necessary steps for the purposes of collecting or recovering payments. But a *person* is not to be treated as administering a regulated mortgage contract merely because he has or exercises a right to take action for the purposes of enforcing the contract (or to require that such action is or is not taken). In the *FSA*'s opinion, the activity of administering a regulated mortgage contract is a continuous activity. Accordingly, it can be carried on in relation to a contract that was not a regulated mortgage contract when it was entered into but which subsequently becomes such a contract. As long as the contract was entered into after article 61 has entered into force a person will be carrying on a regulated activity when he administers the contract after it has become a regulated mortgage contract. Article 61 applies to the administration of a regulated mortgage contract even if the lender is a private individual – see 1.22.4 G.

1.21.7 Professional firms should note that there are no exclusions from the activities included in article 61 (for example, as regards the activities of trustees). However, the issue as to whether there should be some form of exemption or exclusion for professional trustees who engage in regulated mortgage contract business solely for the benefit of trust beneficiaries is currently under consideration by the Treasury. The outcome of this will be made clear to *professional firms* in due course.

1.22 The business test

1.22.1 Under section 22 of the *Act* (The classes of activity and categories of investment), for an activity to be a *regulated activity* it must be carried on 'by way of business'.

1.22.2 There is power in the Act for the Treasury to change the meaning of the business test by including or excluding certain things. They have exercised this power (see the Financial Services and Markets Act 2000 (Carrying on Regulated Activities by Way of Business) Order 2001 ('the Business Order'). The result is that the business test differs depending on the activity in question. This in part reflects certain differences in the nature of the activities:

    (1)   the activity of accepting deposits will not be regarded as carried on by way of business by a person if he does not hold himself out as accepting

deposits on a day to day basis and if the deposits he accepts are accepted only on particular occasions. The frequency of the occasions and any distinguishing characteristics must be taken into account;

(2) except for the trustees of occupational pension schemes, for which special provision is made (similar to that in section 191 of the FS Act), the business test is not to be regarded as satisfied for any of the regulated activities carried on in relation to securities or contractually based investments (or for those regulated activities carried on in relation to 'any property') – essentially, those which currently constitute investment business under the FS Act – unless a person 'carries on the business of engaging in one or more of the activities'. This is a narrower test than that of carrying on regulated activities by way of business (as required by section 22 of the *Act*), as it requires the regulated activities to represent the carrying on of a business in their own right. To give an example, a *professional firm* which makes arrangements, in its capacity as an employer, for its employees to be able to participate in a particular group personal pension scheme or stakeholder scheme is liable to be conducting the activity of arranging deals in investments under article 25(2) of the *Regulated Activities Order*. Unless the firm has a commercial interest in providing the pension arrangements (beyond that of maintaining its workforce and safeguarding their interests) it is unlikely to be carrying on the business of arranging deals in investments (that is, the narrower business test in the Business Order). But the firm would be likely to be carrying on the activities by way of business (that is, the broader test in section 22 of the *Act*);

(3) the business test for all other *regulated activities* is that the activities are carried on by way of business. This applies to the activities of effecting or carrying out contracts of insurance, the activities relating to the Lloyd's market, entering as provider into a funeral plan contract and the activities relating to regulated mortgage contracts.

1.22.3 Whether or not an activity is carried on by way of business is ultimately a question of judgement that takes account of several factors (none of which is likely to be conclusive). These include the degree of continuity, the existence of a commercial element, the scale of the activity and the proportion which the activity bears to other activities carried on by the same person but which are not regulated. The nature of the particular *regulated activity* that is carried on will also be relevant to the factual analysis.

1.22.4 Where the activity of administering a regulated mortgage contract is concerned, a person will require *authorisation* or exemption if he carries on the administration by way of business regardless of whether or not the regulated mortgage contract has been entered into by the lender by way of business.

1.23   General issue regarding exclusions – the Investment Services Directive

1.23.1 The exclusions contained in articles 15 (dealing in securities as principal), 68 (sale of goods and supply of services), 69 (groups and joint enterprises) and 70 (sale of a body corporate) of the *Regulated Activities Order* are not available to a *person* who is an *investment firm* for the purposes of the *Investment Services Directive* and who is providing *core investment services* to third parties on a professional basis (see article 4(4)(b) of the *Regulated Activities Order*).

1.23.2 Any *person* who is providing or is intending to provide *core investment services* as set out in Section A of Schedule 2 to the *Regulated Activities Order*) to third parties on a professional basis in circumstances where the services would not be exempt under article 2.2 of the *Investment Services Directive* will require to be authorised. *Core investment services* are, broadly speaking, dealing in or managing, underwriting or receiving and transmitting orders in investments which are securities or contractually based investments of a financial nature. In this respect, article 2.2(c) of the *Investment Services Directive* exempts firms which provide *investment services* in an incidental manner in the course of a professional activity. The *FSA* regards the 'incidental' test in article 2.2(c) of the *Investment Services Directive* to be equivalent to the test in the Part XX exemption – see 1.10.1 G.

1.24   Other exemptions – appointed representatives and insolvency practitioners

1.24.1 Other exemptions which may be relevant to *professional firms* are provided under the *Act*. These are:

(1)   section 39 of the Act (Exemption of appointed representatives) which exempts an *appointed representative* subject to compliance with the Financial Services and Markets Act 2000 (Appointed Representatives) Regulations 2001 ('the Appointed Representatives Regulations') and which, by and large, reproduce the existing exemption under section 44 of the FS Act; and

(2)   the Financial Services and Markets Act 2000 (Exemption) Order 2001 ('the Exemption Order') made under section 38 of the *Act* (Exemption orders) and which provides miscellaneous exemptions. Of particular relevance to some *professional firms* will be paragraph 39 of the Schedule to the Exemption Order which exempts insolvency practitioners for most *regulated activities*.

1.24.2 As regards 1.24.1 G(1), section 39 of the *Act* and the Appointed Representatives Regulations made under it would, therefore, permit an unauthorised *professional firm*, acting pursuant to an agreement with an *authorised person* who has accepted responsibility in writing for the *professional firm*'s actions, to:

(1)   advise on investments (being *securities* or *contractually based investments*);

(2)   arrange deals in such investments; and

(3)   arrange for safeguarding and administration of such investments.

1.24.3 The exemptions referred to in 1.24.1 G cannot apply to an *authorised person* but are available to a *person* who is relying on the Part XX exemption in respect of his other *regulated activities*.

1.25   Transitional considerations

1.25.1 There are no specific transitional provisions under the *Act* governing the switch from authorised status under the FS Act to the Part XX exemption. Hence, *professional firms* seeking to use the Part XX exemption to avoid the need for *authorisation* will need to ensure that they have ceased to conduct any *regulated activity* to which the Part XX exemption does not apply (and for which they are not otherwise exempt) by 1 December 2001. In this respect, a *professional firm* would not breach section 327(3) of the Act simply by virtue of receiving a payment after 1 December 2001 provided the payment relates to activities carried on before that date.

1.26 **Financial promotion**

1.26.1 *Professional firms* relying on the Part XX exemption or not carrying on *regulated activities* at all will be subject to the restriction on *financial promotion* in section 21 of the *Act* (Restrictions on financial promotion). As *unauthorised persons* they will be unable, in the course of business, to *communicate* or cause the *communication* of an invitation or inducement to *engage in investment activity* (a *'financial promotion'*) unless the content of the *communication* is approved for the purposes of section 21 of the *Act* by an *authorised person* or it is exempt under the Financial Services and Markets Act 2000 (Financial Promotion) Order 2001 ('the *Financial Promotion Order'*) made under section 21(5) of the *Act*. The *FSA* has issued for consultation detailed guidance on the subject of financial promotion (Consultation Paper 104). This is available on the *FSA* website. Paragraphs 1.26.2 G to 1.26.23 G below provide a brief summary of the main aspects of the *financial promotion* régime which will be of most relevance to *professional firms*.

1.26.2 *'Engage in investment activity'* is defined by reference to section 21(8) and (9) of the *Act* and article 4 of and Schedule 1 to the *Financial Promotion Order*. Generally speaking, it covers entering or offering to enter into an agreement the making or performance of which constitutes a *controlled activity* by either party or exercising certain rights conferred by *controlled investments*. Also, it is not necessary that the *controlled activity* be one engaged in for business purposes (it could, for example, be the activity of an individual buying an investment). In broad terms, the definitions of *controlled activities* and *controlled investments* to which they relate are very similar, but not identical, to *regulated activities* and *specified investments* as defined in the *Regulated Activities Order* but, in the case of *regulated activities*, without taking account of any of the exclusions contained in Part II of the *Regulated Activities Order*.

1.26.3 The restriction applies to any form of *communication* whether non-real time (for example, written communications, including websites, e-mails and personal letters) or real time (for example, oral communications, including personal conversations and meetings) as well as advertising and broadcasts.

1.26.4 The scope of section 21 is potentially wide. However, the *Financial Promotion Order* contains a number of exemptions which may be relevant so far as *professional firms* are concerned. Some of these relate to the activities covered by exclusions under Part II of the *Regulated Activities Order*. It is anticipated that many *professional firms* should be able to make use of these exemptions so as to avoid any need to seek approval from an *authorised person*. The main potential exception to this is likely to be brochures which hold out services which are excluded from being regulated activities (see 1.26.12 G(3) for further guidance on this). More detail concerning the relevant exemptions is in 1.26.5 G to 1.26.24 G. It should be noted that the titles given to exemptions are merely indicative of the type of *financial promotion* to which the exemption is likely to apply. The fact that a particular exemption may appear to be appropriate for a particular situation does not mean that use cannot instead be made of another exemption should it not be possible to satisfy the terms of the exemption which may appear to be the appropriate one to use in such a situation. For example, a *professional firm* making a *financial promotion* in connection with introducing *persons* to an *authorised person* may not be able to satisfy the terms of the introducers' exemption in article 15 but may be able to use the exemptions in articles 28 or 28A for one off *financial promotions*.

1.26.5 *Persons* who are exempted under sections 38 or 39 of the *Act* (as referred to in 1.24.1 G) are granted exemption under article 16 of the *Financial Promotion Order* as respects any *communication* (other than an *unsolicited real time financial promotion*) made or caused to be made for the purposes of carrying on the activities in respect of which they are exempt. Article 16 does not, however, apply to a *person* whose activities are exempt under Part XX of the *Act*.

Exemptions for professional firms conducting Part XX exempt activities

1.26.6 Exemptions designed specifically for *professional firms* conducting Part XX activities are provided in articles 55 and 55A of the *Financial Promotion Order*. These exemptions deal, respectively, with *real time* and *non-real time financial promotions*.

Real time financial promotions by professional firms

1.26.7 Article 55 of the *Financial Promotion Order* contains a specific exemption for *professional firms* allowing them to make *solicited* or *unsolicited real time financial promotions* (for example, those made during telephone calls and personal visits or subjects raised in a meeting with a client) provided the *communication* is made:

   (1) by a *person* who carries on a *regulated activity* without needing *authorisation* by virtue of the Part XX exemption; and

   (2) to someone who has already (that is, before the *financial promotion* is made) engaged the *person* making the *communication* to provide professional services.

1.26.8 The article 55 exemption also requires that:

   (1) the *financial promotion* relates to an activity to which the Part XX exemption applies or which would be a *regulated activity* but for the exclusion in article 67 of the *Regulated Activities Order* which concerns activities which are a necessary part of professional services – see 1.20.5 G; and

   (2) the activity to which the *financial promotion* relates would be undertaken for the purposes of, and be incidental to, the provision of professional services to or at the request of the recipient.

1.26.9 The effect of this is that if the *financial promotion* relates to an activity which is not a *regulated activity* as the result of an exclusion in the *Regulated Activities Order*, a *professional firm* using the Part XX exemption cannot make *real time financial promotions* in reliance on article 55 of the *Financial Promotion Order*, unless the exclusion is provided by article 67 of the *Regulated Activities Order*. Neither can a *professional firm* rely on article 55 in order to make *real time financial promotions*, in connection with the provision of professional services to an existing client, where the *financial promotions* are made to a third party, such as prospective counterparties or other advisers, rather than to the client. In such circumstances, another exemption would need to be available. It should be noted that *authorised persons* are not allowed to approve *real time financial promotions* for *unauthorised persons*.

Non-real time financial promotions by professional firms

1.26.10 Article 55A of the *Financial Promotion Order* was added by article 2(b) of the Financial Services and Markets Act 2000 (Financial Promotion) (Amendment) Order 2001 (SI 2001/2633). It exempts *non-real time financial* *promotions* (such as brochures, websites, advertisements, letters and e-mails) where the *financial promotion*:

(1) is made by a person who carries on a *regulated activity* without needing *authorisation* by virtue of the Part XX exemption ('Part XX activities'); and

(2) contains a specified statement and is limited in its content to the matters referred to in 1.26.11 G.

1.26.11 A *financial promotion* made under article 55A must contain a statement in the following terms:

'The [firm/company] is not authorised under the Financial Services and Markets Act 2000 but we are able in certain circumstances to offer a limited range of investment services to clients because we are members of [relevant designated professional body]. We can provide these investment services if they are an incidental part of the professional services we have been engaged to provide.'

The *financial promotion* may also set out the Part XX activities which the *person* is able to offer to his clients, provided it is clear that these are the incidental services to which the statement relates.

1.26.12 The article 55A exemption should enable *professional firms* to issue brochures, websites and other *non-real time financial promotions* without any need for approval by an *authorised person* provided the *financial promotion* does not also contain an invitation or inducement relating to *regulated activities* other than those covered by the Part XX exemption. In this respect, it should be noted that, unlike article 55, the article 55A exemption does not extend to activities which are excluded under article 67 of the *Regulated Activities Order*. The *FSA* takes the following views in relation to article 55A:

(1) it is not necessary for the details concerning the Part XX activities to be set out in one place or adjacent to the statement. A brochure or website, for example, may contain details of Part XX activities in various places so long as it is made clear that they will be incidental investment activities as referred to in the statement (which, as a result, needs to be set out only once in the brochure or website);

(2) the inclusion of contact details would be regarded as part of the description of Part XX activities;

(3) the mere fact that a *financial promotion* made under article 55A may be likely, on occasion, to result in the carrying on by the *professional firm* of activities which are excluded under the *Regulated Activities Order* does not mean that the *financial promotion* must fail to satisfy the terms of article 55A. There will be occasions where a *professional firm* will, of necessity, offer to provide services which may or may not involve Part XX activities or excluded activities. In the area of corporate finance, for example, a *professional firm* may offer its services in relation to the sale of an incorporated business or a substantial shareholding in such a business. It will not be apparent whether the *professional firm*'s services will be Part XX activities or excluded activities until the details of a proposed deal are known. Similarly, a *professional firm* may offer services which, in some instances, will fall under the 'necessary' exclusion in article 67 of the *Regulated Activities Order* but, in others, will be Part XX activities. In practice, it will often be impossible for a *professional firm* to distinguish between Part XX activities and excluded activities at the preliminary stage of a brochure or website offering its services. In the *FSA*'s

view, the article 55A exemption will apply provided the only *regulated activities* held out in the brochure, website or other *non-real time financial promotion* are Part XX activities. It will, of course, be possible for a *professional firm* to make an offer involving excluded activities to a *person* who responds to a *financial promotion* issued under article 55A provided another exemption (such as the one off *financial promotions exemption* – see 1.26.14 G) is available in respect of any subsequent *financial promotions*.

Other exemptions of potential relevance

1.26.13 In making *financial promotions* to which articles 55 or 55A do not apply, an unauthorised *professional firm* (whether or not it is making use of the Part XX exemption) will need to ensure that another exemption under the *Financial Promotion Order* is available or otherwise obtain approval from an *authorised person*. In this respect, it is anticipated that a significant number of *financial promotions* made by *professional firms* are likely to come within the exemptions which correspond to the exclusions in Part II of the *Regulated Activities Order* (such as those for trustees and personal representatives) and the additional exemptions which have been provided, and thus will not need to be approved. In particular, *professional firms* should be able to make good use of the exemptions referred to in 1.26.14 G to 1.26.24 G.

One off financial promotions

1.26.14 Exemptions for one off *financial promotions* are provided in articles 28 (One off non-real time communications and solicited real time communications) and 28A (One off unsolicited real time communications). Article 28 sets out conditions which, if all are met, are conclusive that a *financial promotion* is a one off *financial promotion*. Where only some of the conditions are met that fact will be indicative. Futhermore, article 28 is capable of applying even if none of the conditions are met. Article 28A adds further conditions which must be met by one off *unsolicited real time financial promotions*.

1.26.15 A one off *financial promotion* is, broadly speaking, one which is personal to the recipient (or recipients where they intend to invest jointly – for example, a husband and wife or members of an investment club) and not part of an organised marketing campaign. Article 28 will allow *professional firms* to respond (whether orally or in writing) to requests from clients and to deal with individual clients on a day to day basis provided *unsolicited real time financial promotions* are not made. However, it will not apply to such things as brochures or websites which will represent an organised marketing campaign (to which the exemption in article 55A may apply – see 1.26.10 G). In the *FSA*'s view, *financial promotions* which are part of a series of *communications* made to a particular client are capable of remaining one off *financial promotions*.

1.26.16 It is appreciated that there will be times when a *financial promotion* is made by a *professional firm* to a client and, at the same time, to another *person* who is present (for example, a friend or relative or other supporter or an ex-spouse and their adviser in the case of a matrimonial dispute). Provided the *financial promotion* made in such circumstances remains personal to the client it is the *FSA*'s view that it would continue to be regarded as 'one off' in nature.

1.26.17 There may be situations where, for example, *professional firms* may retain registers of potential investors to each of whom they may send details of investment opportunities from time to time. Such *financial promotions* will not be one off *financial promotions* as they are likely to be regarded as part of an organised marketing campaign. On the other hand, where a *professional firm* has clients and may write personally to those whose individual circumstances and objectives suggest that they may be interested in a particular investment opportunity, such *financial promotions* are likely to remain one off in nature. In the *FSA*'s view, an essential ingredient of a one off *financial promotion* is that the *person* making the *financial promotion* applies his mind to the individual circumstances of the recipient and tailors the *financial promotion* accordingly.

1.26.18 Article 28A was added by article 2(a) of the Financial Services and Markets Act 2000 (Financial Promotion) (Amendment) Order 2001 (SI 2001/2633). It exempts one off *unsolicited real time financial promotions* provided that the *person* making the *financial promotion* believes on reasonable grounds:

(1) that the recipient understands the risks associated with engaging in the investment activity to which the *financial promotion* relates; and

(2) (at the time the *communication* is made) that the recipient would expect to be contacted by him in relation to the investment activity to which the *financial promotion* relates.

The meaning of 'unsolicited' is explained in 1.26.25 G to 1.26.30 G.

1.26.19 In the *FSA*'s view, the article 28A exemption should provide scope for *professional firms* to make *unsolicited real time financial promotions* in various situations, for example, when approaching persons with whom their clients are proposing to do business or those persons' professional advisers. The exemption will not apply where the *financial promotions* are part of an organised marketing campaign. So in cases where a *professional firm* is to contact a number of *persons* on a matter which involves each of them (for instance, where they are significant shareholders in a company for which an offer has been made) it will be necessary for the firm to consider whether the approaches would be an organised marketing campaign. In the *FSA*'s opinion, in accordance with the comments in 1.26.17 G, provided the *professional firm* applies its mind to the circumstances of each recipient and tailors the *financial promotion* accordingly it should be possible for the *financial promotion* to be regarded as one off in nature. Ultimately, however, the matter will remain one of fact.

1.26.20 Whether or not it would be reasonable, in any particular case, to believe that a *person* understands the risks associated with the investment activity to which the *financial promotion* relates or would expect to be contacted about it will be matters to be judged on the particular circumstances. In the *FSA*'s opinion, however, it would be reasonable to believe that a *person* understands the risk involved if he is understood to be a professional, or to be professionally advised, in relation to the investment activity to which the *financial promotion* relates. A *person* may also reasonably be regarded as understanding the risks involved if, for example, he occupies a position in a company which it is reasonable to suppose would require him to have such an understanding (such as a finance director for example).

Follow up communications

1.26.21 Follow up *non-real time* or *solicited real time financial promotions* are exempted under article 14 of the *Financial Promotions Order*. This will allow *professional firms* to make further communications (other than *unsolicited real time financial promotions*) where their initial approach to the recipient was through a *financial promotion* which relied upon an exemption which required that certain information be disclosed or statements made. Examples include the exemptions concerning deposits and contracts of insurance which are not *contractually based investments* (articles 22 and 24 of the *Financial Promotions Order*), those relating to certified high net worth individuals or sophisticated investors (articles 48 and 50) and that for non-real time financial promotions relating to Part XX activities (article 55A). This will mean, among other things, that article 14 will not apply to a follow up of a *financial promotion* which relied solely upon an exemption for one off *financial promotions*.

Communications to professionals

1.26.22 *Financial promotions* made to investment professionals, high net worth companies and individuals and sophisticated investors are exempted under articles 19 and 48 to 50 of the *Financial Promotion Order*. In this respect, *professional firms* will be investment professionals if the *financial promotion* made to them relates to a controlled activity which they may be expected to engage in in the course of their ordinary activities. For example, *financial promotions* made to professional trustees concerning investment of the trust funds are likely to be exempt under article 19 but a *financial promotion* which merely invites professional firms (or their partners) to make personal investments will not do so.

Introducers

1.26.33 *Real time financial promotions* concerning introductions are exempted under article 15 of the *Financial Promotion Order*. This exemption will allow *professional firms* to make communications for the purpose of introducing the recipient to an *authorised person* or an *exempt person* acting in the course of his *exempt activities* provided, in broad terms, that:

(1) the *authorised* or *exempt person* is not connected to the *professional firm*;
(2) the *professional firm* does not receive any form of payment other than from his client; and
(3) the recipient has not sought advice, in his capacity as investor, from the *professional firm* or, if he has, the *professional firm* has declined to give it and has referred the recipient to an *authorised person*.

A *professional firm* cannot use this exemption when making introductions which are excluded under article 33 of the *Regulated Activities Order* where it receives and retains payment from the *authorised* or *exempt person* to whom introductions are made. It is the *FSA*'s view, however, that a *professional firm* may be regarded as not receiving payment other than from his client in circumstances where there is a clear pre-existing understanding between the firm and its client that the firm would account to the client for any payment he may receive from a third party (including where the payment is to be used as part payment for professional fees due to the firm from that client) – 1.9 contains guidance on the meaning of 'accounts to his client'. Neither can a *professional firm* use the exemption for making a *non-real time financial promotion*.

Generic promotions

1.26.24 Article 17 of the *Financial Promotion Order* contains an exemption for generic *financial promotions* being *financial promotions* which do not identify (directly or indirectly) a *person* who provides the *controlled investment* to which the *financial promotion* relates or identify any *person* as being a *person* who carries on a *controlled activity* in relation to that investment. In the *FSA*'s view, this exemption will be of limited use to *professional firms*. It will allow them to make promotions relating to deposits or contracts of insurance which are not *contractually based investments* provided there is no mention of a particular deposit taker or insurer. Such *financial promotions* may identify the *professional firm* as, for example, an adviser on or arranger of such investments as those are not *controlled activities*. *Financial promotions* relating solely to a firm's *professional services* are unlikely to be *communications* to which section 21 of the *Act* applies. However, where a *professional firm* refers to its ability to provide services which include activities which are *regulated activities* or which would be but for exclusions in the *Regulated Activities Order*, it is unlikely the exemption will apply (because the firm will be identifying itself as a *person* who carries on a *controlled activity*).

Meaning of unsolicited communications

1.26.25 It will frequently be important for a *professional firm* to determine whether a *real time financial promotion* it is contemplating making will be solicited or unsolicited as a number of the exemptions do not apply to *unsolicited real time financial promotions* (including, for example, follow up *financial promotions* and *financial promotions* made to certified high net worth individuals).

1.26.26 Article 8(1) of the *Financial Promotion Order* provides that a *real time financial promotion* is solicited where it is made in the course of a personal visit, telephone call or other interactive dialogue which was initiated by, or is made in response to an express request from, the recipient. An *unsolicited financial promotion* is any *financial promotion* which is not solicited.

1.26.27 Article 8(3) of the *Financial Promotion Order* clarifies that a *person* will not have expressly requested that a *financial promotion* be made to him merely:

(1) because he omits to indicate that he does not wish to receive any or any further visits or calls or to engage in any further dialogue; or

(2) because he agrees to standard terms that state that such visits, calls or dialogue will or may take place unless he has signified clearly that, in addition to agreeing to the terms, he is willing for them to take place.

1.26.28 Article 8(3) of the *Financial Promotion Order* also provides that a *financial promotion* is to be regarded as solicited only if it is clear from all the circumstances when the visit, call or dialogue is initiated or requested that *financial promotions* made during the course of the visit, call or dialogue will concern the *controlled investments* or *controlled activities* to which the *financial promotions* which are in fact made relate.

1.26.29 *Professional firms*, in issuing terms of engagement letters to clients may, therefore, consider it prudent to draw specific attention, where relevant, to the possibility of the firm making *unsolicited real time financial promotions* and seek the client's specific acceptance of this as well as his acceptance of the other terms. This could be achieved, for example, by the client providing a separate signature by the side of the relevant term.

1.26.30 In certain situations, a *person* may make a *financial promotion* to someone who has expressly requested that it be made but where, at the same time, it is also made to *persons* who have not requested it, for example, where a *person* answers questions from an audience at a presentation. Article 8(4) of the *Financial Promotion Order* provides that this will represent an *unsolicited financial promotion* made to the *persons* other than the *person* who expressly requested that it be made unless those other persons are:

(1)   close relatives of that *person*; or
(2)   expected to engage in any investment activity jointly with that *person* (for example, a husband and wife or the members of an investment club).

In this respect, the exemption for *unsolicited real time financial promotions* in article 28A of the *Financial Promotion Order* (see 1.26.18 G) may be relevant where, for example, business meetings are concerned.

Approval of other persons' communications

1.26.31 *Persons* who are exempt under Part XX of the *Act* (or for any other reason) cannot approve for the purposes of section 21 of the *Act* the content of a *financial promotion* which is to be made by another *person*.

1.27   Conclusion

1.27.1 *Professional firms* who, having considered their position in the light of this guidance and of the rules of and of any guidance issued by their *designated professional body*, conclude that they need *authorisation* should follow the instructions on how to obtain *permission* under Part IV of the *Act* which are contained in the material accompanying this guidance. Any *person* who remains unsure whether *authorisation* will be needed should consider seeking professional advice. General enquiries regarding the matters contained in this guidance may be made of the *FSA*'s Authorisation Enquiries Department. Enquiries regarding the rules made by a *Designated Professional Body* should be made to that body.

Financial Services and Solicitors: Law Society Professional Ethics information pack (extracts)

GUIDANCE ON THE BASIC CONDITIONS

The Scope Rules set out basic conditions which firms wishing to undertake *exempt regulated activities* must satisfy. These conditions are derived from sections 327 and 332(4) of the Act. The conditions are as follows:

1. **The activities arise out of, or are complementary to, the provision of a particular professional service to a particular client (Rule 4(a)).**

1.1 This is the overriding condition which must be satisfied before a firm, which is not authorised by the FSA, may undertake a *regulated activity*. The effect of this is that it is not possible to undertake a *regulated activity* in isolation for a client, as the basic condition will only be satisfied where the activity in question **arises out of or is complementary to** other professional services provided to a particular client. These professional services must be services which are provided by a firm in the course of its practice and which do not themselves constitute carrying on a *regulated activity*. To satisfy this basic condition, the firm must be able to identify the relevant professional services.

1.2 Listed below are examples of the types of services which *regulated activities* may arise out of or be complementary to:

- Conveyancing work – giving legal advice, drafting documents, dealing with the Land Registry and undertaking the conveyancing transaction.
- Corporate work – giving legal or tax advice, drafting documents, dealing with regulatory or other quasi-legal matters.
- Matrimonial work – giving legal or tax advice, drafting documents, dealing with court proceedings and other related matters.
- Probate work – winding up the estate, giving legal or tax advice, drafting documents and dealing with court procedures.
- Trust work – giving legal or tax advice, dealing with trust property, preparing trust accounts and drafting legal documents.
- Acting as an attorney or as a receiver appointed by the Court of Protection.

1.3 This test is similar to the 'incidental' exception to discrete investment business in the SIBR. Therefore anything which met that exception will meet this test. Otherwise it should not be difficult for firms to apply a common sense approach to this test.

2. The manner of the provision by the firm of any service in the course of carrying on the activities is incidental to the provision by the firm of professional services (Rule 4(b)).

2.1 To satisfy this condition, the *exempt regulated activities* cannot be a major part of the practice of the firm. The FSA considers that the following factors are relevant to this condition:

- the scale of *regulated activity* in proportion to other professional services provided;
- whether and to what extent activities that are *regulated activities* are held out as separate services; and
- the impression given of how the firm provides *regulated activities*, e.g. through its advertising or other promotion of its services.

2.2 This condition is required because of the Investment Services Directive (ISD) which defines those 'investment firms' which are subject to the ISD, and capital adequacy requirements, but exempts *'persons providing an investment service where that service is provided in an incidental manner in the course of a professional activity'*. This test is different to the **arising out of or complementary** test, as it depends on a qualitative judgement about the way in which the services are provided. For example, even if the services can be shown to contribute a minor part of the services provided by the practice as a whole, the way in which the *regulated activities* are advertised and/or presented as a separate business within the overall practice, could be relevant. Firms should, therefore, take care that any advertisement or promotion does not have the effect of holding out the *regulated activity* as a separate business.

2.3 Under the FS Act the Law Society, as a Recognised Professional Body, was not allowed to authorise firms which did not meet the equivalent test. Therefore it is unlikely that this condition will cause any difficulty to firms within the DPB regime. In addition, any advertising or promotional activity which could lead to a breach of this condition may also be a financial promotion under the FPO and therefore could not be issued by a solicitor's firm which is not authorised by the FSA unless it is approved by an authorised person.

3. The firm accounts to the client for any pecuniary reward or other advantage which the firm receives from a third party (Rule 4(c)).

3.1 This condition means that if a firm receives commission (or any financial benefit) from a third party because of acting for or giving advice to a client, the firm must account for the commission (or other financial benefit) to the client. Accounting to the client does not mean simply telling the client that the firm will receive commission. It means that the commission or reward must be held to the order of the client. This is similar to the requirement under Rule 10 of the Solicitors' Practice Rules 1990 (see the Guide to the Professional Conduct of Solicitors 8th edition). The Society believes that solicitors will still account to the client if they have the client's **informed consent** to keep the commission.

3.2 If a firm is charging the client on a fee basis, the firm can off-set the commission against the firm's fees. The firm must send the client a bill or some other written notification of costs to comply with the Solicitors' Accounts Rules 1998.

3.3 The requirement for informed consent would not be met if a firm were to

- seek blanket consent in terms of business to the keeping of all unspecified commissions, or
- seek negative consent.

The firm must be able to demonstrate that the client has given informed consent to any retention of the commission, having had full disclosure of the amount. The FSA Perimeter Guidance (Section 1.9) indicates that the firm should also inform the client, in effect, that the commission belongs to the client.

3.4 There is one important difference between Practice Rule 10 and the condition in Rule 4(c) of the Scope Rules in that Practice Rule 10 includes a *de minimis* provision whereby firms are allowed to keep commissions of £20 or less. **This £20 *de minimis* provision does not apply in relation to Rule 4(c).** Therefore commissions of £20 or less, which arise out of *regulated activities*, must be treated in the same way as commissions of more than £20.

4. The activities are not of a description, nor do they relate to an investment of a description, specified in any order made by the Treasury under section 327(6) of the Act (Rule 4(d)).

4.1 Under s.327(6) of the Act, the Treasury has made the Financial Services and Markets Act 2000 (Professions) (Non-Exempt Activities) Order 2001 (NEAO) which specifies certain *regulated activities* which do not fall within the exemption under Part XX of the Act. The provisions of the NEAO have been incorporated into the Scope Rules and therefore a firm which complies with the Scope Rules will also be complying with the NEAO.

5. The firm does not carry on or hold itself out as carrying on any regulated activity other than one which is allowed by these rules or one in relation to which the firm is an exempt person (Rule 4(e)).

5.1 This condition makes it clear that a firm must not hold itself out as carrying on *regulated activities* which do not fall within the Scope Rules other than activities in relation to which the firm is exempt, for example, activities undertaken whilst acting as an insolvency practitioner (see FSA Perimeter Guidance Section 1.24). The effect of this condition is that a firm which is regulated by the FSA would not be able to be an *exempt professional firm* for the purposes of Part XX of the Act.

6. There is not in force any order or direction of the FSA under s.328 or s.329 of the Act which prevents the firm from carrying on the activities (Rule 4(f)).

6.1 This refers to the FSA's powers under s.328 and s.329 of the Act.

Section 328 – This enables the FSA to make a direction in relation to classes of person or descriptions of *regulated activity* whereby a person within a particular class (or carrying on a particular *regulated activity*) will not be an *exempt professional firm* for the purposes of Part XX of the Act.
Section 329 – This gives the FSA power to make an order disapplying the Part XX exemption from a person named in the order.

7. The activities are not otherwise prohibited by these rules (Rule 4(g)).

7.1 This refers to the other restrictions contained in Rule 5 of the Scope Rules. Further guidance on the effect of these other restrictions in relation to particular areas of work is contained in Section 5.

GUIDANCE ON THE CONDUCT OF BUSINESS RULES

1. Introduction

1.1 The detailed conduct of business rules contained in the SIBR are repealed on 1 December 2001. Most of those rules applied to discrete investment business, i.e. mainstream investment business. However, some rules applied to non-discrete investment business, and some of those have been retained, in an amended form, in the Conduct of Business rules.

1.2 The Society has concluded that the number of special rules which only apply to *exempt regulated activities* should be kept to a minimum as those activities should, as far as possible be covered by the same rules as all other services provided by firms.

1.3 These rules would not apply where firms are operating under an *exclusion* in the RAO. However there may sometimes be a fine line between operating under an *exclusion* and providing services within the DPB régime. It may therefore be easier for firms to apply these rules to all such activities.

2. Application

2.1 These rules apply to all firms within the DPB régime and regulate the way in which they carry on *exempt regulated activities*. However, most of the rules also apply to firms who are authorised by the FSA, in respect of their *non-mainstream regulated activities*. FSA rules distinguish between mainstream activities of solicitors' firms and *non-mainstream regulated activities*. Most FSA rules are disapplied to firms' *non-mainstream regulated activities* – which are the same as the services that non-FSA authorised firms can provide as an *exempt regulated activity* under the DPB régime. The FSA relies on the relevant professional body (i.e. the Law Society) to regulate *non-mainstream regulated activities* and it is, therefore, appropriate that the Conduct of Business Rules are applied to all firms.

3. Status disclosure (Rule 3)

3.1 The FSA Professional Firms Sourcebook (4.1.2R) provides that DPB firms must avoid making any representation to a client that:

(i)   it is authorised under the Act or regulated by the FSA; or
(ii) the regulatory protections provided by or under the Act to a person using the services of an authorised person are available.

This means that firms who are not authorised by the FSA must remove any statement on letterheads that the firm is authorised for the conduct of investment business by the Law Society. The FSA have indicated that firms may use up old stocks of pre-printed stationery provided that the statement is crossed through.

3.2 The Professional Firms Sourcebook (4.1.3R) also requires firms in the DPB régime, before providing a regulated activity, to disclose in writing to a client, in a manner that is clear fair and not misleading, that it is not authorised under the Act. The guidance makes it clear that this information does not have to be contained on stationery and the Society does not consider that such a statement on stationery would be helpful. However, the information can be contained in client care/terms of business/retainer letters.

3.3 The FSA also considers that clients should understand the implications of receiving *exempt regulated activities* from a non-FSA authorised firm and have required the Society, as a DPB, to provide for further status disclosure in the Conduct of Business Rules. Therefore, Rule 3(2) provides that firms should give clients the following information in writing before carrying out an *exempt regulated activity*:

(a)   that the firm is not authorised by the FSA;
(b)   information on the nature of the *regulated activities* carried on by the firm and the fact that they are limited in scope;
(c)   a statement that the firm is regulated by the Law Society; and
(d)   a statement explaining that complaints and redress mechanisms are provided through Law Society regulation.

3.4 Many firms already carry a statement that they are regulated by the Law Society on their stationery, as it is a requirement of rule 11 of the Solicitors' Practice Rules in cases where firms do not have the word 'solicitors' on their notepaper. Having this statement on stationery will ensure compliance with Rule 3(2)(c). Suggested paragraphs that could be included in terms of business to deal with Rule 3(2)(a)(b) and (c) would be as follows:

> 'Sometimes conveyancing/family/probate/company work involves investments. We are not authorised by the Financial Services Authority and so may refer you to someone who is authorised to provide any necessary advice. However we can provide certain limited services in relation to investments, provided they are closely linked with the legal services we are providing to you, as we are regulated by the Law Society.'

> 'If during this transaction you need advice on investments, we may have to refer you to someone who is authorised by the Financial Services Authority, as we are not. However, as we are regulated by the Law Society, we may be able to provide certain limited investment services where these are closely linked to the legal work we are doing for you.'

> 'Sometimes family etc. work involves investments. We are able to provide a limited range of advice and arrangements for which we are regulated by the Law Society. For more complicated matters we may refer you to someone who is authorised by the Financial Services Authority, as we are not so authorised.'

3.5 The Financial Promotions Order, as referred to in Section 1, para 8.2 above, can apply to a firm's own advertising material if the material refers to, broadly, *regulated activities*. However, article 55A contains an exemption for DPB firms, a condition of the exemption requires a certain statement to be included in the advertising material. This statement would also comply with Rule 3(2)(a) and (b), but the firm must ensure that the client has received a copy of the statement. The statement is:

> 'The firm is not authorised under the Financial Services and Markets Act 2000 but we are able in certain circumstances to offer a limited range of investment services to clients because we are members of the Law Society. We can provide these investment services if they are an incidental part of the professional services we have have been engaged to provide.'

3.6 Rule 3(2)(d) does go further than the requirements in the Solicitors' Costs Information and Client Care Code relating to the information that should be given to clients on complaints handling. Firms can ensure compliance with this rule by expanding the paragraph in all client care letters on complaints with this rule by expanding the paragraph in all client care letters on complaints handling, or will have to identify those clients who are most likely to receive *exempt regulated activities* and give a special retainer letter to those clients. A suggested paragraph which could be included in such letters is:

> 'If you have any problem with the service we have provided for you then please let us know. We will try to resolve any problem quickly and operate an internal complaints handling system to help us to resolve the problem between ourselves. If for any reason we are unable to resolve the problem between us, then we are regulated by the Law Society which also provides a complaints and redress scheme.'

4. Execution of transactions (Rule 4)

4.1 Under the DPB regime, solicitors may often be effecting transactions and this rule, therefore, repeats the requirements of the current SIBR that firms should execute transactions as soon as possible unless it believes that would not be in the client's best interests.

5. Records of transactions (Rule 5)

5.1 Rule 5 requires that firms keep certain basic information when dealing with transactions involving *exempt regulated activities*. This obligation applies where the firm instructs another person to effect a transaction, in that the firm should also keep details of the terms of the instructions, the date when they were given and the name of the other person instructed. It is likely that this information will be contained in most files in any case. The rule does not require a separate record to be made nor for it to be kept centrally.

6. Record of commissions (Rule 6)

6.1 Again, Rule 6 repeats broadly what is contained in the current SIBR in that firms are required to keep a record of the amount of commission but this rule also requires a record of how the firm has accounted to the client. It is a basic condition of the DPB régime that firms account to clients for commission (see Section 4). It is also a condition of some of the exclusions in the RAO. Compliance with this Conduct of Business rule should, therefore, help firms to demonstrate compliance with these conditions. The rule is not prescriptive as to how the record should be kept and it is likely that the normal information on the file, e.g. letters to the client, would provide the relevant record. Where the firm has accounted to the client by setting off the commission against the bill, the bill itself may amount to a record for the purposes of this rule.

7. Safekeeping of clients' investments (Rule 7)

7.1 The SIBR contained fairly detailed provisions about the safekeeping (custody) of clients' investments. These provisions are now replaced by this rule which simply requires firms to operate appropriate systems (including the keeping of appropriate records) to ensure the safekeeping of assets entrusted to the firm by clients and others. Most firms of solicitors will operate such systems for all assets and deeds held on behalf of clients whether or not they are investments.

7.2 The rule also contains the sensible requirement that where assets are passed to a third party, the firm should obtain a receipt and that where such assets are being passed to a third party on the client's instructions, the instructions are also obtained in writing.

8.   Packaged products – execution only business (Rule 8)

8.1 The Guidance on avoiding FSA authorisation (Section 5) refers to a number of situations where solicitors can, for example, make arrangements for the disposal of a packaged product on an execution only basis. The condition attached to those exclusions/exceptions requires that it must be clear that the client has not sought advice from the firm as to the merits of entering into the transaction or that if the client has sought such advice and the firm has declined to give it that the firm has suggested that the client seeks advice from an authorised person. Compliance with Rule 8 will assist firms in demonstrating that the conditions in the exclusions/exceptions have been met. The rule requires the firm to send to the client written confirmation to the effect that the client has not sought and was not given advice by the firm, or that the client was given negative advice by the firm, but nevertheless wishes to persist in effecting the transaction. The letter should clarify the fact that the transaction is effected on the client's explicit instructions.

8.2 This rule again replicates, more or less, the requirements in the current SIBR and is retained as it will help in clarifying the position for clients and in establishing that the solicitor is acting within the terms of the exclusions/exceptions.

Index

Accepting deposits *see* **Deposits**
Accounts Rules 1998 5.11
Activities carried on in course of profession 3.32
Administration *see* **Probate and administration**
Advertising
Solicitors' Practice Rules 5.4
see also **Marketing a solicitor's practice**
Advising on investments
additional remuneration 3.29, 3.31
body corporate, sale of 3.33, 13.4
broadcast advice 2.36, 3.19
corporate department 13.1
definition 2.36, 3.19
generic advice 2.36
insurance policies 2.36
litigation department 14.1
newspaper advice 2.36, 3.19
off-the-cuff advice 2.36
personal representatives 3.29, 3.30, 3.31
powers of attorney 10.4, 10.10
private clients 15.1
probate and administration 8.3, 8.9, 8.15, 8.21
receivers 11.6
regulated activity 2.36
regulated mortgage contracts 2.36
statutory exclusions 3.19, 3.29
trustees 3.29, 3.30, 3.31, 9.4, 9.11, 9.17, 9.24
Appointed representatives
definition 1.4
exempt person, as 1.4
Solicitors' Practice Rules 5.9
Arranging deals in investments
arrangements by company for purposes of issuing own shares or share warrants 3.15

arrangements not causing a deal 3.11
authorised person, arranging deals with or through 3.12
body corporate, sale of 3.33, 13.4
commission agreements 2.30
definition 2.30, 3.10
finance, provision of 3.13
generally 2.29, 2.30
introductions 3.14
pecuniary reward or advantage 3.12, 3.14, 3.25, 3.31
personal representatives 3.25, 3.30, 3.31
powers of attorney 10.5, 10.11
probate and administration 8.4, 8.10, 8.16, 8.22
receivers 11.7
statutory exclusions 3.10–3.15, 3.25
trustees 3.25, 3.30, 3.31, 9.5, 9.12, 9.18, 9.25
Attorney *see* **Powers of attorney**
Authorisation
conditions for 2.1
exclusions 3.1
FSA Guidance 3.1, 3.9, 3.16, Appendix C1
generally 1.1, 2.25, 3.1
Authorised persons
advice given to client by 3.5, 3.7
contractually based investments 2.28
corporate department 13.5
criminal offences 1.6
dealing as agent 3.5, 3.6, 13.5
definition 1.3
litigation department 14.4

Bank deposit accounts 2.24
Beneficiaries
financial promotions 7.18
probate and administration 8.25

287

Body corporate
  activities in connection with sale of
    3.33, 13.4
Bonds 2.6, 2.7
Branch offices 16.5
Building society accounts 2.24

Certificates of deposit 2.6
Civil remedies 1.7
Client care
  Solicitors' Practice Rules 5.10
Client money
  interest on 2.26, 5.11
  Solicitors' Accounts Rules 5.11
COB Rules *see* **Solicitors' Financial
  Services (Conduct of Business) Rules
  2001**
Collective investment schemes
  definition 2.10, 2.34
  establishing 2.34
  unitised property fund 2.24
  units in 2.10
Commission
  arranging deals in investments 3.12,
    3.14
  claw-back 15.5, 16.8
  dealing in investments as agent 2.29,
    3.9
  FSA Guidance 3.9, 3.31
  introductions 3.14
  Law Society guidance 3.9
  life office, from 15.5
  management of investment business
    16.8
  personal representatives 3.31
  private clients 15.5
  records of 6.6
  renewal commissions 15.5
  retention of 15.5
  Solicitors' Practice Rules 3.9, 5.8
  third parties, from 3.9, 5.8
  trustees 3.31
Commission agreements 2.30
Commodity futures 2.15
Complaints procedures 6.3, 6.11, 16.7
Compliance
  Conduct of Business Rules *see*
    **Solicitors' Financial Services
    (Conduct of Business) Rules 2001**
  corporate department 13.13
  generally 5.1
  litigation department 14.10

Money Laundering Regulations
  business relationship 5.12
  generally 5.12
  identification procedures 5.13
  insurance business 5.13
  internal reporting procedures 5.15
  one-off transactions 5.13
  penalties 5.17
  record-keeping requirements 5.14
  reinvestments 5.13
  relevant financial business 5.12
  training 5.16
powers of attorney 10.13
probate and administration 8.26
property department 12.16
receivers 11.9
Solicitors' Accounts Rules 1998 5.11
Solicitors' Investment Business Rules
  1995 5.18
Solicitors' Practice Rules
  basic principles 5.3
  client care 5.10
  fee sharing 5.7
  generally 5.2
  introductions 5.5
  investment business 5.9
  offering services other than as
    solicitor 5.6
  publicity 5.4
  receipt of commissions from third
    parties 5.8
  referrals 5.5
  trusts 9.28
Compliance officer 16.6
Contracts for differences 2.16
Contracts of insurance *see* **Insurance
  contracts**
Contractually based investments
  authorised persons 2.28
  contracts for differences 2.16
  corporate department 13.7
  definition 2.12
  exempt regulated activities 4.22
  funeral plan contracts 2.18
  futures 2.15
  generally 2.3, 2.23, 3.4
  insurance contracts 2.13, 2.22, 12.4
  litigation department 14.6
  Lloyd's syndicate capacity and
    syndicate membership 2.17
  options 2.14
  property department 12.10–12.12

rights under insurance contracts 2.13
safeguarding and administering *see*
**Safeguarding and administering
investments**
Scope Rules 12.12, 13.7
Corporate department
advising on investments 13.1
authorised person 13.5
compliance 13.13
contractually based investments 13.7
corporate finance 4.24, 13.10
financial promotions 13.14
FSMA, Part XX régime 13.7
insolvency practitioners 1.4, 13.12
introductions 13.3
necessary exclusion 13.6
packaged products 13.8
pension policies 13.9
regulated activities 13.1
safeguarding and administration
13.11
sale of body corporate 13.4
securities 13.7
statutory exceptions 13.2–13.6
Corporate finance
Scope Rules 4.24, 13.10
Credit unions
shares in 2.5
Criminal offences
authorised persons 1.6
due diligence defence 1.6
financial promotions 1.6
generally 1.1, 1.6
penalties 1.6
reasonable precaution defence 1.6
regulated activities 1.6
Custodian services 6.7

Dealing in investments
agent, as
authorised person 3.5, 3.6, 13.5,
14.4
advice given to client by 3.5,
3.7
body corporate, sale of 3.33, 13.4
client has not sought advice of
solicitor as to merits etc. 3.5, 3.8
corporate department 13.5
generally 2.28, 2.29, 3.5
litigation department 14.4
pecuniary award or advantage, for
2.29, 3.9

sale of body corporate 3.33
statutory exclusion 3.5–3.9, 3.33
trustees 9.2, 9.18
body corporate, sale of 3.33, 13.4
contractually based investments 3.4
definition 2.28
funeral plan contracts 2.28, 2.29, 3.4
holding out 3.30
insurance contracts 2.28, 3.4
principal, as 2.28, 3.4
body corporate, sale of 3.33, 13.4
personal representatives 2.28, 3.24
powers of attorney 10.3, 10.9
receivers 11.5
sale of body corporate 3.33
statutory exclusions 3.4, 3.24, 3.33
trustees 2.28, 3.24, 9.2, 9.12, 9.18,
9.23
probate and administration 8.4,
8.10, 8.16, 8.22
securities 3.4
trustees 9.25
dealing as agent 9.2, 9.18
dealing as principal 2.28, 3.24,
9.2, 9.12, 9.18, 9.23
Debentures 2.6
Dematerialised instructions, sending
generally 2.33, 3.18
personal representatives 3.28
powers of attorney 10.6, 10.12
probate and administration 8.6,
8.11, 8.17, 8.23
receivers 11.8
statutory exclusions 3.18, 3.28
takeover offers 2.33, 3.18
trustees 3.28, 9.7, 9.13, 9.19, 9.26
Deposits
acceptance of 2.26, 3.3
certificates of deposit 2.6
definition 2.20
interest on client money 2.26
Differences, contracts for 2.16
Discrete investment business 1.1
Due diligence defence 1.6

Endowment policies 12.4, 12.12
Exempt regulated activities
appointed representatives 1.4
complementary to other professional
services 4.13
contractually based investments 4.22
corporate finance 4.24

Exempt regulated activities (continued)
  criminal offences 1.6
  designated professional bodies 4.1
    control or management by
      members of 4.3
    membership of 4.3
    rules of 4.6
  discretionary management 4.23
  FSMA, Part XX, under 2.1, 4.1–4.8
  generally 1.1, 1.4, 2.25, 4.1
  manner of provision of service 4.5,
    4.14
  meaning 2.1, 4.1, 4.2
  non-mainstream regulated activities
    4.8
  packaged products 4.20
  pecuniary reward or advantage 4.4,
    4.15
  personal pension schemes 4.21
  Scope Rules 4.9–4.25
    see also **Solicitors' Financial
      Services (Scope) Rules 2001**
  securities 4.22
  Treasury orders 4.7, 4.16
Exemption order 1.4

Fee sharing
  Solicitors' Practice Rules 5.7
Financial futures 2.15
Financial promotions
  beneficiaries of trust, will or
    intestacy 7.18
  brochures 7.20
  certified high net worth individual
    7.15
  communications 7.1
    members of profession, by
      7.4–7.10
        non-real time promotions 7.10
        real-time promotions 7.4–7.10
  controlled activities 7.1
    regulated activities distinguished
      7.1
  controlled investments 7.1
  corporate department 13.14
  criminal offence 1.6, 7.1, 7.3
  cross-selling to existing clients 7.21
  engaging in investment activity 7.1
  exemptions 7.3–7.18
  follow-up communications 7.13
  generally 1.5, 7.1
  high net worth companies 7.16

  intestacy, beneficiaries of 7.18
  introductions 7.14
  litigation department 14.11
  marketing a solicitor's practice
    7.19–7.22
  non-real time promotions 7.2
  one-off promotions 7.11, 7.12
  oral communications to non-clients
    7.22
  personal representatives 7.17
  powers of attorney 10.14
  probate and administration 8.27
  property department 12.17
  real time promotions
    definition 7.2
    non-solicited 7.2
    solicited 7.2
  receivers 11.10
  settlors 7.17
  trustees 7.17
  trusts 7.18, 9.29
  types of 7.2
  unincorporated associations 7.16
  websites 7.20
  will, beneficiaries of 7.18
Financial Services Act 1986 1.1
Financial Services Authority 1.1
  functions 1.1
  powers 1.1
Financial Services and Markets Act 2000
  appointment representatives 1.4
  authorised persons 1.3
  civil remedies 1.7
  collective investment scheme 2.10
  criminal offences 1.6
  exempt persons 1.4
  financial promotions 1.5
  general prohibition 1.2, 1.7
  generally 1.1, Appendix A1
  Part XX Appendix A2
    corporate department 13.7
    exempt regulated activities 2.1,
      4.1–4.8
    litigation department 14.6–14.9
    powers of attorney 10.7–10.12
    probate and administration
      8.18–8.23
    property department
      contractually based
        investments 12.12
      regulated mortgage contracts
        12.9

shares in management or
service company 12.15
receivers 11.4–11.8
trustees 9.21–9.27
*Financial Services in the United
Kingdom: A New Framework for
Investor Protection* 1.1
Funeral plan contracts
contractually based investments, as
2.18
definition 2.18
entering as provider 2.38
generally 2.28, 2.29, 3.4
Futures 2.15

General prohibition 1.2
Government securities 2.7
Gower Report 1.1

Industrial societies
shares in 2.5
Insolvency practitioners 1.4, 4.17, 13.12
Insurance contracts
acknowledging indebtedness 2.6
assignment of 2.28
contractually based investment, as
2.13, 2.22, 12.4
definition 2.13, 2.22
effecting and carrying out as
principal 2.27
endowment policy 12.4
general insurance contracts 2.22,
2.27, 13.4
generally 2.6, 2.22, 3.4, 12.4
long-term insurance contracts 2.22,
2.27, 12.4
mortgage protection policies 12.4
pension policy 12.4
property department 12.4
rights under 2.13
term assurance 12.4
Introductions 7.14
commission 3.14
corporate department 13.3
litigation department 14.3
Solicitors' Practice Rules 5.5
Investment business
definition 1.4
discrete 1.1
non-discrete 1.1
providers of 1.1
Solicitors' Practice Rules 5.9

**Investment Management Regulatory
Organisation** 1.1
Investments
registration of title 6.7
rights and interests in 2.23
unregulated 2.24
see also **Advising on investments;
Arranging deals in investments;
Dealing in investments; Managing
investments; Safeguarding and
administering investments**

Land
unregulated investment 2.24, 12.2
Law Society
commission, guidance on 3.9
corporate department, and 13.14
Professional Ethics information pack
Appendix C2
receivers, statutory exclusions for
11.3
Recognised Professional Body, as 1.1
Litigation department
advising on investments 14.1
authorised person 14.4
compliance 14.10
contractually based investments 14.6
financial promotions 14.11
FSMA, Part XX régime 14.6–14.9
introductions 14.3
necessary exclusion 14.5
packaged products 14.7
pension policies 14.8
regulated activities 14.1
safeguarding and administration 14.9
Scope Rules 14.6–14.9
securities 14.6
statutory exceptions 14.2–14.5
Lloyd's
activities relating to 2.37
advise as to membership 2.37
syndicate capacity 2.17
syndicate membership 2.17
Loan stock 2.6, 2.7

Management of investment business
branch offices 16.5
commissions 16.8
complaints procedures 6.3, 6.11, 16.7
compliance manual 16.9–16.16
compliance officer, appointment of
16.6

Management of investment business
(continued)
generally 16.1
organisation of investment business
16.4
policy decisions 16.2–16.8
types and extent of investment
business 16.3
Managing investments
definition 2.31, 3.16, 10.1
discretionary management 2.31, 3.16
additional remuneration 3.26,
3.31
day-to-day decisions 4.23, 10.2
exempt regulated activities 4.23
personal representatives 3.26
routine decisions 4.23, 10.2
trustees 3.26
FSA Guidance 3.16
generally 2.31
holding out 3.26, 3.30
personal representatives 3.16, 3.30,
3.31
powers of attorney 2.31, 3.16, 10.1,
10.2, 10.8
probate and administration 3.16,
8.2, 8.8, 8.14, 8.19
receivers 3.16, 11.2, 11.4
statutory exclusions 3.16, 3.26
trustees 3.16, 3.30, 3.31, 9.3, 9.10,
9.16, 9.22
Marketing a solicitor's practice
brochures 7.20
cross-selling to existing clients 7.21
generally 7.19
oral communications made to non
clients 7.22
Solicitors' Practice Rules 5.4
websites 7.20
see also **Financial promotions**
Money Laundering Regulations 1993
business relationship 5.12
generally 5.12
identification procedures 5.13
insurance business 5.13
internal reporting procedures 5.15
one-off transactions 5.13
penalties 5.17
record-keeping requirements 5.14
reinvestments 5.13
relevant financial business 5.12
training 5.16

Mortgage protection policies 12.4
Mortgages
private, administration of 2.39
see also **Regulated mortgage contracts**

N2 1.1
Nominee companies 9.20
Nominees
exclusions applicable to 3.23
use of 6.7
Non-discrete investment business 1.1

Open ended investment companies
shares in 2.5, 2.10
Options 2.14

Packaged products
COB Rules 6.8
corporate department 13.8
execution only business 6.8
litigation department 14.7
Scope Rules 4.20, 12.12, 13.8
Pension policies
corporate department 13.9
litigation department 14.8
property department 12.4
Pensions
advising private clients 15.2
Personal Investment Authority 1.1
Personal pension schemes
Scope Rules 4.21, 12.12, 13.9
Personal representatives
additional remuneration 3.25, 3.26,
3.27, 3.29, 3.31
arranging deals 3.25
dealing as principal 2.28, 3.24
probate and administration 8.20
dematerialised instructions, sending
3.28
discretionary management 3.26
exclusions applicable to 3.23–3.31
financial promotions 7.17
holding out 3.26, 3.30
investment advice 3.29
managing investments 3.16
probate and administration
acting for external PRs 8.13–8.17
acting as PR 8.8–8.12, 8.19–8.20
acting as or for PRs 8.21–8.23
safeguarding and administration 3.27
Powers of attorney
advising on investments 10.4, 10.10

arranging deals in investments 10.5, 10.11
compliance 10.13
dealing as principal 10.3, 10.9
dematerialised instructions, sending 10.6, 10.12
drafting 10.1
financial promotions 10.14
FSMA, Part XX régime 10.7–10.12
generally 10.1
managing investments 2.31, 3.16, 10.1, 10.2, 10.8
safeguarding and administration 10.6, 10.12
Scope Rules 10.7–10.12
statutory exclusions 10.2–10.6

Private clients
advising on investments 15.1
charging
fee-paying basis 15.4
generally 15.3
remuneration certificate 15.4, 15.5
retention of commission, by 15.5
generally 15.1
pensions 15.2
school fees 5.2
tax 15.2

Probate and administration
advising on investments 8.3, 8.9, 8.15, 8.21
arranging deals in investments 8.4, 8.10, 8.16, 8.22
beneficiaries 8.25
compliance 8.26
dealing in investments 8.4, 8.10, 8.16, 8.22
dematerialised instructions, sending 8.6, 8.11, 8.17, 8.23
financial promotions 8.27
FSMA, Part XX régime 8.18–8.23
managing investments 3.16, 8.2, 8.8, 8.14, 8.19
personal representative
acting as 8.8–8.12, 8.19–8.23
activities undertaken by other members of firm 8.12
dealing as principal 8.20
external, acting for 8.13–8.17
regulated activities and the estate 8.1–8.6
safeguarding and administration 8.5, 8.11, 8.17, 8.23

Scope Rules 8.18–8.23
statutory exclusions 8.7–8.17
will trusts 8.24

Profession
activities carried on in course of 3.32

Property department
compliance 12.16
contract of insurance 12.4
contractually based investments 12.10–12.12
FSMA, Part XX régime 12.12
statutory exclusions 12.11
financial promotions 12.17
generally 12.1
land 12.2
regulated mortgage contracts 12.3, 12.7–12.9
FSMA, Part XX régime 12.9
statutory exclusions 12.8
shares in management or service company
excluded activities 12.14
FSMA, Part XX régime 12.15
generally 12.5, 12.13

Provident societies
shares in 2.5

Public securities 2.7

Publicity
Solicitors' Practice Rules 5.4
stationery 6.3
see also **Marketing a solicitor's practice**

Reasonable precaution defence 1.6

Receivers
advising on investments 11.6
arranging deals 11.7
compliance 11.9
dealing as principal 11.5
dematerialised instructions, sending 11.8
financial promotions 11.10
FSMA, Part XX régime 11.4–11.8
managing investments 3.16, 11.2, 11.4
safeguarding and administration 11.8
Scope Rules 11.4–11.8
statutory exclusions 11.2–11.3

Recognised Professional Body 1.1

Records
commissions, of 6.6
Money Laundering Regulations 5.14

Records (continued)
title documents, of 6.7
transactions, of 6.5
Referrals
Solicitors' Practice Rules 5.5
Registration of title to clients'
investments 6.7
Regulated activities
ancillary to professional activities 1.1
appointed representatives 1.4
a business 2.2
collective investment scheme,
establishing 2.34
Conduct of Business Rules *see*
Solicitors' Financial Services
(Conduct of Business) Rules 2001
contracts for differences 2.16
contractually based investments
2.12–2.18
definition 2.12
corporate department 13.1
criminal offences 1.6
definition 2.2
dematerialised instructions, sending
2.33
deposits 2.20
acceptance of 2.26
exempt *see* **Exempt regulated**
activities
funeral plan contracts 2.18, 2.28,
2.38
futures 2.15
generally 1.1, 2.1
insurance contracts 2.22
effecting and carrying out as
principal 2.27
insurance contracts, rights under 2.13
investments
advising on 2.36
arranging deals in 2.30
dealing as agent 2.29
dealing as principal 2.28
managing 2.31
rights and interests in 2.23
litigation department 14.1
Lloyd's, activities relating to 2.37
Lloyd's syndicate capacity and
syndicate membership 2.17
options 2.14
regulated mortgage contracts 2.21,
2.39
securities *see* **Securities**

specified investments 2.3
stakeholder pension scheme,
establishing 2.35
Regulated mortgage contracts
administering 2.39, 3.20
advice on 2.36
assisting acquisition of 3.10
definition 2.21, 2.39, 3.20
entering as lender 2.39
generally 2.21, 2.23, 2.39
property department 12.3, 12.7–12.9
Scope Rules 12.9
statutory exclusion 3.20
trustees 9.8, 9.27
Remuneration certificate 15.4, 15.5

Safeguarding and administering
investments
additional remuneration 3.27, 3.31
corporate department 13.11
excluded activities 2.32
generally 2.32, 3.17
holding out 3.30
litigation department 14.9
personal representatives 3.27, 3.30,
3.31
powers of attorney 10.6, 10.12
probate and administration 8.5,
8.11, 8.17, 8.23
qualifying custodian
arrangements with 2.32, 3.17
definition 3.17
receivers 11.8
statutory exclusions 3.17, 3.27
trustees 3.27, 3.30, 3.31, 9.6, 9.13,
9.19, 9.26
Safekeeping of client's investments 6.7
Sale of body corporate
activities in connection with 3.33,
13.4
School fees
private clients 15.2
Scope Rules *see* **Solicitors' Financial**
Services (Scope) Rules 2001
Securities
bonds 2.6, 2.7
certificates of deposit 2.6
certificates representing certain
securities 2.9
corporate department 13.7
debenture stock 2.6
debentures 2.6

definition 2.4
exempt regulated activities 4.22
generally 2.3, 2.23, 2.28, 3.4
government securities 2.7
instruments creating or
    acknowledging indebtedness 2.6,
    2.7
instruments giving entitlement to
    investments 2.8
litigation department 14.6
loan stock 2.6, 2.7
open ended investment companies,
    shares in 2.5, 2.10
public securities 2.7
rights under stakeholder pension
    schemes 2.11
safeguarding and administering *see*
    Safeguarding and administering
    investments
Scope Rules 13.7
shares 2.5
units in collective investment schemes
    2.10
warrants 2.8
Securities and Futures Authority 1.1
Securities and Investment Board 1.1
Self Regulating Organisation 1.1
Settlors
financial promotions 7.17
Share options 2.14
Shares
body corporate, in 3.33
credit unions, in 2.5
generally 2.5
industrial societies, in 2.5
management or service company, in
    12.5, 12.13–12.15
open ended investment companies, in
    2.5, 2.10
provident societies, in 2.5
Solicitors' Accounts Rules 1998 5.11
Solicitors' Financial Services (Conduct of
    Business) Rules 2001
complaints 6.3, 6.11
custodian services, firm's
    responsibilities in relation to 6.7
execution of transactions 6.4
generally 5.19, 6.1, 6.2, Appendix B2
monitoring 6.11
nominees, use of 6.7
packaged products, execution only
    business 6.8

records 5.14
    commissions 6.6
    title documents 6.7
    transactions 6.5
registration of title to clients'
    investments 6.7
regulated activities 6.3–6.9
safekeeping of client's investments
    6.7
solicitors authorised by FSA, non
    mainstream activities 6.10
status disclosure 6.3
waivers 6.9
Solicitors' Financial Services (Scope)
    Rules 2001
application 4.10
contractually based investments
    12.12, 13.7
corporate department 13.7
corporate finance 4.24, 13.10
discretionary management 4.23
effect of breach of rules 4.25
generally 4.9, Appendix B1
litigation department 14.6–14.9
other basic conditions 4.12–4.19
packaged products 4.20, 12.12, 13.8
personal pension schemes 4.21,
    12.12, 13.9
powers of attorney 10.7–10.12
probate and administration 8.18–8.23
prohibited activities 4.11
receivers 11.4–11.8
regulated mortgage contract 12.9
securities 13.7
trustees 9.21–9.27
Solicitors' Investment Business Rules
    1995 5.18
Solicitors' Practice Rules 1990 (as
    amended)
appointed representatives 5.9
basic principles 5.3
client care 5.10
fee sharing 5.7
generally 1.4, 5.2
introductions 5.5
investment business 5.9
offering services other than as
    solicitor 5.6
publicity 5.4
receipt of commissions from
    thirdparties 3.9, 5.8
referrals 5.5

Specified investments 2.3
Stakeholder pension scheme
establishing, operating or winding up 2.35
rights under 2.11

Takeover offers
dematerialised instructions, sending 2.33, 3.18
Tax
private clients 15.2
Term assurance 12.4
Trustees
acting as 9.10–9.14, 9.21–9.23
or for 9.24–9.27
activities undertaken by other members of the firm 9.14
additional remuneration 3.25, 3.26, 3.27, 3.29, 3.31
advising on investments 3.29, 3.30, 3.31, 9.4, 9.11, 9.17, 9.24
arranging deals in investments 3.25, 3.30, 3.31, 9.5, 9.12, 9.18, 9.25
compliance 9.28
controlled trustee 5.11
dealing in investments 9.25
agent, as 9.2, 9.18
principal, as 2.28, 3.24, 9.2, 9.12, 9.18, 9.23
dematerialised instructions, sending 3.28, 9.7, 9.13, 9.19, 9.26
discretionary management 3.26
exclusions applicable to 3.23–3.31
external, acting for 9.15–9.19
financial promotions 7.17, 7.18, 9.29
FSMA, Part XX régime 9.21–9.27
holding out 3.26, 3.30
managing investments 3.16, 3.30, 3.31, 9.3, 9.10, 9.16, 9.22
nominee companies 9.20
regulated activities and trust funds 9.1–9.8
regulated mortgage contracts 9.8, 9.27
safeguarding and administration 3.27, 3.30, 3.31, 9.6, 9.13, 9.19, 9.26
Scope Rules 9.21–9.27
statutory exclusions 9.9–9.19
will trusts 8.24

Unregulated investments 2.24

Warrants 2.8
Will trusts 8.24